EFFIE GRAY
By G. F. Watts, R.A.

Other books by Admiral Sir William James

THE BRITISH NAVY IN ADVERSITY
(A study of the War of American Independence)
(Published by Longmans)

BLUE WATER AND GREEN FIELDS
(Published by Methuen)

ADMIRAL SIR WILLIAM FISHER
(Published by Macmillan)

PORTSMOUTH LETTERS
(Published by Macmillan)

THE BRITISH NAVIES IN THE SECOND WORLD WAR
(Published by Longmans)

THE ORDER

OF RELEASE

THE STORY OF
JOHN RUSKIN, EFFIE GRAY
AND
JOHN EVERETT MILLAIS
TOLD FOR THE FIRST TIME
IN THEIR
UNPUBLISHED LETTERS
EDITED BY
ADMIRAL
SIR WILLIAM JAMES, G.C.B.

*

LONDON

JOHN MURRAY

1948

First edition January, 1948
Reprinted February, 1948

PRINTED IN ENGLAND AT THE CURWEN PRESS

Dedication

This vindication of their sister is dedicated to the memory of George Gray, Albert Gray, Melville Gray, and especially Alice Stibbard.

29th viii 1946

Contents

LIST OF ILLUSTRATIONS

[1] *In the possession of Sir Ralph Millais, Bt.*
[2] *In the possession of Admiral Sir William James, G.C.B.*

Author's Note

THE publication of the truth about John Ruskin's marriage to Effie Gray will, inevitably, throw into relief the licence that certain authors of books and articles have allowed themselves when accounting for its disastrous course.

But those who have seen the film depicting Ruskin as best man at the marriage of Millais and Effie Gray, or read that Ruskin was never in love with his wife, or that Millais ran away with Mrs. Ruskin, or that Effie Gray's father contrived the marriage as a step towards obtaining financial help from Ruskin's father, should not judge too hastily the authors of these canards.

Ruskin's married life was shrouded in mystery by his principal biographers, Cook and Collingwood, and the fictitious stories spread abroad by Ruskin's parents and friends served to accentuate the mystery.

His admirers may therefore be forgiven for preferring versions of the story that accorded with their conception of that great genius to versions that discovered some clay in the feet of their idol.

If the cellar at Effie Gray's old home at Bowerswell and the loose board in the study of John Ruskin's last home at Brantwood had revealed their secrets forty years ago, authors of books on the period when John Ruskin and the Pre-Raphaelites flourished would not have had to strain their imaginations to unravel a story that seemed so full of contradictions and Effie Gray's family would have been spared much pain. But it is evident from the letters that passed between members of her family during those forty years that the annulment of the marriage, though sanctioned by Church and State, was considered a subject to be avoided in conversation, that resort to the public press to contradict apocryphal stories about Effie Gray was not countenanced, and that remonstrance by private letter was the only acceptable weapon for the defence of her good name.

There must, however, come a time when those who have the necessary personal knowledge of a sequence of events to speak with authority pass away and a story, already garbled, becomes still further mutilated because no voice is raised in defence of the victim of unintentional misrepresentations.

The justification for this book is that, in the case of Effie Gray, that time has now come.

The authenticity of the 633 letters from which a selection has been made has been verified by handwriting, dates on letters, and postmarks on envelopes. If the envelope has been missing the date on a letter has been checked by a concurrent event, e.g., the death of the Duke of Wellington, the arrival of the first hippopotamus at the London Zoo, Jenny Lind's first appearance at Covent Garden.

The original punctuation is retained in the letters quoted in this book.

THE ORDER OF RELEASE

CHAPTER I

Introduction

THIS is a story of two men of genius and a beautiful woman, a story that has been often told and retold in biographies and in less ambitious books with varying degrees of inaccuracy to fulfil the purpose of the author.

The true story is here told for the first time, based on hitherto unpublished letters.

My grandmother, Effie Gray, was married in 1848 at the age of twenty to John Ruskin, already famous as an art critic and author. The marriage was annulled six years later, and Effie Gray (she resumed her maiden name) married John Everett Millais, then in the front rank of English painters and the most gifted member of the Pre-Raphaelite Brotherhood, which had been founded by Holman Hunt, Rossetti and himself.

It was inevitable that a social drama in which two such men were involved should attract a large and attentive audience. It was also inevitable that Ruskin would find champions who would fix the blame for his disastrous marriage on his wife.

The account offered to and accepted by readers of books about Ruskin and the Pre-Raphaelites is that Ruskin's mother, in her desire to hold her famous son, chose for him a wife who would be safe and manageable, that her choice unfortunately fell on a shallow and unaffectionate girl, and that, in his greatness of heart, Ruskin freed her to marry Millais, with whom she had fallen in love.

More extravagant versions are that Effie Gray's father contrived her first marriage as a step towards obtaining financial assistance from Ruskin's father, and that Millais and Effie Gray ran away together when Ruskin's conduct became unbearable.

The high-water mark of embellishment was reached a few years ago in an American film which depicted John Ruskin as best man at Millais's wedding.

The caption on the advertisement for this film, called *The Love of John Ruskin*, was:

'The ideals and ideas of some of the most prominent men were exceedingly strange and past finding out. John Ruskin, poet and littérateur, held very strange views on the subject of marriage, as displayed in the surrender of his wife to his friend, Sir John Millais. Ruskin became acquainted with his wife through a loan which he made to her father, and his noted generosity no doubt appealed to her, and it seems that she married him more out of gratitude than actual love. Be that as it may, the fact remains that when Millais met her, he and she fell desperately in love with each other. Ruskin observed this; not at once, however. His mind was absorbed in his literary effusions, and at first he paid little heed to it, but eventually he woke up to a realization of their mutual affection. Ruskin loved his wife intensely, but he was not demonstrative. His heart was bowed down with a great sorrow, he would not deny his wife that love which he could not enjoy himself. He willingly gave her freedom and released her from her marriage vows. He not only consented to the marriage with Sir John Millais, but acted as best man at their wedding. Congratulating them and bidding them a fond farewell, he remained a friend to them always, retiring to his home lonely and sad.'

All these fantastic stories, which will now be dispelled to the four winds, have sprung from three sources, the two standard biographies of Ruskin and the malicious accounts of their son's married life which were assiduously circulated by his parents after the annulment.

Ruskin's biographers, Cook and Collingwood, were not incompetent; on the contrary, they understood their work only too well. They realized that the British public are exceedingly frightened of any form of sexual abnormality and that to admit that Ruskin lived for six years with a beautiful woman, in intimacy at first lover-like, and yet refused to consummate the marriage, would be presenting him as an abnormal being and probably frighten away a large number of readers and damage his publicity value.

Cook only makes a brief reference to the annulment. He

quotes Mrs. Carlyle as joining in the lively gossip and aiming pointed shafts at both parties, and says he does not propose to engage in the chatter. He adds that the true romance of Ruskin's life was yet to come.

Collingwood is not nearly so restrained:

'His readers and the public were intensely puzzled when she left him. To his acquaintances, however, it was no great surprise, though, with one exception, they took his part, and fully exonerated him from blame. He, with his consciousness of having fulfilled all the obligations he had undertaken, and with an old fashioned delicacy and chivalry which revolted alike from explanation and from recrimination, set up no defence, brought no countercharges, and preferred to let gossip do its worst.'

In support of his contention that no blame attached to Ruskin he records that his friends stood by him and that Miss Mitford had no qualms in introducing him to the Brownings!

In *Ruskin's Complete Works*, edited by Cook and Wedderburn, the whole episode is described in one sentence:

'Ruskin's wife left him in April 1854, and from May to October he was in Switzerland with his parents.'

It is not surprising that subsequent writers have sensed some mystery when Ruskin's biographers left in doubt what actually happened, and by so doing fostered an implication that he was not at fault, but the biographers would, no doubt, be surprised to see the advantage their successors have taken of their silence, and the rein given to surmises and imagination.

Nor was any check to imagination ever imposed by either Ruskin or Effie Gray. He avoided any mention of his marriage in his books, and no word of her six years' martyrdom ever passed her lips.

Moreover, J. G. Millais, in his *Life of His Father* makes no mention of his mother's first husband, only inserting a footnote to the effect that Miss Gray had been previously married, that the marriage had been annulled on grounds sanctioned by Church and State, and that the circumstances attending the annulment were better left in obscurity.

Whilst Effie Gray was alive she was protected by the law of libel, but there is no law of libel to protect the dead, and stories about her have been published with a freedom and confidence which would have seemed unbelievable in her lifetime.

After her death the defence of her reputation was undertaken by her brother, Sir Albert Gray, and her daughters, Lady Stuart of Wortley, and Mary Millais, but it was of a negative nature, buying letters which without the context might damage her memory, and overtaking false statements after publication. It was Albert Gray who extracted a promise from Sir William Rothenstein that he would take out of his second and subsequent editions of *Men and Memories* the statement that Effie ran away with Millais; it was at his instigation that W. M. Rossetti published in the *Athenæum* of 2 July 1904, a withdrawal of two statements in his book *Rossetti Papers* that Ruskin, subsequent to the annulment, paid money to Effie and her parents. Albert Gray exonerated Rossetti from intentional misrepresentation, but thought him very gullible to draw any facts from Howell, of whom Cook and Wedderburn wrote:

'his adventures lost nothing in the telling of them',

and Ford Madox-Brown called:

'the Munchausen of the Pre-Raphaelite Circle'.

Albert Gray also prevented the publication of Ruskin's account of his married life which he gave to his proctor a fortnight before the case for annulment came before the Court, and thereby hangs a strange story.

He learnt in 1924 that the widow of the last survivor of the firm of solicitors who had acted for Ruskin had the document in her possession and, anticipating that its contents in the hands of an unscrupulous person might gravely damage his sister's reputation, he approached the widow with a view to obtaining possession.

He found that she had already been informed that she could sell the document for a considerable sum in the United States, but when she was made aware of the harm it might do to an innocent woman she accepted his offer.

As the document had lain unclaimed for seventy years in the solicitors' office and the Ruskin family had died out, he was much surprised when, three months later, Ruskin's literary executor claimed it, quoting legal authorities.

Albert Gray was then Counsel to the Chairman of Committees in the House of Lords and, after consulting the authorities, disputed the executor's legal right to possession, but eventually agreed to hand over the original whilst retaining a copy for the protection of his sister against any further calumnies that might be published.

On his death his Ruskin papers were, in accordance with his instructions, sent to the Bodleian Library with the proviso that none of them were to be published for thirty years. It must, therefore, suffice here to say that the statement was written in a petulant mood, that it does not traverse Effie Gray's account of her married life which will be found in her letters to her father and to her mother-in-law, but, of course, throws all the blame for the strange happenings on the wedding night and after on his wife. Its publication could only harm its writer.

The voices of those who knew Effie Gray well are no longer heard in her defence; there is no one now to keep a watchful eye on the extravagances of authors of books and articles about the period; but fashions in art are constantly changing and public interest in the great Victorians is from time to time fanned by some writer who makes a new approach to their achievements. However powerful the influence of new schools of painting, the day is still far distant when visitors to the Tate Gallery will hurry past 'The Order of Release' or cease to be arrested by the face and figure of Effie Gray.

Not only is there no longer any justification for withholding from prospective authors the true facts of Ruskin's marriage, but Effie Gray's descendants would certainly be lacking in chivalry if they allowed to go by default any attempt to tarnish her reputation.

It is possible that a more positive line of defence by publishing the whole truth was for so long avoided because of the odium that might follow accusations against a popular hero. But those who, through personal acquaintance, might have borne animus against Ruskin are no longer alive, and the truth can now be told without incurring a charge of prejudice.

Millais, who had more reason than most men to bear animus against Ruskin because he saw at close quarters Ruskin's treatment of his wife, only used accusatory language during the few months that elapsed between his awakening to the truth at Glenfinlas and Effie Gray's return to her parents. He was then a much troubled man. But after that he never belittled or berated Ruskin.

He fully recognized the genius of Ruskin; he greatly admired Ruskin's works; he always made full allowance for Ruskin not being as other men, and grieved that such an intellectual Colossus should have been fated to play out the tragic farce of an unnatural marriage. It is in that spirit that this book is written. It will, too, be abundantly clear as the story unfolds that much of Ruskin's conduct was directly inspired by his parents.

But for them his marriage might have endured with a semblance of harmony, because Effie always said that she could have borne the unnatural physical conditions if only an urge to be cruel had not possessed her husband, an urge that originated with the sly suggestions of his parents, who stopped at nothing to recover full possession of their son.

All through the pattern there runs a morbid and at times grotesque thread which is the Innkeeper's daughter who brought a genius into the world, and a smaller, wobbling, menacing thread which is the pompous, wordly Wine Merchant whose father had committed suicide in the room where Effie Gray was born.

It will become abundantly clear that Effie Gray led a blameless life throughout her six years of martyrdom.

That she was a beautiful woman is evident in Millais's famous picture 'The Order of Release', and in G. F. Watts's pencil drawing when she was eighteen, both of which are reproduced here.

That she was a woman of the highest integrity is evident from her conduct when the Ruskins endeavoured to drive her from the path of rectitude and thereby terminate an unnatural and miserable union by divorce proceedings which would not reveal the son's extraordinary treatment of his wife. That she was also a woman of great courage is testified by her decision to face the publicity of annulment proceedings in an age when matrimonial rifts were only discussed in whispers, and when annulment, however solid the grounds, brought social stigma. Indeed, it was then a generally held view that a wife had no right to complain of the conduct of her lord and master, however outrageously he behaved.

After Effie Gray left Ruskin, Millais wrote:

'I have heard that Thomas Carlyle is very boisterous in the question of asundering, his judgement is that no woman has any right to complain of any treatment whatsoever, and should patiently undergo all misery.'

Queen Victoria refused to allow Effie to be presented as Lady Millais until Millais was on his death-bed. She only relented when in response to her inquiry if she could do anything for him, he replied, 'Yes, let her receive my wife'.

Effie Gray's letters to her parents throw new light on the strange, morbid family at Denmark Hill, and leave no doubt that there was a streak of insanity in Ruskin, which manifested itself in calculated cruelty to a girl he married under false pretences. Of particular interest are a letter to her father and her last letter to Mrs. Ruskin in which she abandoned her proud reserve and disclosed that immediately after her marriage Ruskin told her that for physical and religious reasons she would only be his wife in name until she was twenty-five, when he would reconsider the matter, and that when she reached that age he told her that he had no intention of altering their unnatural mode of life as she was mad and unfit to have children.

These letters provide the missing chapters in the lives of Millais and Ruskin.

The great beauty and charm of Ruskin's passionate love-letters during his engagement show how completely he had lost his heart to the 'Fair Maid of Perth', and her letters, though less passionate, reveal her wholehearted response.

The incongruity of his statement after the annulment that he was never in love with Effie will now be apparent. So, too, will the oft-repeated statements that Millais ran away with

Effie seem grotesque when read with Millais's letters during the months preceding Effie's escape from thraldom, and her letters written during her new-found freedom in which she expresses her fears of tempting providence again.

Only a portion of the letters used in this book are directly concerned with the more intimate aspect of Effie's married life, the remainder are used to sketch in the background.

That Effie Gray was a woman of great intelligence and wide knowledge is evident from her letters to her mother and to Rawdon Brown, the 'Doge of Venice'. Her critical and informative comments on art and music, and on the religious and political questions of the day, reveal a richly stored mind. It is not surprising that those who welcomed an opportunity of a talk with her ranged from the Duke of Wellington to the Master of Trinity to the Dean of St. Paul's.

Not the least interesting passages in her letters are those in which she describes her travels abroad with Ruskin when he was collecting information for his major works, and those in which she comments shrewdly on the London social world into which she was thrown after marriage. She met all the giants in the Literary and Artistic world and the Society leaders of the day. One day she is at a great social gathering and noting the dresses and behaviour of the Duchesses; the next day she is visiting Turner in his bare and miserly room and is shown his picture of 'a steamer drawing a wreck and such a sunset as you never see in pictures but his own' and ready to pawn her all for it only to be told that someone has already offered £1,000 for the '*Old* Temeraire'; the next day she is taken into dinner by Gladstone, and the next she is discussing the religious questions of the day with Carlyle.

Space only allows the inclusion of a small selection of the letters describing the Social, Political and Arts world of London, and life in Venice in the middle of the last century, which is a matter for regret because they undoubtedly are a contribution to our knowledge of the period.

My cousin, the Hon. Clare Stuart-Wortley, spent many years collecting, annotating, and establishing the authenticity of the letters relevant to the history of John Ruskin and Effie Gray from which a selection has been made for this book.

The majority of the 633 letters were found in the archives at Bowerswell, where Effie Gray was born, married, and died. Some, including Ruskin's love-letters, were bought by two of Millais's daughters, Lady Stuart of Wortley and Mary Millais, from a Mr. Telford of Grasmere, an antique dealer, who had bought them at an auction of the contents of Brantwood, Ruskin's residence in later life; it was a Mr. Sharp, who had been educated at Ruskin College and was a Ruskin admirer, who, on seeing the letters, realized their importance and wrote to Mary Millais. Three which had gone to America before Mary Millais could act, were recovered.

They were hidden under the floor-boards in Ruskin's study and were found when a bookcase was moved revealing a loose board. Of the remainder some were bought at sales and some given to Clare Stuart-Wortley.

As a young man, Millais's boon companions were John Leech, the famous *Punch* artist, Edward Lear, whose *Book of Nonsense* is a classic, Wilkie Collins, the novelist, his brother Charles Collins, the water-colour painter, and Holman Hunt.

All these men had much in common. All found a tremendous zest in being alive. All were gifted with an exceptionally keen sense of humour.

A further bond of friendship between Millais and Leech was their love of hunting and fishing. They never missed a day's sport or the opportunity planning the day gave them for exchanging notes illustrated with pen and ink drawings. Millais's membership of the Garrick Club widened his circle of close friends. Lord James of Hereford wrote this account of the Club in those days:

'Being elected a member of the Garrick Club, I found Millais one of the foremost amongst the distinguished men frequenting the old Club-house in King Street. Night after night some twelve or fifteen men gathered in the smoking room of the Club. Thackeray, Dickens, Anthony Trollope, John Leech, Robert Keeley, Shirley Brooks and others equally well known in different callings formed a group it was pleasant enough to associate with.'

Millais's niece, Mrs. Lear, lent me a number of letters

B

written to him by his friends and some of them find an appropriate place in this book.

I have relied for background on the standard biographies of Ruskin, on J. G. Millais's *Life and Letters of Sir John Everett Millais*, and the letters themselves.

I have used a few letters that have already been published to weld the story together; the source of these letters is given in each case to differentiate them from the new letters.

My links with the principal characters are, of course, slender but none the less unforgettable.

As a boy I was often at my grandfather's house in Palace Gate, and was for long periods at Bowerswell under the care of my great-grandmother, Mrs. Gray.

I have a vivid recollection of the last time I saw my grandfather, shortly before he died, and I find in Lord Rosebery's letters the reason for the freshness of my memory.

'Even on his death-bed my recollection is one of divine beauty and patience. Has any likeness been preserved of him as he lay dying? I was urgent that this should be done, for I never saw so beautiful a sight, putting its pathos on one side.'

A year later I spent the last weeks of my leave before joining my first sea-going ship with Effie Gray at Bowerswell. Despite the ravages of time and illness that was soon to prove fatal, it was still plain to see why she had once been called the 'Fair Maid of Perth'.

As a young man I spent most of my leave periods at Bowerswell with her brother, George, whose mind remained unimpaired up to his death at the age of ninety-five, and in that house of so many strange memories I imbibed much information about the people and times with which this book is concerned.

This was the concluding paragraph in an obituary notice in *The Times:*

'For the last 40 years Mr. Gray lived a quiet life at home, dispensing a generous charity and a wide hospitality. At one time or another it would have been possible to meet under his roof guests or visitors such as John Bright, Matthew Arnold,

Lord James of Hereford, Sir William Harcourt, Arthur Sullivan, Frederick Walker, Arthur Cecil Blunt, Sir Johnstone Forbes-Robertson, and Mrs. Kate Perugini. During his last years the affliction of blindness, borne with uncomplaining patience, hardly affected the charm given to his conversation by an unfailing humour and a well-stored memory of which both lasted to the end.'

If the principals in this story could revisit Bowerswell today they would find little changed.

The chatter and laughter of many children would be very familiar to Mrs. Gray, though she would be disappointed and surprised to hear that they were not little Grays, but evacuees from towns attacked by Germans.

The flowering shrubs flanking the long walk, where Millais pleaded with Effie Gray to forget the past and make a new life with him, are perhaps a little less shapely; the beech tree under which Ruskin poured out his passionate love for Effie Gray has gone, but the seat remains; the high holly hedge and terraces are just as Millais painted them in the 'Vale of Rest'; the dining-room, where Ruskin fascinated the company with his rich, rolling phrases, and Millais, with lightning sketches, made merry over his latest adventures with rod and gun at Murthly, is unchanged; Mrs. Gray's stick and workbox are still in their proper place.

CHAPTER II

Young Genius

EFFIE GRAY was born on 7 May 1828, at Bowerswell, Perth, in the room where her future husband's grandfather, John Thomas Ruskin, described as being of unstable disposition, committed suicide; a coincidence that was to gratify the superstitious and have a strange influence on her future mother-in-law when she realized that her son was taking more than a friendly interest in the young visitor from Perth.

In deference to the Scottish tradition, she was baptized Euphemia Chalmers to perpetuate the names of her maternal grandmother.

Her father was George Gray, a Writer to the Signet. He was not a wealthy man, but his business was sufficiently extensive to send all his sons to public schools and his daughters to young ladies' seminaries of good repute, and eventually to build a new house on the site of the original Bowerswell to house his large family. He bought Bowerswell from John James Ruskin, father of his future son-in-law, with whom he was on terms of close friendship for many years, and it was with the Ruskins that his two eldest children, Effie and George, stayed in London on their way to and from school.

Though a shrewd business man he was one of the many thousands who invested money in the new railroads, anticipating a steady rise, and for a period was in serious financial difficulties. This caused the first rift, as Mr. Ruskin plied Mr. Gray with long verbose letters on the iniquities of speculation:

'Long since indeed I used to say that from speculative propensities I believed to prevail in Perth, I did not in a business point of view value any gentleman there as to property at 3 months purchase . . . John knows my severity in money matters . . . I am so upset myself at hearing of any speculation,' and much more in the same vein, which incensed Mr. Gray.

He would have been much more incensed if he had known

GEORGE GRAY, SENIOR, 1876
By Sir J. E. Millais, BT., P.R.A.

then that Mr. Ruskin would one day spread abroad outrageously distorted stories about his temporary embarrassment. That he should have regarded investments in Railway Stock as wild speculation seems very strange today.

Effie's mother was the daughter of Andrew Jameson, Sheriff Substitute of Fife, and the progenitor of a long line of Scottish legal luminaries. His son, Andrew, became Sheriff Principal of Aberdeenshire; his son, also called Andrew, was Sheriff of Perth and as Lord Ardwall, a Judge of the Court of Session, was described by John Buchan in *Memory hold the Door* as the last of the great 'characters' on the Scottish Bench and a figure who might have stepped out of a Raeburn canvas; Lord Ardwall's son, John, is now Sheriff Substitute of Midlothian and Haddington.

The Scottish Judges of those days would have raged furiously at the suggestion that a woman should plead before them, but even if a legal career had been open to women, Sophia Gray would have found little time to study for the Bar, as between 1828 and 1855 she brought fifteen children into the world.

Next after Effie came George, who spent his early life in Australia and died at Bowerswell at the age of ninety-five; then came four boys and three girls who fell victims in childhood to epidemics which today only cause temporary discomfort and little anxiety. Undeterred by this grim experience, little Grays continued to arrive in the world periodically. Sophia, who was born in 1843, was, whilst still a child, a shrewd observer of the Ruskin family at Denmark Hill and, as we shall see, helped to open her eldest sister's eyes to their true character.

Alice, born in 1845, was one of the lovely children in Millais's 'Autumn Leaves', and two years later again appeared on the walls of the Royal Academy in 'Apple Blossoms'; when she was nineteen, Millais chose her as model for 'Swallow, Swallow', and four years later for his famous picture 'Rosalind and Celia'.

Four boys came next. John, who spent his life in Australia; Melville, who spent his early life in New Zealand and his later life at Bowerswell, where he died in his ninety-eighth year in 1946; Albert, who became Counsel to the Chairman of Committees in the House of Lords; and Everett who founded the well-known Stock Exchange firm of Vivian, Gray & Co. The Ruskins occasionally visited their relations in Perth, and it was during one of these visits that Mrs. Gray saw her future son-in-law for the first time, then a boy of eight.

He was, she used to say, a remarkable looking child with beautiful blue eyes and fair curls, and already had a surprising knowledge of botany, which his proud mother drew out as they walked round the garden.

The details of the visit were also long remembered because of the strange conduct of Mrs. Ruskin, who, though paying a social call, flatly refused to enter the house where her father-in-law had committed suicide. It was not, however, till she was twelve, that Effie met John Ruskin, when she was stopping for a few days with his parents on the way to school.

The eager young botanist was now twenty-one, and already causing a considerable stir in the Literary and Artistic world.

His early education had taken an unusual course. Up to the age of ten he had been taught by his mother, who had been educated at a fashionable day school, and, being proud and ambitious, had since her marriage with her prosperous cousin lived down being the daughter of the landlady of the King's Head Inn at Croydon and her sister's marriage to a baker.

When he was ten his mother handed over his education to tutors, but the most important part of his education was the annual summer tour on the Continent with his parents. His father was a partner in a firm of wine merchants, Ruskin, Telford and Domecq, and though his son tells us that Domecq contributed the sherry, Telford the capital, and Ruskin the brains, it was Ruskin who frequently travelled abroad. He combined business with pleasure which he found in the picture galleries, the architecture and the scenery and a love of beautiful things which was fully shared by his young son.

So whilst other boys were learning Latin grammar and Greek verbs, John, with his father and mother, was travelling by easy stages through Germany, Italy, France and Switzerland, stopping at one place to examine minerals, already a subject of keen interest, at another place to study a famous collection of pictures, and, when drawn by the beauty of the countryside, wander and sketch, heedless of time.

To the son these journeys were a continual delight from the day his parents decided the date of departure:

'The beginning of delight was in choosing the carriage, and in arranging cunningly what was to be virtually the travellers home for many weeks. Then came the rapture of starting—the first trot through Camberwell—the sense of pity for all the inhabitants of Peckham who weren't going, like the pity of lovers on their wedding-day for everybody who is not being married; the change of horses at Dartford, feeling that the last link with Camberwell was broken, that we were already in a new and miraculous world.' (Cook)

They travelled in great luxury, four horses to draw the carriage, a postilion and a courier, and always occupied the best rooms in the best hotels. In the *Stones of Venice* Ruskin lamented that those peaceful, instructive Continental tours, which were a feature in the education of those who could afford them, were a thing of the past:

'These were the olden days of travelling, now to return no more, in which distance could not be vanquished without toil, but in which that toil was rewarded partly by the happiness of the evening hours when, from the top of the last hill he had surmounted, the traveller beheld the quiet village where he was to rest, scattered among the meadows beside its valley stream, or, from the long-hoped-for turn in the dusty perspective of the causeway, saw for the first time the towers of some famed city, faint in the rays of sunset.'

Meanwhile he made no young friends, and his mother never let him out of her sight.

Though, as he wrote in *Fors Clavigera*, 'nothing was ever promised me that was not given, nothing ever threatened me that was not inflicted, nothing ever told me that was not true', he realized in later years that he had nothing to love, nothing to endure, and was never taught 'precision or etiquette of manners'. In *Præterita* he says:

'My parents were—in a sort—visible powers of nature to me, no more loved than the sun and the moon; . . . still less did I love God. Not that I had any quarrel with Him or fear of Him; but simply found what people told me was His service, disagreeable; and what people told me was His book, not entertaining. I had no companions to quarrel with neither; nobody to assist, and nobody to thank— .... When affection did come, it came with violence utterly rampant and unmanageable, at least by me, who never before had anything to manage.'

The first of these storms burst on him when he was seventeen. Mr. Domecq came to stay with the Ruskins with his four daughters,

'the first well-bred and well-dressed girls I have ever seen—or at least spoken to . . . a most curious galaxy or southern cross of unconceived stars, floating on a sudden into my obscure firmament of London suburb.'   (*Præterita*)

He fell violently in love with Adèle-Clotilde, the eldest girl, 'a graceful, oval-faced blonde of fifteen', but 'a combination of the single-mindedness of Mr. Traddles with the conversational abilities of Mr. Toots' made him a poor suitor for the hand of the elegant and sophisticated young Parisian who, in any case, being a Roman Catholic, was entirely unacceptable to his mother.

He must have endured agonies:

'My own shyness and unpresentableness were further stiffened or rather sanded by a patriotic and Protestant conceit which was tempered neither by politeness nor sympathy, so that while in company, I sate jealously miserable like a stock fish—on any blessed occasion of tête-à-tête I endeavoured to entertain my Spanish-born, Paris-bred and Catholic-hearted mistress with my own views upon the subjects of the Spanish Armada, the Battle of Waterloo and the Doctrine of Transubstantiation.'

In an effort to save the situation he tried to dazzle her with literary offerings, but she did not appreciate their merit or their author, and returned to Paris, leaving him bewildered and aware that he had cut a foolish figure.

In October 1836 he matriculated at Oxford, and in the following term went into residence at Christchurch but was still, and for his whole time at the University, under the watchful eye of his mother, who took lodgings for the period of each term.

He devoted much of his time to writing verse, and after two unsuccessful attempts won the Newdigate prize in 1839 with a poem on 'Salsette and Elephanta'.

He had appeared in print when only fifteen with his 'Enquiries of the causes of the colour of the Rhine' and 'Considerations on the Strata of Mont Blanc' which were published in the *Magazine of Natural History*; when eighteen he wrote 'The Poetry of Architecture', papers which laid down the line of study he afterwards pursued in the *Seven Lamps* and *Stones of Venice*; and during 1838 an important series of articles by him entitled 'The Convergence of Perpendiculars' appeared in the *London Architectural Magazine*. But though absorbed in his work he could not forget Adèle-Clotilde and was still hoping to win her when, in his third year at Oxford, he was told that she was engaged to a young French nobleman.

This unmanageable and rampant storm left him prostrate, and for the next two years he travelled in search of health.

Such was the remarkable young man who Effie Gray met for the first time in the summer of 1840 when on her way to school.

Her hostess would certainly have talked to her about her already famous son, and she, no doubt, gazed with awe at the sad but striking-looking young man. He, on his side, though utterly dejected and seriously ill, was captivated by her beauty and intelligence and wrote for her the charming story, *The King of the Golden River*, which was illustrated by Doyle of *Punch* fame, and was one of the most popular of his minor works.

It was translated into German, Italian and Welsh, and was adopted as a Board School prize book in England, and a lesson book in the United States.

Ruskin, in his *Præterita*, said it was 'a fairly good imitation of Grimm and Dickens, mixed with a little true Alpine feeling of my own'.

At the age of twelve people do not leave a great impression, but this brilliant young man who had talked to her and taken an interest in her drawing and music cannot have easily been forgotten.

The memory of that meeting remained fresh with young Ruskin, and as soon as her education was completed he begged his mother to ask her to pay them a visit in London.

By then he had mounted far on the ladder of fame. Infuriated by the reception of Turner's pictures in 1836, he had, though only seventeen, constituted himself the painter's champion, and in 1843 the first volume of *Modern Painters* was published and had an immediate success. He travelled far and wide to collect his material, always with his parents, and in 1846 the second volume appeared, to confirm and establish his fame.

Millais, it may be noted, had the year before exhibited his first picture in the Royal Academy, 'Pizarro seizing the Inca of Peru', painted when he was sixteen, having at the age of nine won the Gold Medal of the Academy for a series of drawings in an open competition.

CHAPTER III

Strange Wooing

IN the spring of 1847, just before her nineteenth birthday, Effie Gray left Bowerswell for her first grown-up visit to the Ruskins at Denmark Hill. John Ruskin was now twenty-eight.

Her previous visit in October, when for the last time her father came south to take her home from school, had not been a success. The Ruskins had given them a cold reception, and they had cut short their visit.

It was not until he received Mr. Ruskin's letter in April, quoted below, that Mr. Gray knew why his friends had behaved so strangely and, in the meanwhile, Effie had received a warmly worded invitation to Denmark Hill.

The story current at the time, and accepted with few exceptions ever since by Ruskin's biographers, was that his mother, alarmed for her son who had recently suffered a second disappointment in love, and believing that he would never choose a wife for himself who would leave unimpaired her hold on her son, invited Effie Gray to Denmark Hill with every intention that John should marry her.

Another story, current after the annulment, was that Effie Gray's father manœuvred the visit because he was in financial difficulties and could, if the young couple fell in love, approach John's father, now a very rich man, for help.

Ruskin's biographer, Cook, summed up the situation with:

'They saw in a marriage with Euphemia the means by which they might gain a daughter and not lose a son,'

and other writers have stated that Ruskin was never in love with Effie, and that his parents pressed him so hard that he eventually capitulated.

The truth was that Effie was only asked to Denmark Hill when Mrs. Ruskin could no longer refuse her son's persistent requests; that she endeavoured to stave off any attachment forming between her son and Effie by telling her that John was engaged; that when it was obvious that John was falling in love with Effie, Mr. Ruskin wrote to Effie's father asking that her visit be cut short, and that Mrs. Ruskin was throughout influenced by her morbid superstition about Perth and Perth people. All this is abundantly plain in the letters that follow.

Ruskin's own feelings at this time are clear from a letter he wrote to Effie during their engagement:

'The fact is—I have felt the loss of my own youth so dreadfully that I grudge every hour now that keeps your youthful company back from me—and—impatient though I am—I should not be fretful about the mere putting off the thing—if you and I could be—five years hence—18 and 28—I could wait like patience on a monument. . . . But time won't wait—and do you know—I was taken in, a year—When my mother said to me in October—last year—Only wait this winter, John—and then you shall see her—I consented (though sulkily) because I thought you were only seventeen; you know you corrected me only on your birthday—if I had known or thought of the truth—I wouldn't have waited an hour and much suffering I should have saved myself, and a little perhaps to you—for, I don't know whether you *were* or not—but you really *looked* distressed that night you left me at Denmark Hill. But were it not that I have deep cause for thankfulness that things have ended thus—and sooner than I *once* thought possible—and that you have been preserved to me against so many adverse chances—I *could* feel very bitter—comfortless regret at having lost the precious intercourse of promised and increasing affection—and the sight of you—in your *girlish* beauty—which I might have had for three years back.'

Though as will be seen from the letters in the next chapter Ruskin wrote this when his love for Effie Gray was 'rampant and unmanageable', his imagination would not have ramped so wide as to tell his future wife apocryphal stories about his difficulties with his mother.

Effie had only been a few weeks with the Ruskins when her host and hostess, observing that John was taking more than a friendly interest in their young visitor, regretted their surrender to their son's importunings and decided that the two young people must be separated.

Mr. Ruskin accordingly wrote in April to Effie's father:

London,
28 April 1847

'We have been friends for so many years standing that I hope our communications with each other may assume a more frank and easy and confidential form than those betwixt ordinary acquaintances usually do—We have had the very great pleasure of your Daughter's company for these few days past and what we think of her will best appear from the subject of this letter.—You know that my Son is at home—I cannot arrive at the purpose of this letter better than by giving you a short sketch of his past life—

'In 1836 when he was 17 I happened to have my Partner the late Mr. Domecq residing with his Daughters for three months in my house—I believe I have already told you that most unexpectedly to us my son became strongly attached to the eldest Daughter of Mr. Domecq. Her Father was full of affection for his own child and for mine and expressed entire approval of their being united, offering to make his Daughter a protestant. I felt this a great kindness and concession but we could not sanction a union with romanism even though professing to cease to be so and the ample fortune belonging to the Lady, though always an agreeable accompaniment, was no inducement to run such a risk as his Mother thought existed of her Son becoming a Roman catholic, the character of the young Lady's mother was also objectionable—The passion however was powerful and almost threatened my son's life—various journies abroad have scarcely dissipated his chagrin nor repaired his health—The only young Lady we have had about us since from whom any thing was to be feared I will admit is your own Daughter and because both Mrs. Ruskin and myself were persuaded that no young man of taste and feeling could long look upon her with indifference we felt called upon immediately to consider all consequences. For myself I am of course most deeply anxious for my son's happiness but whether it was derived from Paris or from Perth, from small fortune or from great, I was disposed to let matters take their course trusting that my son would not commit any very fatal mistake

if left to his own guidance in such an affair—I ascertained
however that not only to romanism but to Scotland and most
especially to Perth Mrs. Ruskin had an insuperable dislike—
she has had so much misery herself in Perth that she has quite
a superstitious dread of her son connecting himself in the most
remote degree with the place—With knowledge of these
objections in his Mother's mind and of the power of the
presence of such a young creature as Miss Gray I felt there was
no safety but in flight—We *did not* fly from you last year but
we gave you I fear a very cold reception and your stay was very
short—Since you took Miss Gray to Scotland last year my son
has been abroad and since his return he has in the society he
has fallen into found a young Lady who has engaged his
affections and to whom he has made proposals the result of
which is not yet known—To you as a Father I make such dis-
closures as under similar circumstances I should desire to be
made to me.—I would not presume to say that Miss Gray cannot be daily with my son without the smallest danger to herself
but I deem it more than possible from what I already see that
both may fall into some danger and that very great embarrassment might arise to all of us should the favourable impression
wh. each may be already making on the other proceed to take
a more definite form—I repeat that as far as I am concerned I
lay no restraint nor prescribe any course to my son—He may
follow his own inclinations but as he has committed himself
for the present and as his Mother, if he had not, seems so
averse to Scottish alliances I cannot help giving expression to
my apprehensions that both you and I are placing our young
people in danger and that we should at least adopt every
measure of caution and safety in our power. I beg to apologise
for this long letter and for saying anything you may consider
uncalled for but I might have saved my son from many a pang
had I once been as early in my fears and precautions.
    'We join in kindest regards to you and Mrs. Gray.'

    The young lady who had engaged John's affections and who,
according to his father, might soon be expected to give her
answer to a proposal of marriage, was Charlotte Lockhart,
daughter of Sir Walter Scott's son-in-law and biographer.

Ruskin had met her at Lady Davy's house, where men of letters frequently gathered for dinner and afternoon parties, and described her as a 'Scottish fairy, White lady and witch of the fatallest sort, looking as though she had just risen out of a stream'.

She caused no unmanageable storm. Ruskin says that he never could come to any serious speech with her, which was not surprising as Charlotte, who was in love with another man, carefully avoided him.

In view of Effie's comments in her letters to her parents, which appear later, it is difficult to believe that Ruskin's father and mother thought that their son's affair with Charlotte was still prospering, and Mr. Ruskin's letter produces a strong impression that he exaggerated in order to implement his wife's determination to separate the young couple.

On receiving the letter, Effie's father took immediate action:

Perth
1 May 1847

'I only received your esteemed favor of the 28 ulto. this morning and lose not a moment to reply—

'Believe me that I fully appreciate the kind feeling which has induced you to enter so frankly into your family matters with the view of preventing an unhappy attachment arising betwixt your son and my Daughter and you may be assured that knowing as I now do the position in which your son stands with respect to another Lady and, irrespective of this, the feeling of Mrs. Ruskin to a Scotch alliance and particularly with a native of Perth, I shall use such means and influence as is within my power immediately to separate the parties which I trust will be quite sufficient to prevent the renewal of any penchant the one may have ever felt for the other—Accordingly by this post I have written my friend Mr. Gadesden who kindly requests me to allow Phemy[1] to pay him a visit asking whether it would be convenient for him to receive her now and I have no doubt he will send for her directly—On the 18th I believe it is arranged she goes to Mrs. Paget who is then to be in London—It strikes me forcibly that Mrs. Ruskin could have

[1] Effie was called Phemy until she grew up.

quietly given Phemy a hint that John was under engagement
that this would have completely served every purpose we have
in view—If I know anything of Phemy at all I think she
would at once have acted on such a hint and without betraying
confidence kept her affections disengaged on (as the case might
be) any advance from the other side—

'I know well that Phemy has always expressed herself
favourably of John as a person for whom she had a high respect
as a man of talent and refined manners but I know also that
she has a great deal of good sense and maidenly pride and
is the very last person in the world that would either give
her affections to one in John's present position or were he
entirely free accept of him at the expense of wounding his
mother's feelings—No happiness could ensue from such a
connection and therefore do I feel the more obliged to you
for the unreserved communication you have made me which
I sincerely hope may be the means of putting an end to
all our fears—I have considered it my duty to shew your
letter to Mrs. Gray and she intends when writing Phemy to
touch upon the subject very gently as we are both persuaded
that is all we require to do—I return your letter as desired
and with the assurance of our kindest regards to Mrs. Ruskin
John and yourself.'

Though, without a moment's delay, he took steps to remove
his daughter from contact with John, he must have thought
that his old friends were behaving very oddly. They had known
Effie since her childhood, they knew she had grown into a
beautiful girl, they knew only too well their son's dynamic
temperament, and yet they had welcomed her to their house
for her first visit to London.

But Mr. Gray must have been even more surprised when in
reply to his letter Mr. Ruskin wrote this:

London
3 May 1847

'I have your kind letter of 1 instant for which I return my
sincere thanks but I regret you should have written to Mr. G.
or taken any steps to shorten Miss Gray's visit.

'Mrs. R. since I wrote to you has I find told Phemy of John's situation and, even before doing so, we had no grounds whatever to think that Miss Gray was in the least interested about my son beyond the interest of one young person for another on a renewed acquaintance—If it entirely depended on the Lady I think so much of her judgement and womanly discretion that my fears would be few, but my son's poetical temperament comes rather in abatement of his Discretion—Were your Daughter a person of ordinary Character or appearance I might have been saved the pain of troubling you but I confess I dread the danger of a second and deeper impression being made where one already exists and which has led to consequences he could not escape from—My son would be shocked at my even dreaming of a possibility of his being capable of acting dishonourably and I trust in God he never will, but both his Mother and myself see every day that he is too sensibly affected by Miss Gray's presence for his own peace—Still no sudden steps can be taken without too much wounding his feelings and showing a distrust in his strength of mind which not knowing his own Danger, he would ill brook from any one—I hope with your knowledge of the Circumstances and Miss Gray's great good sense, we may let the visit take its course—At all events you can be kind enough to leave the matter in our hands, until I write to you again.

'P.S. I had written above in the City but thought I would see Mrs. R. before sending it. She wishes me after seeing your letter very strongly to impress upon you that her ideas about Perth are not of recent growth and can have no personal relation to Miss Gray, indeed I think that so much does Mrs. Ruskin love her that were nothing else in the way, she would herself endeavour to bring about what in Imagination she seemed to dread—I can add in Justification of her feelings about Perth and in proof of their having no reference to any family in particular, that since we left it in December 1827 she has never changed her sentiments. We came to Scotland I think in 1838 but I could not get her to Perth and although we have all wished to visit the Highlands, we have not made it owing to

C

these Impressions. During twenty years she has refused to go
to your beautiful neighbourhood—and never I believe in her
life would now visit it.'

One of the strangest features of the story of Ruskin and
Effie Gray is this sudden change of front which took place in
the course of one week.

It is hard to believe that it was caused solely by the discovery
that Effie was not particularly interested in John; it is much
more likely that they dared not risk the effect on their son of
severing abruptly his new attachment, and also very probable
that John himself intervened when he was told that Effie's visit
was to be cut short.

That they accepted the position with bad grace is evident
from one of their son's letters written a few months later.

22 December
1847

'You are a good girl to speak so of my father and mother—
though how you should think them the kindest people you
ever knew I can't understand—for when you were here last—
they *could* not be kind to you—they were afraid for you—more
for me—afraid to ask you to stay—afraid to let us be together—
much vexed with themselves—angry with me—and a *little*
with you—every way uncomfortable—my mother especially
at first—my father at last—I thought them thoroughly *un*kind
—and I believe still that you have mistaken idea of them—and
that whatever good you may think of them—you will find that
you get on with them *far* better than you expect—but of
course there will be trials now and then.'

Effie, unaware that she was living in the calm centre of a
circular storm, was meanwhile enjoying her first experience
of London society, and getting not a little amusement from
John's so-called love affair with Charlotte.

She perhaps began to realize that John was taking some
interest in her when on her birthday—four days after the
Ruskins decided to allow her to stay—she received these verses
from him, which were afterwards published under the title
'For a birthday in May' and reprinted in *Præterita*:

'Thorn, and meadow grass, sweet sister,
Twine them as I may,
Deemest thou a darksome garland,
For thy natal day?
Thou thyself art fairer, sister,
Than all flowers of May,
Had I brought thee buds and blossoms,
Shamed were I and they,
Think not of their grace, sweet sister,
Nor their colours gay,
Since their utmost glory, sister
Is to pass away.

'Grasses of the field, sweet sister
And the wreaths they bind,
Though they deck the depth of summer,
Dread no winter wind,
Through the thrilling frost, sister,
Through the sleet storm blind,
These to earth and all her creatures,
Are for ever kind.
And let us remember, sister,
With a quiet mind,
Even thorns are fair, sister,
With the heaven behind.

'May that happy path, sister,
Ever more be thine,
Through the mighty shepherd's pasture,
And by streams divine,
May all earthly sun, sweet sister,
On thy journeying shine,
Though perhaps there may be, sister,
Shadows upon mine,
Kindly he for all, dear sister,
Will the end design,
Who for both our sakes, sister,
Brooked the spear and spine.'

On the same day that Mr. Ruskin was writing to suggest her visit should be cut short, she wrote to her mother:

Denmark Hill
28 April 1847

'I am enjoying myself exceedingly although in a quiet way, Mr. Ruskin is as kind as ever and as droll—Mrs. Ruskin is the same but I think she is beginning to feel old age a good deal, she sleeps so badly during the night that she falls asleep in the evenings, she is always saying she is afraid I will weary with her, but we get on admirably and she is always giving me good *advices* which I would repeat had I not so much news to tell you. John I see very little of excepting in the evening as he is so much engaged but he seems I think to be getting very celebrated in the literary world and to be much taken notice of; on Saturday he was at a grand reunion of Sir R. Peel's where everyone was, the Duke of Cambridge was there boring everybody with his noise, Sir Robert and Lady Peel were there the whole time and extremely affable. On Friday John is going to a private view of the Royal Academy, the ticket is sent to him by "Turner" who is one of the 50 Academicians who have a ticket at their disposal so that it is the highest compliment paid to any man in London. They have got home a very fine Picture by the above artist yesterday of Venice which is the largest they have and which must have cost *something*.

'On Monday we went to the new Society of Watercolours which is very fine this year. You will read an account of it in last week's Athenæum, those by Topham are beautiful also those by "Vacher". We went early and there was no one in the room but Mr. *Prout* who is the famous artist a nice old man who walked round with us. In the afternoon we had to dinner Messrs. Severn, Vacher, Newton, Richmond, Munro. Mr. Severn I talked much to, and liked as much. He has been painting a large hall at Gatten in frescoes for the Countess of Warwick, and he told me a great deal about her; he lives much amongst those people, his wife being granddaughter to the late Marquis of Ailsa. He played and sang very nicely.

'Mr. Vacher[1] is a very nice young man of 25 and very merry not at all like an artist. He told me a great deal about the society he liked in Rome and I was much amused with him— you will see in the Athenæum about his pictures. Mr. Newton sat by me at dinner, the same extraordinary man saying queer things, but as he was talking to me all the time of dinner John did not bring him out which I regretted; he sat all the evening looking at something or nothing, so odd. Mr. Richmond[2] I did not speak to.

'Mr. Munro, a son or nephew of Sir Hector Munro, a queer uncouth-looking being asked me to come and see his pictures of which John says he has a very fine collection. Lord Eastnor was breakfasting here the other morning—he is very talented and John and he are proposing to go to Italy in two months, they are great friends and the former is a beautiful drawer, he is eldest son I think of Earl Somers, also rather fond of queer things, such as he wanted to see a Massacre and went some months ago to Algiers where he saw two or three very good ones and has come back quite satisfied. Yesterday Mrs. Ruskin took me to call on Mrs. Cockburn but she was out, we drove on to Greenwich and saw the Hospital with which I was much pleased, the Painted Hall is very fine and all the pictures of the Admirals. I saw the coat and waist-coat Nelson wore at the Battle of Trafalgar the latter spotted with blood lately presented to the Hospital by Prince Albert. It was very interesting to see the nice old men going about in all directions, we saw their tea laid out and their ornamented little cabins and etc. This morning Mr. Harrison was here at Breakfast and was very amusing making a great many puns.'

W. H. Harrison was a great admirer of Ruskin's and as Editor of *Friendship's Offering* had published his early poems. It was to him that Ruskin entrusted the final revision of his books, and, according to Cook, he kept 'a stern eye upon Ruskin's grammar and punctuation'.

[1] Vacher, Charles (1818–83), water-colour painter.

[2] Richmond, George (1809–96), portrait painter; painted Effie after her marriage.

The first reference to John's love affair appears in a letter written two days before her birthday:

Denmark Hill
5 May 1847

'I have not heard from Mr. G. yet but we drive every day and Ewell is a very short drive from here. Mrs. Ruskin wishes me to make this my headquarters and will not hear of it being otherwise—she desires me to tell you this with her love and as she will not let me make any arrangements for myself I find it best to allow her to settle things for me as she likes so that do not trouble yourselves about me as I will tell you all my plans in my letters.

'Mrs. Ruskin told me of John's affaire the first night I came but I did not tell you as I thought she perhaps did not wish it to be known, but she did not tell me who the Lady is and John never hints of her, he is the strangest being I ever saw, for a lover, he never goes out without grumbling and I fancy the young lady cannot be in London. Mrs. R. says "if my John gets her he *will* have a treasure as she is very elegant and high-bred". Mrs. R. tells me she has never seen her and that she is in a higher rank of life than they are but she knows her well by character.

'John is such a queer being he hates going out and likes painting all day and Mrs. R. reading, he is drawing me just now which amuses me very much as he destroys a fortune in paper and paint and I have to sit in all manner of positions, he won't let me see how he gets on, until he is finished which I don't think he will ever be. He is just gone to breakfast with Rogers the poet, he then lunches at the Dean's Dr. Buckland, he then goes to Sir Stratford Canning's and dines at Mr. Ellis's. Mr. Newton came out here last night and slept here, he amused us beyond expression and went on with John this morning, he is a great genius. Talking of geniuses Mr. and Mrs. Liddell came the other day, she is a lovely girl of 19 with sparkling black eyes and hair dressed in a black and blue checked silk, a beautiful upper dress of Polka form of blue velvet fitting to her figure trimmed with rich black lace and large buttons, a gray chip bonnet lined with pink crape and pink ribbon outside and in yellow kid gloves etc., etc., she is very fashionable and dines often with her Majesty, Mr. L. is Headmaster of Westminster school and one of the Queen's chaplains. I don't like Mrs. L.'s manner and she has not a sweet voice.

'Mrs. Ruskin's sight is so bad that she does not know London at all. Mr. Telford and Mr. H. Watson dined here, we had some nice music. John dined at Mr. Ellis's and met Mr. T. B. Macauly (*sic*) who he says is very clever but talks too much and makes a great noise. They talk of sitting late in Perth but at Mr. Ellis's they did not rise from the dinnertable till half past two. As we passed the Opera House at five the street was crowded with people going in to the house to get good seats to hear Jenny Lind,[1] the first night of her singing, she was expected at the Palace the night before but did not go, they say her voice is very uncertain and she is very nervous at times.

'John talks of taking me to the Opera some night but I don't think I will be able to go as Mrs. Ruskin won't go herself and I suppose she would not let me go without a lady.

'The bonnets this season are quite round in front and not at all large at the ears. I see a great many cloaks of pale glacé silk with ruished (*sic*) frills round them.'

On her birthday she sent some more news to her mother about John's love affair. It is clear that she had not yet given a thought to John as a suitor for her hand, and that his mother's apprehensions seemed to her absurd.

Denmark Hill
7 May 1847

'I have this moment got a kind note from Mr. Gadesden saying he is sorry I cannot come today but that it is only a pleasure deferred and that I may come whenever I like and they shall be delighted. How Papa came to say that I was to be off to Leicestershire I cannot think as I shall certainly not be there till about the 20th of June which was my original plan.

'Mrs. Ruskin, John and I went to the Dulwich Gallery to-day but could not get in. We drove on to Peckham and took a long walk, John and I went into a Chalk Pit, the only one I ever saw, and the country is looking most exquisitely beautiful the shades of green and the long hedgerows are beyond

---

[1] *Jenny Lind* made her début in London on 4 May in *Roberto il Diavolo*.

anything I ever saw. John has gone to dine with Rogers the Poet and is to meet Edwin Landseer and other eminent men. He and Mr. & Mrs. R. very kindly gave me presents to-day. Mrs. R. amuses me by telling everybody that they have no idea how fond she and I are of each other. I declare John will be quite and is quite jealous of me. Mr. Ruskin has taken a box at the Opera for Tuesday night to hear Jenny Lind. Mrs. Ruskin does not approve of the Opera and won't go but Mr. R., John and I and Mr. Richmond the painter make the four. I have not yet had the courage to ask John who his Lady-*Love* is, of the last syllable I suspect there is little, it is an extraordinary affair and I could astonish you were I at home to tell you about them. I suspect from what is said that the Lady has a fortune and that love must come after marriage. Mr. and Mrs. R. are always talking about marrying from reason, rather odd, isn't it. I much doubt if John will ever marry her as he has not asked her yet. I cannot understand the affair, nor I suppose can you, but at any rate if I tell you anything about them I trust you will keep it entirely to yourselves as Mr. Ruskin never told me he had written to Papa about it, in fact Mrs. Ruskin tells me that nobody knows and she only told me in case, as she says, that John and I should *love each other*. Wasn't it good, I could not help laughing but thanked her for her caution which however I *did* not *require* as I consider him the same as married and should never think of such a thing—however I think this little gossip will amuse you but be sure it goes no further as I should dislike it exceedingly and Papa *must* be particular in writing or saying nothing that I write.'

Holman Hunt, one of Millais's greatest friends, was led by Mrs. Ruskin to believe that it was always her intention that John should marry Effie. 'Effie' he wrote, 'played up as Mrs. Ruskin had hoped, and soon showed untiring interest in the art questions which John was pursuing.'

Effie was a shrewd observer of the family life at Denmark Hill, and it was not long before she realized the extent to which John was dominated by his parents. From the next letter it also appears that John had begun to take her into his confidence about his affaire.

Denmark Hill
14 May 1847

'I am going tonight to hear Jenny Lind in "La Somnambula"
Mr. Ruskin, John and I with Mr. Richmond the Painter, it was
put off from Tuesday till this evening which I was glad of, but
it has prevented me going to Mrs. Paget's. I am going however
tomorrow to stay till Saturday night, as it was quite impossible
my going to Ewell to call. I have written to say I will go on
Tuesday for a week if convenient. Mrs. Gardner has not been
here yet. John is going tomorrow to the Exhibition with the
Duke and Duchess of Manchester and Mr. Macdonald of St.
Martin's after which Mr. M. comes here till Saturday. I am
sorry I shall miss meeting him. Lord Stavordale and his sister
come here on Saturday forenoon, I should like to have seen
them. Yesterday we were in St. James's Palace seeing the
large picture of the Queen and Prince Albert with the
children by Winterhalter, the children looked very nice but it
did not seem to me well painted. A gentleman takes in by
order. On coming up St. James's Street by great good luck I
passed the Duke of Wellington on horseback, I looked out after
him and saw him touching his hat to the people as he passed.
What you say about J's affaire is very true, if he marry the
Lady it is from prudence and a false notion of duty, he has
only seen the young Lady six times at parties in his whole life
and does not love her a bit, but believes they have each
qualities to make the other happy were they married. Did you
ever hear such philosophy? I think Mr. and Mrs. R. are doing
wrong, at least they are wishing for their son's happiness and
going the wrong way to work. He adores them and will
sacrifice himself for them, as I see too easily. Private!'

References to the 'affaire' gradually disappear from Effie's
letters but there is nothing in her letters up to the time she returned home to suggest that she and John were anything more
than good friends. Indeed in one of her last letters written on
18 June, a few days before she left Denmark Hill, she tells her
parents that they need not expect to see John at Bowerswell,
though he will be spending the autumn with his friend Mr.
Macdonald at St. Martin's Abbey, only six miles away.

That John's parents, whatever their fears for their son,

spared no pains to entertain their young visitor can be seen
from the full accounts of her doings and the people she met, in
her long and frequent letters home, some of which are quoted
below. She was evidently supremely happy until the middle of
June and her sudden eagerness to cancel further visits and
return home may well have been due to a growing awareness
that John was in love with her.

Denmark Hill

18 May 1847

' After calling on Mrs. Ewart I went on to Regent Street where
I found the Pagets and Parkers in a body glad to see me; we
went and saw Brunetti's model of Jerusalem, the new Water
colour Exhibition, and in the evening Mr. John Parker,
Messrs. George and Arthur Paget, Mr. Burnside, Louie Jane
and I went to the French Theatre and enjoyed it exceedingly.
The acting was beautiful and I understand French better than
I thought I did so I could quite follow them. I saw there close
to us Prince Louis Napoleon, Marquis of Worcester, the Hon.
Mrs. Norton etc. On Saturday we went and saw the new
Houses of Parliament which are gorgeous in the extreme—
after coming out all the party went to Dulwich Gallery
excepting Louie and Mr. Burnside who went one way shopping
—Mr. Arthur Paget and I went through the Green Park and
up Rotten Row as it was early and no one there—by good
chance we met Prince Albert and Col. Bouverie, the Prince
bowed to us and looked very well. We walked a little further
and met the Duke of Wellington who touched his hat and
looked uncommonly well, he is in mourning and does not look
at all feeble. Mr. Arthur Paget and I went lounging through
Regent Street and looking at all the carriages and people which
amused me exceedingly as I had not walked before. We were
going through the Burlington Arcade when we came past a
gentleman finely dressed whom I thought I knew. It proved to
be Mr. Athole Burnet walking with a lady—he did not speak
but I bowed, Louie and the rest were so vexed at not having
seen him. In the evening, some went to hear Jenny Lind and
the rest of us with Mr. Parker to the Colosseum[1] which I left at

---

[1] In Regent's Park. Commenced 1824, completed 1829. Exhibited
panoramic views of London, Paris, etc.

nine and came home here, Anne having come for me. I was
dreadfully tired seeing and walking so much. I am sorry to go
today to town as Mr. and Mrs. Stuart Wortley and Lady
Davy,[1] Sir Humphrey's widow, are coming to lunch. John is
very sorry that I am going as he says I miss all his friends. John
was dining at Sir R. Inglis's on Saturday and sat next Sir James
Graham who was speaking to him against Penitentiaries and
said if they would flog in the first instance it would be better.
Mr. Ruskin is going to town so adieu. I was hearing Jenny Lind
last Thursday, I never heard such a singer, all they say of her
is true.'

*   *   *

Ewell Castle
27 May 1847

'Yesterday we had a great treat we drove up to town in the
morning and remembered quite by chance that this was the day
for the grand Fancy Fair for the Irish in the Regent's Park; we
went there and paid 5/- to get in. The sight of the ladies was
splendid but you will read an account of it in the Times—few
people seemed to be buying, but moving about I saw only two
beauties selling, Lady Clementina Villiers and another—the
former was in mourning and plainly dressed; the old Countess
of Jersey was behind a horrid old woman. The Duchess of
Sutherland looked well and handsome but is getting very stout
—she was in black with quantities of point lace and a cap of the
same with two rows of large pearls round her neck she looked
very goodnatured—the Marchioness of Londonderry was
beside her in pink tarleteine (*sic*) over white, so fat, but with
such splendid diamonds on her fingers and on her neck—the
Duchess of Bedford was in white figured satin with jewels
round her waist, an ugly old woman. Viscountess Combermere
looked very well in black silk with her hair crimped all over her
head, she has a handsome face, but I was disappointed in the
looks of most of them being plain in face although perfectly
dressed. The Queen's Maids of Honour had a stall and a
plainer set I never saw, one with bright red hair. The Queen

[1] A prominent figure in the society of Rome and London.

and Prince Albert had just left when we got there. The arrangements were admirable, no crushing or pushing about and next to the room a large Marquee was spread for refreshments and two bands of the Life Guards played alternately. After we had left we walked about shopping. I met Andrew Aitken and he walked a little way with us. I forgot to tell you I met him by accident last week in Covent Garden Opera where Mr. Ruskin and John with myself had gone to hear Grisi in Lucrezia Borgia, I was quite charmed and think that but for Jenny Lind this Opera is superior.

'Bye the Bye, I have heard a little more about John Ruskin's affair and if he has got into a mess it is his own fault as Mr. and Mrs. Rn only wish for his happiness, a fact which is proved by their refusing a lady with £50,000 but then she was a Catholic, but I have not yet found out who the present lady is as they don't talk about it.'

*   *   *

Denmark Hill
2 June 1847

'Yesterday I went with all the Ruskins to a monthly lecture on Horticulture where by accident I met all the Gadesdens. I introduced them to the Ruskins and they were mutually pleased with each other. Mr. G. says he is going to take me to hear the "Creation" in Exeter Hall on the 10th which will be a very fine thing, it is for the Scotch you will see it advertised. Mrs. Gardner also called and I went there yesterday—I am going to them on the 15th. They were very anxious for me to go with them tomorrow to Ascot Races, Mrs. G. said her son had quite set his heart upon my going, but I have no doubt he will survive the disappointment. I pleaded as excuse a dinner-party here which I would have been sorry to lose, Mr. Turner dines here also Messrs. McDonald, Richmond, Leslie, and a number of other eminent artists who John was so kind as to ask that I might meet them.

'I enclose for your perusal a little sonnet sent to me yesterday through John from Mr. Harrison whose professed admiration for me amuses us all excessively—he has sent me a book as a remembrance of him so pray keep the poem till I return—he is a kindhearted good man. You ask about my dress and purse. I am almost daily subject to slight headaches from the warmth of my clothes as excepting my pink muslin nothing is wearable from the heat and when I go to the Gardners where it is much warmer I really think I will require some more clothes. I have four pounds left and I have been as economical as possible, but the heat is dreadful, and Mr. Ruskin advises me to get a crinoline that I may leave off my flannel petticoat. '

*   *   *

Sussex Gardens
15 June 1847

'Here I am writing to you half asleep in my bedroom at half-past eleven o'clock which I am sure you will say is very foolish and wish me in bed instead but, as we are going tomorrow morning to a great Review in honor of the Grand Duke Constantine in Hyde Park, unless I write you now I shall not be able to do so till Friday when it will be too late. Mrs. Ruskin brought me here today at 5 o'clock when I immediately dressed for dinner, and Mr. *William* Gardner's room being next to mine and the walls very thin, that young gentleman to show I suppose his extreme joy at my arrival, executed various *Pas* to his own whistling much to my amusement as I formerly believed him incapable of any great exertion of bodily strength or mental power. After dinner we went out in the carriage to see the Queen go in state to the Opera to see Jenny Lind in Norma, it was a most splendid sight and so many carriages being full of gentlemen in uniform, the Queen looked very well and the Ladies seemed beautifully dressed, this being the night of the Caledonian Ball which they are to attend afterwards.

'The chief reason for my writing you tonight is to ask you if you have any objection to my returning home from here. You will I doubt not think this a strange request but I have *many reasons* for writing it, one of which is the *extreme* impropriety of my travelling alone homewards from Leicestershire and down to Mrs. Paget's. The last time I went it was quite different as I had company the whole way there, and nearly all the way coming home. I do think Mrs. Paget will be disappointed but that is nothing to what some people will think of your permitting me to travel alone. If you have no *decided objection* I can get home very easily from here which will save you a great deal of trouble and expense on my account, besides I think I have trespassed quite long enough on my mother's kindness and yours in allowing me to stay already as long as you have done. I will however be guided entirely by you but I hope you will consider the objection which I offer *well*. When I was younger it did not signify so much but now I consider it very improper. Were you here you would see it in the same light as I do and I have been considering of it for some days and today I thought I must make up my mind or it would be too late. I hope you will answer me by return of post and if you allow me to return by Dundee I must write Mrs. Paget, but if you do not wish me to come home you must tell me what your plans are for me.

'Unless you have some particular reason for my staying, pray let me come home. My wish even allows me to think with patience of a sea voyage which of all things on Earth I consider the most insufferable.'

*   *   *

11 Sussex Gardens
18 June 1847

'John Ruskin will certainly be in Scotland to stay with Mr. Macdonald but you need not expect to see him at Bowerswell. He cannot come for various reasons and as you know Mrs. Ruskin would be miserable every moment he was in Perth or under our roof which would be much worse; it is extraordinary to me how a woman of her powers of mind and extreme clearness of understanding can be so superstitious. Mr. Ruskin has imbibed the same absurd ideas but their prejudices must give way some day or other surely as long as she keeps from Perth the thing will grow on her.'

That John had fallen in love with Effie during the last few weeks of her stay at Denmark Hill is clear from the letter already quoted: 'If I had known or thought of the truth (*about her age*) I wouldn't have waited an hour' but as she had given no sign that she regarded him as anything more than a friend, and he still believed she was younger than she was, he refrained from visiting Bowerswell during August and September though Effie was within easy driving distance. Instead he kept touch by writing to Effie's mother.

Crossmount, Pitlochry
1 September 1847

'You cannot but have thought it not a little strange that I should have passed through the main street of Perth and never waited on you—but I trust that you will not think I did so without cause, or without regret. You may suppose that I could not re enter Perth after the lapse of twenty years—and the various dispersion of all my *then* dearest interests in its many lovely localities, without feelings of pain which I should have been sorry to have intruded upon my friends—and indeed, the place and its neighbourhood have been to *me* so peculiarly and constantly unfortunate that I would not willingly associate any of my present pleasures with its hitherto ill boding scenes. I could hardly even express this to Mr. Gray —for I felt severe pain at the thought of either staying in Perth—or quitting it so abruptly—and I was hardly able to speak either to him, or to Mr. Melville Jameson—whom I was fortunate enough to meet in my short stay—nor did the depression leave me until some days afterwards—compelling me even to leave Dunkeld—where I had intended staying for a day or two—but where I found old recollections still too strong for me—Since I have been here I have only delayed writing to you in order that I might be able to tell you more decidedly how far I was able to appreciate your Scotland. I thought Dunkeld, and its woods, of singular loveliness,—being not a little surprised at finding laurels and Spanish chestnuts mixed with its birches and larches—nor was I less struck with the banks of the Tummel at Pitlochrie and Killiecrankie—and thoroughly bowed down before the perfect beauty of the *bell* heather—which does not grow in Switzerland—and whose opalescent softness and depth of colour are I think more lovely than the fuller flush of the Alpine Rose. But will you be so kind as to say to Miss Gray that I have only found five *Gentians* all

this time—and those of a most pitiful and disconsolate character
—and that I am therefore persuaded nothing but *her* care and
kindness could have brought my pet flower to anything
approaching the perfection with which she assured me it
adorned Bowers Well—and that I am content it should grow
under such auspices—provided it refuse—as it seems to me
very proudly and positively to do—to flourish any where else—
or without such peculiar favour and encouragements.

'I am afraid I must not say any more about the Scottish
mountains (as they are—by courtesy, I think, styled—) lest I
should get into disgrace like Mr. Harrison,—and—as I am not
sure whether my peace is yet made in the matter of Celimene
—I dare not run any farther risk.

'I can hardly say at present how long I may stay here—it will
depend on Mr. Macdds. movements whether I remain in the
east—or return by Ben Nevis—Loch Lomond, and Glasgow—
but—even if I should pass through Perth again—you must not
think ill of me if I pass in the same way. I sincerely hope we
may have the pleasure of seeing you all in England—or perhaps
that my father and mother may be able to persuade Miss Gray
to pay us another visit—and you to let her come.

'Miss Gray spoke of *honeysuckle* on Kinnoul. For all I can see,
the bees get all their honey *here* out of the *thistles*—'

In the middle of September he changed his mind and wrote
to Mrs. Gray:

Crossmount, Pitlochry
15 September 1847

'I should have answered your very kind letter before now, but
have been waiting until I could tell you whether I should be
able to return by Perth. I have determined to do so—and as I
do not think that my superstitious or painful feelings will be so
strong on a second visit as to compel me to run away from my
kindest friends, I must trust to you to tell me whether you
could conveniently receive me for a day in the course of the
week after next. I am afraid I may have some difficulty in
telling you the day, exactly—for I have some memoranda to
complete at Pitlochrie which make my stay there dependent on

BOWERSWELL HOUSE
A drawing by John Ruskin

the weather,—but I should not, I hope, be later than the close
of that week—Saturday the 2nd,—unless some accident should
intervene—or the weather be more ordinarily unfavourable—
Mr. Jameson mentioned to me some thoughts you had of coming
to Edinburgh—if the time I have named should interfere with
any arrangement of this kind—I should hope for the pleasure
of seeing you in Edinburgh.

'I have—people say—been unfortunate in my September
weather—and, assuredly, I have not found it available for any
sedentary out-of-door work.—and perhaps my impression of
the Highlands is somewhat more bleak and damp than by
rights it should be—I see that Miss Gray in her letter to my
mother, speaks of my blindness to the beauty of the *blue hills*—
I have seen only brown morasses. There is an ugly heap of peat
earth with stones in it, behind the house here, which takes
two hours work to get up, which they call Schehallion—and
the view to the westward from the top of it is very good—the
Glencoe ranges looking proud, and precipitous—but for the
rest—I have seen nothing in the way of hill which is not so
round and pointless—and nothing in the way of valley which
is not so mossy and treacherous—that I am getting a little tired
of a country where I can neither fix the top, nor find the
bottom. My admiration of the heather continues undiminished,
though the fire of it is fast going out—fading—like Miss Gray's
riband—(please tell her that she must at any rate grant me it
was ill chosen for *wear*—for there is certainly not sun enough
in Scotland to affect the health of a riband with anything like
a constitution) but I find a bell or two very bright still, here and
there, and hare bells, (rabbit bells for the most part, I think,
for the hares keep the hill top) very blue and graceful—and
another flower which I had not seen before—a white star with
a single heartshaped leaf—not to speak of Eglantines with hips
so bright as to answer most of the purposes of roses—and
barberries—which however—I can get better and brighter—
and I fancy sooner, in the south.

'The crags down beside the Tummel are very beautiful—
only they have an awkward, up setting way of standing on
edge—like an old saw—so . . . .
which renders the exercise of walking one of considerable

D

nicety—and small convenience—An Alpine torrent allows of
no such capriccios in its neighbour crags—but rolls and roars
them down into obsequious polish—so that the effect of the
Tummel crag scenery is, to me, a good deal like the paste-
board gulphs which they drop the extra bandit into, at the end
of an opera—I never can believe it is real:

'Pray—if you are thinking of going to Edinburgh—do not
let me interrupt any of your plans even for a day—as my time
is very much at my own disposal—If you are only going for a
few days, I would wait at Pitlochrie until you returned—for I
have a great deal to study about Killiecrankie, and the Highland air is good for me, though I should like it quite as well if—
occasionally, the supply of it were somewhat more limited—I
thought—last night, it would have blown the water out of the
Tummel, and the top off Schehallion.

'I am afraid—on reading my letter over—that Miss Gray
will be very angry with me—and will not accept my kindest
regards—but really—her Scotland has treated me very ill—
and if I were not "a good creature" I should say worse of it.'

He gives one reason for departing from his original intention
not to see Effie during the autumn in a letter to her father
written after they were engaged.

Princes Street, Edinburgh
17 March 1848

'As we were returning yesterday—together from Craig-
millar Castle, she touched upon a subject which has (most
unnecessarily as far as I am concerned)—caused of late much
uneasiness to both her and you. Had even the communication
which she made to me, been entirely unexpected by me, it
would have produced no other impression upon me than one of
gratitude for the candour and courage of the avowal—(accompanied of course—by such concern as I must ever feel for
whatever cause of anxiety may occur to you or Mrs. Gray). But
it was fortunate, as it happened, that I was able to set Effie's
heart at rest at once, by assuring her that I had known of the
unfavourable posture of your affairs at the time of my first

proposals to her: and even previously, and although not
certain of the extent of your losses—I had always been prepared
for, and partly believed the worst.

'I cannot state to you the exact time at which the reports on
this subject first reached my father: but he immediately
warned me that they were such as he could not distrust, and
this *before* my visit to you last Autumn. It was partly owing to
this information that I departed from my first intention of not
visiting Perth at that time,—and I find that I was right in
attributing, as I did, Effie's change of manner to me, in some
degree to this cause, though, not knowing how far she was
acquainted with the state of your affairs I could not venture to
question her, or endeavour to arrive at any certain conclusion
on the subject—My offer to her was however made sooner, on
this ground, than it would otherwise have been.'

The story, current after the annulment, that Effie's father
had kept secret his financial position, hoping for assistance
from John's rich father after the marriage, is thus shown to be
no more true than most of the stories circulated by the Ruskins
and their friends.

John had not disguised his feelings from his parents who had
by now not only abandoned their earlier attitude towards Effie
but, knowing the danger of frustrating their emotional son,
were eager to further his marriage with a girl who had, by her
beauty and character, won a warm place in their hearts during
her London visit.

Mrs. Ruskin could not, however, approve of her son's
proposal that Effie should accompany the Ruskin family on a
Continental tour so that, being continually in her company, he
could win her love, and wrote to him in September:

Denmark Hill
11 September 1847

'I think what your father has written to day ought to put you
entirely at rest regarding Effie's connections, as far as your
father and I are concerned I have not the slightest misgiving
on the subject. I have always heard from all acquainted with
them that Mrs. Gray's family in all its branches were highly

respectable and estimable, you know your cousin was some
weeks in Mrs. Gray's house and she always has spoken of Mrs.
Gray as a sweet, quiet, and sensible person, an excellent manager without bustle or conceit (I think her letter well and
judiciously written) and of Mr. Gray as thoroughly good
natured open and hospitable with excellent temper and warm-
heartedness, he has also shown that he possesses no small share
of common sense and judgement in the way he has improved
his fortune and brought himself and family into the best
society his neighbourhood affords—he has I believe at present
been overpersuaded by friends and brought himself into some
difficulties with Railroads—but he is very prompt—knows
business, and I have great hopes will see his way and pursue it
with steadiness and may not be so great a loser in the end.

'I think Effie considering her age inherits in no small degree
these good qualities with much of her Mother's sweetness—or
she never would have borne with such temper your attack on
her taste in the matter of the ribbon—never have continued to
wear what she was told did not become her—never have
maintained her opinion so stoutly against yours—there is more
of character shown in this matter than I think you are aware of
because you do not know how such things operate on female
minds generally—I hope to make you sensible of this soon to
your great satisfaction. Your father some years ago when Effie
was a mere child (the time she repeated your lines on Ch. Ch.)
dined with Mr. Gray at Bowers Well, and was much pleased
with the Style of everything (much superior to his sister's he
said) with the manners and appearance of both parents and
children—I think it is quite proper that you should see as you
return Mr. & Mrs. Gray in their own house, you could not leave
Scotland without seeing them and *Miss Gray*. I am going when
I write of her to give her sometimes her just title. We say
Effie and Effie until without knowing it we may lessen her real
value and consequence in our minds. To me she is a being of no
small importance when looked upon in connection with you.
My desire that you should marry is so strong that you may
hesitate to place any confidence in my judgement in this
matter. I need not tell you how much, and how deeply, it has
occupied my thoughts, and it is my fixed, decided, opinion that

your enjoyment and usefulness will be infinitely greater if you marry, than if you remain single, and that it is most improbable, you will in any class, ever meet with another possessing the qualities and gifts necessary for the comfort and happiness of a mind and character like yours in the same degree or at all equal to those which Effie really possesses—I will allow of your selfishness if you wish it, but that will neither prevent your being a good husband and a good father if God should bless you with children—As for your being like any of the persons you have named it is altogether out of the question. Both father and mother will be different and there is no fear but she will soon come up to your standard, after she is your wife unless you are unreasonable indeed. I do not know that there would be any thing very improper in Effie's going abroad with us unmarried, but neither am I satisfied that the doing so would be either proper or wise. If I were younger, or you had a sister, it would appear less marked. Another objection to this plan, in my opinion, is that you would be spending part of that happiness, which ought to be kept for your married life. You will see what your father writes on this subject, I do not like that he should be disappointed, and I do not like that your happiness should be deferred, I will do what you both wish, I think if Effie were sure of your regard and that you were not like to be parted again for any length of time she would be satisfied to remain quietly with me when I could not go about with her—Still it would be very different if you two could go about together with propriety in such excursions as were too much for your father and me.'

A Continental tour was not, however, necessary to bring to an end John's anxieties and doubts. They were dispelled when he visited Bowerswell in October.

On the third day he wrote to his friend, W. M. Macdonald: 'I love Miss Gray very much and therefore cannot tell what to think of her, only this I know, that in many respects she is unfit to be my wife unless she also loved me exceedingly. She is surrounded by people who pay her attentions, and though I believe most of them inferior in some points to myself, far more calculated to catch a girl's fancy. Still Miss Gray and I are old friends. I have every reason to think that if I were to try I could soon make her more than a friend and if, after I leave her this time, she holds out for six months more, I believe I shall ask her to come to Switzerland with me next year.'

His efforts to make her more than a friend were successful and the strength of his passion for the girl he had at last won will be seen in the letters written during their engagement which appear in the next chapter.

CHAPTER IV

Affection Rampant

WHEN Ruskin left London for his visit to his friend, Macdonald, his emotional state of mind was undermining his health but he returned home in the highest spirits with his health restored and for the next six months poured out his heart to Effie in a continual stream of passionate letters.

Ruskin's statement to Mr. George Macdonald that he had never been in love with Effie and that, not being in love with his wife, he had not claimed the usual relations because he believed he had no right to do so, and a statement in a recently published book that during the months he was writing the letters he was saying that it was impossible that he should love Effie and that not only did he not love her but loved someone else, can now be revalued.

The first of the letters that follow was written early in November and the last in March.

Denmark Hill
November

'I'm really a little vexed about the hair; but don't touch it—perhaps it will come all right again—better any way than artificial—I don't believe a word of what mama says about people's not caring for looks after marriage—I am only afraid—(only wait, and don't judge me till I have modified this confession) of caring too much. I am sure however that I shall be like Wordsworth in my *mode* of caring. See his two sonnets "to a painter"—"the visual powers—which hold their sovereign empire in a faithful heart".—You know I couldn't possibly help answering your letters to *me*—received at Leeds —though I felt as you do about the place—but though I had got one before, with E.C.G. this one was "Effie"—and I could never have borne to have received *two* without answering.

'Are you reading French. You know we shall want it next year, God willing.—I wonder what you will think of Couttet, —my friend and guide—and what he will think of you—I hope

you will come up to his idea in one respect—I was speaking to
him one day of a lady's having gone over a high snowy pass—
incredulously—"Qu'est ce que c'a fait? said he—elle est
nouvelle mariée—la première année, elles passent partout—
après—il leur faut une voiture! I really must'nt scrawl any
more—Dearest love.'

*   *   *

Denmark Hill
9 November 1847

'My own Effie—my kind Effie—my mistress—my friend—
my queen—my darling—my only love—how good of you—
and I can't answer you a word today. I am going into town with
my mother in half an hour—and have all manner of things to
do, first—but I am so glad that you have my letter speaking
about this very thing—Indeed I *never* will be jealous of you—
and I will keep that purer form of jealousy—that longing for
more love—within proper limits—and you will soon find out
how to manage this weakness—and perhaps to conquer it
altogether; I can't enter into details today—but indeed it was
anxiety and weakness of nerve which made me so fretful when
you were here—natural enough I think—and even then, I was
only jealous of *some* people—and that because I was hurt
by your *condescension*—it was, I think—at the root—more
pride than jealousy—I was speaking of large parties to my
mother yesterday for you—she said ''You would'nt like to see
her surrounded by a circle of gentlemen like Mrs. Liddell?''
''Indeed I should,'' I said.'

*   *   *

Denmark Hill
11 November 1847

'My Dearest Euphemia,
    'What a pretty name you have—I like to write it full, some-
times, it puts me in mind of old times—Do you recollect the
first time I ever called you ''Effie''—when I was frightened at
finding you practising in the cold drawingroom and stopped,
and begged pardon—and your giving me leave an evening or

two afterwards—What a luxury it was to call you Effie—and is—By the bye—you haven't told me anything about Captn. C.—and the happiness he looked forward to—Grant him *that* —but—I'm very sorry—I can't help it—don't be angry with me—I *would* rather he did'nt call you Effie any more! *please!*

'How difficult it is to be quite true—There was I, yesterday —making a great *merit* of telling you all that you asked—and if pretending that I ought to be rewarded for it—as if I were not dying all day long to tell you everything I am doing and thinking—and only too happy to be asked or to be listened to! My Mother bade me say—last night—when I read her the passage in your letter about her coming—that you would not have to wait so long for her blessing—for she blesses you and prays for you every day of her life.

'I think fortune is in my favour. You know we cannot be married in Lent—and Lent begins 8th March—or thereabouts—So that—don't think me selfish or without a conscience—you know *I* can't help Lent's coming in the way— nor the necessity for our leaving England in April—It's very terrible—but indeed you will have to fix some day before the 8th March—and I shall have to come to Scotland in February. My own love—Only two whole—unbroken—interminable months between us—if God permit.—

'You know—I often speak depreciatingly of myself. To show you that this is not affectation—I will tell you that—as I was talking with Sir W. Ross in the Academy—last Tuesday— I came to the conclusion that I was worth *three* of him—both in sense and in feeling—only he is a goodnatured person—and I like him, in a general way.

'That's all I can tell you today—I have letters to answer by the dozen—but shan't answer them, except by sixes and sevens.

'Evening. My Mother gave me a message for you yesterday —which I forgot! an important one, too, that you must not— though—of course—you will know this without her telling you —but it may be as well to remind you—that any dresses you may be buying for next year, had better be of the plainest kind— for travelling—of stuffs that will not crush—nor spoil, nor be bulky in a carriage—for you know we shall be *four*—and very simply made—you will only want one of any more visible or exhibitable kind—in case we might go to opera at Paris—or be seen a day or two here, before leaving. You may guess there is no *dressing* at Chamouni—the higher the rank commonly the plainer the dress—and it would be no use to leave handsome dresses behind you here, merely to find them out of fashion when you come back. You will not need them very warm— the climate of Chamouni is much about the same as that of Perth—morning and evening—but with hotter sun in the middle of the day—but have them close up to the throat—for fear of ice chills—*notice* this—which is *my* advice especially— and also—not to have the flounces *too* full—nor too *long*—it will not do to be exposed to chance of treading continually on your dress in going up hill—and the Swiss hills are steep, mind;—you had better have one dress quite cool—Geneva and Vevay are often as hot as Italy. For the rest—I need not say to you—knowing your good taste—not to have even your best dresses *fine* or expensive—Your beauty is conspicuous without the slightest adornment—and the least *over* dress would appear as if you *wished* to draw all eyes to you—it should be your study to dress if possible—so as to *escape unobserved*—while yet the dress—when it *was* observed—should be perfect of its kind —becoming—graceful—perhaps even—now and then—a little piquant—but never conspicuous. I don't know—but I have a great fancy that I shall ask you sometimes to put on your finest dresses when we are alone—and always your simplest when we are going into public.

'When we are *alone*—You and I—together—Mais—c'est inconceivable—I was just trying—this evening after dinner— to imagine our sitting after dinner at Keswick—vous et moi.— I couldn't do it—it seemed so impossible that I should ever get you all to myself—and then I said to myself "If she should be dull—if she should not be able to think but of her sweet sisters —her deserted home—her parents—giving up their chief joy —if she should be sad—what *shall* I do—And—if she should *not*—what shall I do—either—how shall I ever tell her my gladness—Oh—my own Love—what shall I do indeed—I shall not be able to speak a word—I shall be running round you— and kneeling to you—and holding up my hands to you as Dinah

does her paws—speechless—I shan't do it so well as Dinah
though—I shall be clumsy and mute—at once perfectly
oppressed with delight—if you speak to me I shall not know
what you say—you will have to pat me—and point to something for me to fetch and carry for you—or make me lie down
on the rug and be quiet—or send me out of the room until I
promise to be a good dog; and when you let me in again—I
shall be worse—What *shall* I do?

'Friday evening. I have been correcting the last sheets of M.S.
and am so tired. I couldn't do anything—except write to you—
I feel quite rested directly.

'I read the last page—no—stop—the one about the dress—
to my mother—and got quite into disgrace—she asked me how
I could possibly be so impertinent as to think you didn't know
everything you ought to get—that she only meant me to hint
that you needn't get dresses to be left at home—and that she
begged pardon for hinting so much as that—She said "you
would be thinking that we were afraid of your dressing too
highly"—and that it was very wrong of me to say anything—
But I don't think it was. I don't see how you could get your
dresses with comfort to yourself—unless you had some idea of
what I should like—and as you knew that I always *liked* to see
you in full dress—it was just possible that you might have
indulged me in this a little, contrary to your own taste—yet
now that I read it over—it does read abominably impudent—
I beg your pardon a thousand times, dear Effie: dress as you
think best—I never saw you but well dressed, yet—though—
for best of all bests—I am divided between the velvet knots,
and the plaid over the head,—in the garden, you know—
when you first came— No—the best of all bests was—that
night—the *wave*—but that won't do on *all* occasions.

'Mama desires me to say that, far from being able to tell
you how to dress, she wants you to come and tell *her*. She can't
please herself, and she wants you for a thousand things
besides.

'We are all going to Folkestone for a week—I shall hardly be
able to write you a word tomorrow—though I hope for a
letter—but after this—I trust I shall be free.

'I am a little ashamed of speaking so much of your fair face

—Effie—but indeed, when I search into my heart—it is not the features that I care for—it is the sweet—kind—half pensive—depth of expression which is the great charm. I have been intending a long time to tell you this—but reserved it for the philosophical letter—only I am afraid of your again beginning to think that I only love you "because you are pretty".

'Saturday. I have your precious letter—my love—I will write about March from Folkestone—D.V.—when I have thought over the matter a little to find out all that may be said in its favour—But how *can* you think of our "quarrelling"—or make resolutions in case of such a contingency.

'I am sure it is *physically impossible*—and this I say seriously. Fools may quarrel even when they love each other—or wise people quarrel, when they don't;—but we are not fools—: I think we are both reasonable people—with something more than the average of sense—and then we love each other—how deeply? Tell mama she may just as well think of our quarrelling *before* marriage—as after it.—I expect it is the likelier—or rather the less inconceivable—and I think we are just as likely to give each other up altogether, as to do *that*—

Ever my dearest—fairest—kindest Effie

Yours beyond all telling.'

*   *   *

Folkestone
21 November 1847

'My Dearest, Kindest Effie,

'I had your good—affectionate—condescending letter this morning and read it with deep thankfulness. My beloved lady—how *could* you think I would ever press you in anything painful to you—for my pleasure—All that I said about March was only in the event of my father's being obliged to travel early.—if he can delay his journey, I not only will not press you, but even should agree with you in thinking it better to delay our marriage till April—lest you should suffer from travelling in cold weather. I should be dreadfully anxious and frightened. We shall be better able to determine matters when we know more of his business arrangements—meantime take

my fondest thanks for your goodness to me. I felt, when I got
your Thursday's letter much like an unwise general—who
having pressed an advantage too hotly and too far, receives an
attack in front which compels him not only to abandon all that
he has gained—but his own position besides. You were not so
far wrong in your guess, neither. I *was* beginning to think—
"*February* is only just before March—if she would make me a
present of her hand on my birthday—how nice it would be!"

'I believe—my fairest—that when we are seen together in
public—I do not say that *all*—but that *most* of the felicitation
will be to *me*; and that I shall be thought far more fortunate of
the two—those who know us in private will, I sincerely trust
have come to congratulate us both—(as I am sure Uncle
Andrew and Aunt L. will. Aunt is an amusing aunt—is she
not? to find out that in two evenings only—and one of those a
great dinner—when I was talking art all the time—But I am
better at talking art than using it). But I am quite sure my
dearest, that no woman can help taking such pride in her
husband as would—if he loves her—stimulate him to eager
exertion—and that this fresh excitement acting on a mind
naturally fond of praise like mine would lead to great harm,
unless the feeling were checked in both by a strong sense of
principle—and of the falseness and hollowness of worldly
praise. Think over this subject. I have not the slightest idea
whether you are—at heart—ambitious or not—perhaps you
hardly know yourself—vulgarly or commonly ambitious I know
you are *not*—I am, or have been, at least—and I am particularly afraid of the embers of this unworthy flame being
rekindled. I do not mean to speak unworthily of a true—
earnest—humane—honourable ambition—that, I trust we
have, both of us; but I mean the mere love of selfish distinction
and praise. But pray—whatever you do—don't banish me to
those dreadful parties merely to have the pleasure of seeing me
look happy when I come home again—I won't go anywhere
where you don't go with me.—(I beg your pardon for writing
on these scraps—but I have nothing but foreign paper, besides
these—and I don't like to write on that—it tires the sight so—
in reading). So I must bid you goodnight—the rather too—that
I have read nothing yet, this Sunday—I must not make an

idol of you—and forget Him by whose favour I found you.
'I do believe that the most delightful hour of all the journey is
that of hope—the *first* stage *from Calais*. The two hours passed
rapidly among the breezy downs with their spots of sheep and
their rich brown cattle standing sideways on the slopes to
graze—their hides shining in the sun like—I don't know what
—something between velvet and polished old mahogany. I just
got back in proper time for afternoon service. The old vicar—a
sad example of the worst sort of monkish—sensual—idle—unable clergyman, gave us and bungled a boyish rhapsody which
made me angry. When I got out—the sun was just setting—
the sky was clear in the east—and I ran down to the beach to
soothe myself by seeing the moon rise. It rose large over the
sea, beside Shakespeare's cliff—nearly as large as the great cliff
itself;—the tide—its great worshipper—was rising with it—
and sobbed out its subjection—the sea gulls shrieked as if they
didn't know what to make of it—or thought the moon had got
into mischief—and had no business to be so low down—as low
as they, right down on the waves.

'It was half past four when I got in. I dressed—there was no
time to sit down to write before five.

'So I dined—and drawing close to the fire—with a book
in my hand—a book your Uncle Andrew had given me—I
began thinking whether I should write to my father or you
first. A little grave reflection determined me on the former—
and induced me to write rather a longer letter than I otherwise
should—lest I should feel—or he should *say*—that I neglected
him—now I had you to write to.

'That done—I looked for note paper—found the two scraps
only—filled them—thought it wrong to read nothing all day,
read some of Uncle Andrew's book—then some of Milner's
Church History,—over which I am grieved to say—I fell
asleep.

'I was waked by the winds shaking the window and wanting
to get in. I rose and looked out. The moon was oppressed
among fast flying cloud—and cast only a dim light on the sea—
whose surf was roaring and sighing alternately—like a thun-
dercloud with an asthma. I thought of going out to look at it—
and thought I had better not—thought of reading some more

history—and found I couldn't, then thought of going to bed, and did.

'It's past five—and I can't write any more now till I have read the new letter.

'$\frac{1}{4}$ to six—I've drawn the armchair and table close in, to the fire—and arranged the *candles*. Now for it. My Dear—dear— dear—dear Girl—I've found the leaf—only that, yet—and kissed it nearly to pieces—but what a letter—My Beloved. Now! I'm going to read it right through and I can't interrupt myself—even to write thanks—till I've done.

'I've only read half the first page—and here I am again— Oh my love—you are—how very—very—very—above all good—you are just an angel, and that's the least of it. Not to scold me for my querulous letter and to promise to tell me all! God bless you. It's a little thing to take so seriously—but you have made me *so* happy. Do you know—I'm almost crying. I've got down the second page now—but I haven't any more words—and if I gave you tears—I couldn't see to read—so I must try not.

'I've read it all, now, and its enclosures. I can hardly write a word—my hand—or heart I think it is,—trembles so—I have so much to say—and feel so feeble—My Dear Euphemia— your's would not have been the first letter that expressed sad thoughts in its joy—if I had not destroyed one that I wrote you about a fortnight ago—in which I spoke of *myself* with something of the same fear. And indeed there is no happiness which this earth can give—which has not such contingency of distress attached to it as might make us miserable from mere fear, if our hope were on this earth only—But if we have no certain hope beyond it—and an uncertain hope is I think the same as no hope, (in sacred things), the best that this life can give us is valueless—its end will come, and that a bitter one— And if we *have* a certain hope how little does it matter what happens to us here. I often think that even real Christians are deficient in power of realizing to themselves the utter insignificance of *Time*, as far as its happiness or suffering is concerned. Every moment brings with it a *duty*—whose performance—or neglect will be subject of joy or sorrow—perhaps endless—but for the pleasure of this life—think how much it

matters to us *now* what toys we lost or broke when we were
six years old—and then think what a different proportion a
score of years to six—and youth to childhood—bear from that
of eternity to 70 years—and of a glorified spirit to a mortal. I
really can hardly doubt that when men have become fanatical
it was not from over considering—or from too acutely perceiving, the difference between time and eternity—but from
misunderstanding what God required of them in *acting*.

'Tuesday morning. So far I had written yesterday—when
your loved letter—and loving—came in—but Ay di mi, how
far am I from realizing or believing anything of what I have
been writing—your letter set me on a throne—and put a
crown upon my head—I did not forget the Great King—for I
knelt down to Him—but it was to thank Him for the Throne
and the Crown—more, I am afraid, than to ask Him for
strength to please Him.

'You know—Lady Mine, we none of us believe these
things—at least to me it seems not—*I* do not,—cannot. If we
believed them—I do not know how we should act in this life—
we should *care* for nothing—neither ought we—but we should
be miserable in seeing those about us—those near and dear to
us—thoughtless:—And yet I know not—if we felt that God
had chosen us—and given us strength to do his will—we should
acquiesce in that will—not without doubt and sorrow indeed—
but with a conquering trust and gladness. But—I do not know
how it is with others, but with me the great obstacle is not so
much Unbelief of Heaven—as the want of desire of Heaven.
And herein by the bye, my parallel fails somewhat—for I have
supposed the Joys offered by the King to his servants to be
visible to them, and comprehensible by them. But the Joys
of Heaven are only feebly to be comprehended—and, even
feebly, only by those who have already begun to look to them—
One must begin to labour for them before one can desire them.
And—for me—I have no heavenly desires—I do not want to
leave this world. I have had too much of good in it, perhaps,
but I believe with many others the root of irreligion is the
same—they do not want heaven. I find no promise in the Bible
that excites my longing—All the happiness I have here is in
exertion—in progressive knowledge—accompanied by pain—

I cannot conceive an unlaborious happiness—a state of perfect knowledge as being happy—All the mystic descriptions of clouds and golden streets and glorified creatures have no charms for me—I had rather have an immortality among the snowy mountains and sweet vallies of this world.—And then when one's doubtful ideas of happiness are mixed with all the horrors of *certain* death,—and with the artful motives of disbelief which Satan sets before one continually, it is a *hard* thing to believe—Well might our Lord say "this is *the* work of God, that ye *believe* on him whom he hath sent."

'Evening. I have written too long of these things for one letter—it is becoming a sermon instead of an epistle—but I know you will not think me tiresome. I have been reviewing your letters tonight—I have got one, already—for every year of your life—and that's a *great many*, you know love—! though you are not so *very* old, I will allow. I believe the mistake I made—for I knew you were 12 when I first saw you—was in thinking that it was in '41 instead of in '40. As to your defence of yourself by saying that you are 10 years my junior—it is quite in vain—for I consider myself an *old gentleman*.—

'As a philosopher, I should wear a beard, by rights,—not a ferocious one—but a venerable one, curling at the ends. I only don't, because in the present disorganised state of society, beards are not generally indicative of wisdom.

'I have been thinking how long it will be before I know all your letters by heart. Not long—Yet I should *so* like to have them printed, in a little pocket volume—to carry about with me always. And so—love—you did not know how to tell me how heartsick you were! Do not you think that for once you might have told me to judge you by *myself*. Think—my Effie—what a difference between you—with brother and sisters—and many many—countless, friends about you—not to speak of Papa and Mama;—and me—alone here on the sea beach—. May not you—when you are heartsick another time tell me that you feel a little—a very little—as *I* do?

'I really must not go on. I never intended to write at night at all—and yet I cannot be happy till I have said a word or two. You say—you wish you could make me more happy—Have

E

you ever felt yourself *un*able to make me so—when you chose?—Very little will do it—Effie—*So* little!—a kind word— a touch of the hand—a little commission to fetch or do something—so it be for you—a single look—a smile—nay the mere sight of you—(Except when you are sitting in a corner— reading history—or with that peculiar expression about the Lips). Oh—Effie—that's what I have been going to ask you this month—Do tell me what that expression means! Do! It used to come on so suddenly, sometimes—Qu'est-ce que c'a veut dire! Goodbye. Only pray tell me what it means—or I shall be *so* frightened when I see it lest it should mean that I have been naughty.'

*   *   *

Folkestone
30 November 1847

'My Beloved Effie

'I never thought to have felt time pass slowly any more— but—foolish that I am, I cannot help congratulating myself on this being the last day of November—Foolish, I say—for what pleasure soever may be in store for us, we ought not to wish to lose the treasure of time—nor to squander away the heap of gold even though its height should keep us from seeing each other for a little while. But your letter of last night shook all the philosopher out of me. That little undress bit! Ah—my sweet Lady—What naughty thoughts had I.—Dare I say?—I was thinking—thinking, naughty—happy thought, that you would soon have—some one's arms to keep you from being cold! Pray don't be angry with me. How *could* I help it?—how can I? I'm thinking so just now, even. Oh—my dearest—I am not so "scornful" neither, of all that I hope for—Alas—I know not what I would not give for one glance of your fair eyes.— your fair—saucy eyes. You cruel, cruel girl—now that was *just* like you—to poor William at the Ball. I can see you at this moment—*hear* you. "*If* you wanted to dance with *me*, William! *If*!! You saucy—wicked—witching—malicious —merciless—mischief loving—torturing—martyrizing—unspeakably to be feared and fled—mountain nymph that you

are—"If!" When you knew that he would have given a year
of his life for a touch of your hand. Ah's me—what a world
this is, when its best creatures and kindest—will do such things.
What a sad world. Poor fellow,—How the lights of the ball-
room would darken and its floor sink beneath him—Earthquake
and eclipse at once. and to be "if'd" at by you, too; Now—I'll
take up his injured cause—I'll punish you for that—Effie—
some time—see if I don't—*If* I don't. It deserves—oh—I
don't know what it doesn't deserve—nor what I can do.

'I think I shall never be able to tell you what I intended—
how I hoped you might find pleasure in helping me—I must
tell you now—that you may find some way of atonement for
your "ifs" by doing good to somebody—As for poor William—
you can do *him* none now—there is but the coup de grace to be
given—the sooner the better—and the flower of Love lies
bleeding: to be borne in his bright plume—How long? Well—
this was what I thought—only I should tell you first—that as I
had confessed in my last letter to being fretful, and as I think
you have heard me say of myself that I was certainly not to
be put out of temper—I set myself diligently this morning
when I woke in the dark, to consider and determine the
difference between being "fretful" and being "out of temper".
I found however the distinctions run so much finer than I
liked—and the bounds of the parish so difficult to beat, in some
places, that I determined I wouldn't be fretful any more—if I
could help it—lest other people should say I was "out of
temper". This then was my thought—Methought—that your
exceeding fondness of, and acquaintance with, History, might
lead you to take some interest in the histories and associations
connected with the various edifices we should see abroad,—or
indeed anywhere. That, while I was drawing or measuring—
or going up on leads and tiles—and such places where you
couldn't come—(Such scrambles as I have had—Effie—Next
to an Alpine summit—an old church roof is the most exciting
thing in the world) you—in the aisle below—might be examining for me such written traditions of the place as were most
interesting—and that from doing this—you would gradually
come to take an interest in the expression—style and sculp-
tured histories, of the Architecture itself. Keen sighted as you

are, I think you would soon find great delight in deciphering inscriptions—interpreting devices—and unravelling enigmas. —Gradually I think you might become far, far my superior in judging of dates and styles—and from your interest in these disputable questions—you would gradually be led to examine and to feel the relative beauty—propriety—or majesty of this or that manner. I think the pencil which would at first be in your hand to copy a broken letter—or note the order of a series of sculptures—would gradually come to make its own unpretending little memoranda of a capital here—an ornament there—a quaint piece of costume—or a graceful line of mosaic—I think you would probably see me take up these memoranda with avidity—carry them farther—and make use of them—that you would gradually be encouraged to carry them further yourself—and that in a little time—no very distant one—things might even come to such a pass as that I should be able to say to you—"Effie—I want those three capitals—and a bit of that frieze—will you, *please*, do them for me while I go up to examine the vaulting?" And that you would do them for me with great pleasure to yourself, and with more neatness and accuracy than any architect!

'Now mind I do not *expect* this in the least—I do not wish you to try for it—nor to do anything in the least painful or that costs you an effort—In fact—if it were done with an effort, it would be ill done—I shall not even be grateful to you— (added) fancy! Not grateful! if it so happens—because I would not have it happen unless it gave you pleasure—But that if it should happen, you would be of the greatest service to me on a thousand occasions—and that we should have a subject on which our sympathy would procure us a thousand pleasures— is most certain, and I think it is *likely* to happen also—For you will have often to wait for me while I am examining cathedrals, by the *hour*—you may do it at the Inn—but in most cases—when it is not cold, I imagine it will be in the church— that you may see what I am about—see me getting my coat all white over, and creeping into crypts on my hands and knees, and into rood lofts and turrets by inexplicable stairs etc. Well, you will soon find—however much you may be delighted with the sensation of the thing at first—that one cathedral,

carelessly seen—is much the same as another—you will be
tired of sauntering up and down aisles—hearing fat priests
chanting dull bass discords—or watching old women mutter
over their beads. You will begin to ask me what I find so
interesting to keep me all that time. I shall instantly stop and
show you—as long as you will attend—I shall give you something to find out or to count—or to read for me—You will be
interested—whether you will or no—you will notice the same
thing when you see it in another church—you will find the
other church more interesting in consequence—so the thing
will go on—at least I think it most likely that it will. But if
not—you will have to pass many an irksome hour—for you
know I must go on with my *profession* and—while for a certain
time of the day—I shall always be entirely *yours*—to go and
be with you where you choose—yet for another part of the day,
and that—usually the largest—you will have to be *mine*—or
to sit at home.—So now you see what a thoroughly *selfish*
motive—besides many an unselfish one, I had for asking you
to take care of your sight.

'Wednesday. I was reading some of Kotzebue this morning—
a bad translation of what I thought a vile original. There, at any
rate is one thing, my love, in which you will often and often be
of use to me. I can read translations of German books *now*, and
when I come to a bit that I want to comment upon—I shall ask
you if it be rightly translated and get you to give it me better
from the original.—Ah—how happy it will be.

'I had a long long walk along the brow of the cliffs today.
Thinking of many things—among others of a letter of yours
that I was reading again last night—that good, sweet letter—
(what letters of yours are not?) where you say—"you *do* feel
happier when you are nicely dressed." How proud of you I
shall be—Fancy us—at the Opera again, together—We two—
and you with a little,—just a bud,—of orange blossom in
your hair—no more—And I shall see every one gazing at you—
and think—"Yes—you may look as much as you please, but
she is *mine* now, *mine*, all mine." And I shall have just the
little finger bent into mine where the hand falls where nobody
can see—and now and then you will turn away from the
stage and from the house and from all the world—and give

me, just one little look—for half a second?—And shall not I watch for it? and what shall I say for it when it comes? and shall not I look very much at the stage!—and shall not I know a great deal about the opera when it is all over?

'So I thought of that until I was ready to dance—partly with delight and partly with impatience—but dancing did no good —and in fact was much more likely to do a great deal of harm —seeing that I was on the edge of a chalk cliff some 300 feet above the beach—Ah—my sweet—here's another—dear— dear letter—The sun is setting softly over the sea, and rosy clouds are seen beyond the blue of it. I'll read it at once. Bless me—mortar coloured wax again! Ah—the sweet little round seal with the E—One kiss—and then—no, I won't break it— round it with the penknife—Ah mine own Effie—I have read it all through, quite to the end—and it seems as if you had been here for five minutes, and had gone away again—as the sun has set—and left me here, so sad—I really think your letters do me nearly as much mischief as good—I feel so blank and heavyhearted when I come to the end, and think—now it must be three long days before I get another.

'And this one is so very very kind and sweet: and yet it makes me so anxious. It's almost impossible you should escape that frightful influenza—and I must not come—yet—to nurse you—I can't say take care—for I do believe, with that thing, taking care is no use, and that you are just as likely to escape it by standing in the cold to read rambling letters—and taking showerbaths on the bridge—as any other way—But what *shall* I do—if I hear you have it!—If I hear you are in your room— can't write to me? I shall be coming down—certainly—so you had better not—And that frightful Hill of Kinnoul—Pray don't go up it again without someone—take Mr. Tasker or anybody—How curious—that we should both have the same foolish feeling about *twenty*. Do you know I had actually written something—a beginning of a sentence—about it—in one of these letters—and scratched it out—you will find the place if you look—The fact is—I have felt the loss of my own youth so dreadfully that I grudge every hour, now that keeps your youthful sympathy back from me—And—impatient though I am—I should not be fretful about the mere *putting*

off the thing—if you and I could be—five years hence—18 and
28—I could wait like Patience on a monument. But Time
won't wait—and do you know—I was taken in, a year—When
my mother said to me in October—last year—Only wait this
winter, John—and then you shall see her,—I consented
(though sulkily) because I thought you were only seventeen;
you know you corrected me only on your birthday.—if I had
known—or thought—of the truth—I wouldn't have waited
an hour—and much suffering I should have saved to myself,
and a little, perhaps to you—for, I don't know whether you
were or not—but you really *looked* distressed that night you
left Denmark Hill—And I was going to have said something
of this to you in my letter—and then I thought it would vex
you—and scratched it out. But were it not that I have deep
cause for thankfulness that things have ended thus—and
sooner than I *once* thought possible—and that you have been
preserved to me against so many adverse chances—I *could* feel
very bitter—comfortless regret at having lost the precious
intercourse of promised and increasing affection—and the
sight of you—in your *girlish* beauty—which I might have had
for three years back. Neither can I say to myself—as people
commonly do—that "all is for the best." That depends entirely upon the circumstances of the misfortune coming from
one's own fault or not—there is much in this world which is
not for the best—which is permitted as a punishment for folly
or for sin—and which—though it may be right receiving of it,
turned to good—is for the present assuredly evil. But I comfort
myself—not only by thinking how far more fortunate I am
than thousands—(think of poor William—losing you altogether, and that for no *fault* of his own—no folly either—but
because he *cannot* ask you.) and not only by thinking how
absolutely and without need of comparison fortunate I am in
winning you yet so young—when it is still time, I hope—to
recover by your kind influence that morbid tendency in me
which has come upon me by being without such a hope so
long—but also by endeavouring to convince myself of that of
which I spoke to you the other day—the slightness and worth-
lessness of all earthly pleasure—forgive me for speaking this
way—as if I had met with a great *misfortune*—I hardly know

how great a misfortune it may *yet* turn out to be—that I was
not permitted to engage myself to you long ago—it would at
any rate have saved me from much loss of health—a loss which
I think it unlikely I shall ever altogether recover—and it
would have given me two or three years of happiness—which—
come what may now, are *lost for ever*—irremediably lost—and
three years of human life—spent thus—or thus—in Paradise—
or in thorny ground and barren—*are* something—humanly
speaking—But divinely speaking—and in God's sight, they are
not. They are *nothing*—and so I strive to consider them—first
because it does no good now to regret them—secondly—
because it is right and just so to think—and that was what I
began to think—and that was what I began to meditate upon
this morning after terminating my dance upon the top of the
cliff—very seriously—and I was going to have taken up your
denial of the propriety of my word "scornful"—and tried
whether I could not hold my own in that matter—and so I
will, tomorrow—but I am at the end of my third sheet—and
have been serious long enough—Only—whatever philosophy
I may bring to my aid, of this severe and stoical kind—pray do
you still maintain the other side of the question—and act as
if I were no philosopher at all—by receiving me—that is—at
Bowers Well as soon as you and Mama *possibly* can—and by
naming a day as close as close can *possibly* be upon Easter
Sunday. For you know my Father's birthday is the 10th of
May, and we must—God willing—be at Denmark Hill for
that—Therefore *yours*, which is Sunday, will be the last day
we can spend among the lakes—Monday and Tuesday we
must allow for getting home—so—even at the best we cannot
have more than a week among the lakes, and that is very
little—however we shall have better hills and lakes in
prospect, and perhaps a week—or—including travelling days—
a fortnight, is as long as it would be wise in us to trust
ourselves with each other alone—at first—lest we should
quarrel!

'Then we may stop in Switzerland—or go on to *Venice* if we
like—I said I should be afraid—just as I said in almost my first
letter that I would not take you abroad alone—The new
happiness, new anxiety,—and excitement of travelling, are too

much for most people—and in the course of my travelling on
the continent I have heard—of oh—such and so many sad
things happening on these bridal tours. Still if I find that I have
my senses about me at all (which I do not think likely)—and
that you are strong and well, I do not say I will not—but it will
depend upon your feelings, and my Mother's advice. Mama's
plans about Chamouni are just mine. You must always have a
mule, and Couttet—Couttet is engaged already for the summer—Then I walk beside you—and we go to all manner of
happy places—You could not go about without a mule—not
but that there are some places where I hope to take you where
you can't go *with* one—but not many. I am afraid my *high*
climbing is over—I could not be happy now—even if I were
not kept—as I shall be, by my love—to your side—I should
now be nervous and fearful—for your sake—in places which I
should have thought nothing of, last year—and when one is
once nervous—c'est fini.—Besides I really should not like you
to see me coming down from the high snows—my face *burned*,
literally scarlet—You may well talk of the Kalydor—but it
must be for *me* there—that it is wanted. Then the costume:
Fancy—first—me with a huge pair of dark blue—double
glassed—spectacles. Over these—over the whole face, a green
gauze veil—doubled, and fastened down in the waistcoat—
Then a broad straw hat on the top of all—tied tight down with
its flaps *over the ears*—by a handkerchief over the crown of it—
tied under the chin! Many a hard days walk have I had—
so accoutred—enough to frighten anything in the world
but Alpine Sheep—whom nothing frightens—How pleased
you will be the first time you see them trotting from far
away over the snow to come to you and poke their noses into
your hand.

  'What can keep you from sleeping my pet—All night—
too! Now pray—pray don't—it is very bad indeed of you—
what are you so anxious about—one would think you were
miserable at the thoughts of April. But do not write me long
letters after sleepless nights—I don't know what you call
rambling—I think you never wrote me such a sweet one—so
close written too! But don't—after these bad nights. If you go
on that way—I shall come in March—! Send me the imitation

Brussells lace, please. Love to poor little Alice; tell her I hope she will soon be better.

'Ever—dearest dearest Effie, My Effie:

'—Your wearying—happy—devoted servant,

'J. Ruskin.

'—Ah—my mysterious girl—I forgot one little bit of the letter—but I can't forget *all*, though "a great many things."

'My heart is yours—my thoughts—myself—all but my memory, but that's mine. Now it is cool—as you say—to give me all that pain—and then tell me—"Never mind, I won't do it again." Heaven forbid! How could you—puss? You are not thinking of saying that you have "been thinking about it—" or "writing to a friend"—and that you won't have me now! Are you?'

*   *   *

Denmark Hill
15 December 1847

'My Dearest Effie,

'Two whole days—and the greater part of a third—without writing a single *word* to you! What *will* you think. However— you were once four days without saying anything to me—I mean, even without preparing the least bit.

'I had to write to mama today to thank her—why did you let her have pen and ink, Effie!—I am frightened out of my wits—Indeed she should not have written such a letter so soon. But it *was* such a delightful one, dear Effie. It says you are looking so well—and so happy,—and that you love me very much; and it says that mama has no fear for you in giving you to me, and that she would let you come and visit us now—if it were right! I think I could say something in my cause—and against the general principle of caring what people would or will say—what would it matter what they said—but I could not now ask you, seriously, to expose yourself to the winter sea and winter nights, merely to indulge my impatience. I don't at all know how I could bear the thought of your being at sea— alone—now—I should be thinking of Paul and Virginia—and all manner of fearful things—But let me come soon, love—

EFFIE GRAY
At the age of eighteen. A pencil drawing by G. F. Watts, R.A.

will you? Uncle Andrew has a little redeemed his character in
a letter I got a day or two ago—for he seems never to have
thought that I should *stay away* from you—though he *did*
think the *marriage soon*. He says he used to think himself
"half killed" when he was three weeks away. I believe the
man has some human feeling about him, after all. I begged
mama to thank you for your last letter—it is all just as I
thought it would be.—and—for your comfort—you may think
yourself happy if you get out of Perth without doing any more
mischief—and really, now, it is *not fair*. So long as a young
lady has her hand free, if people like to run the risk of coming
near her—she cannot help it—they have their chance,—and
have no right to complain if they lose it. But you know, *now*,
my sweet, you are neither more nor less—stay—I don't mean
that—for more you are—and a great deal more—but still you
are a very sufficient and entire *man-trap*—you are a pitfall—a
snare—an ignis—fatuus—a beautiful destruction—a Medusa
—I am sorry to think of anything so dreadful in association
with such a dear creature—but indeed—people ought to
approach Bowers Well now as Dante did the Tower at the gate
of the city of Dis.

'They should never venture, unless they have a friend to
put his hand over their eyes—or they are lost men—. To be
blindfolded at the bottom of the hill is their last chance,—their
only one. I would not jest with you, but that I think you must
have had quite enought sorrow lately—believe me I feel for
you—you must have suffered very much in being compelled to
give so much pain and in parting from your old friends—and
I feel for *them* still more—you may well say how much some
people have to suffer in comparison with others. Still, I believe
that most people have their share some time—if not in priva-
tion or bodily suffering, it comes in discomfort or discontent—
or in sorrows of the affections—. How enviable most people
would think *me*—yet you know I have had some share of acute
pain, and in general feeling, *before* you took pity on me—my
boy George was the happier of the two. It made me question
myself very seriously when I heard of these two grieved
hearts—whether it was in my power to trust that the one
which you had chosen was worth the sacrifice—I wonder if

you will ever look back—and think that—. No—that you will
not, I am sure—and it needs nothing to make me try to be all
that I can be to you and for you—indeed I will do my best.

'Thursday morning:—We had your delightful letter to
Mama this morning—Never write, my pet, when you are the
least tired—I will never think you are forgetting me—but I
must claim the same faith from you,—for I cannot write so
much here as I could at Folkestone.

'And so poor Harvey Duncan is really gone.—Now are you
not a terrible creature, Effie—to serve Aunt Jessie's[1] three
brothers so—one after another—Kill them off by computation!
—I don't know anything dreadful enough to liken you to—
You are like a sweet forest of pleasant glades and whispering
branches—where people wander on and on in its playing
shadows they know not how far—and when they come near
the centre of it, it is all cold and impenetrable—and when they
would fain turn, lo—they are hedged with briers and thorns
and cannot escape, but all torn and bleeding—You are like a
wrecker on a rocky coast—luring vessels to their fate—Every
flower that you set in your hair—every smile that you bestow—
nay—every gentle frown even—is a false light lighted on the
misty coast of a merciless gulph—Once let the ships get fairly
embayed and they are all to pieces in no time—You are like a
fair mirage in the desert—which people follow with weary feet
and longing eyes—until they faint on the burning sands—or
come to some dark salt lake of tears—You are like the bright—
soft—swelling—lovely fields of a high glacier covered with
fresh morning snow—which is heavenly to the eye—and soft
and winning on the foot—but beneath, there are winding
clefts and dark places in its cold—cold ice—where men fall, and
rise not again—And then you say you "don't know how it
is—"—No—there's the dreadfulness of it,—there's the
danger—Ah, Effie—you have such sad, wicked ways without
knowing it—Such sweet silver under-tones of innocent voice—
that when one hears, one is lost—such slight—short—inevitable—arrowy glances from under the bent eyelashes—such
gentle changes of sunny and shadowy expression about the
lovely lips—such *desperate* ways of doing the most innocent

[1] Effie's aunt, Mrs. Jameson

things—Mercy on us—to hear you ask anybody "whether they take sugar with their peaches"?—don't you recollect my being "temporarily insane" for all the day afterwards—after hearing you ask such a thing—and then all *that* is the least of it—but you are such a good girl, too—and so sorry for all the harm you do—and so ready to like everybody, in reason,—and so surprised when you find they don't understand reason—and so ready to promise after you've half-killed them or driven them mad, that if they won't mind that *once*, you "won't do it again", and so everything that you ought to be, and can be—, that I think you ought to be shut up in an iron cage—or in one of those things which you have got in the Perth Tolbooth— and not allowed to speak to or see anybody—until you are married. A strict convent might do—bye-the-bye—if there are any near Perth.

'Evening. Thursday.—I should have written more to you to-day—but—as usual was interrupted.

'I have been trying to find mama's book—and putting my bookcase in order to-day,—not much done—nor anything found, yet—but I find myself sadly *put out* by my new plans, Effie—I don't exactly know where I am to live, now—and what books are to go to the furnished house—or what is worth while to do here—I know not—I wanted you so, to help me— Certainly I have not room here for half my things—unless you can show me some better way of keeping them. I am always going to be orderly, some day—when I am "older and wiser" —for, though you reject with so much scorn the idea of ever being either the one or the other, I can't help admitting the probability of the first—and expediency of the second. I feel just about as I ought to have felt at 18. If I didn't know how old I was, I should guess that—Ah—my dear Effie—you say we can't expect to be always taken care of—I know we can't— and that's just why I want to be, while we *can*. It is *so* nice, Effie, not to have to take care of oneself. And yet, I must confess to you, that I have had more misgivings since I came home this last time, than before, about your being *quite* so happy as I had hoped—until we are indeed alone—There are little things which often sadden me now, in my father and mother—Still—I am always happiest when I am most dutiful

—and although you may be assured, Effie love, that I will not sacrifice my wife's comfort in any degree to an exaggerated idea of filial duty—still, I think you will find you can give so much pleasure on this journey by very little self-denial, that you will not in the end have reason to wish it had been otherwise planned. Kind they will be to you—as to me—and they will have the same feeling towards us both. My mother was saying but the day before yesterday that she was glad we should by this delay till the end of Lent—be enabled to have the pleasure of seeing the exhibitions—etc—"and taking our child with us" meaning you. The little things that will be drawbacks will be little disputes which we shall not be able to prevent, not with us, but between the old people—about what there ought to be—or ought not to be—and such little wants of sympathy as you can better fancy than I describe—however much they love us and yield to us, and that they will—almost everything. And remember love—we owe them *a little*—all our present happiness—and our future.

'Friday morning—My dearest girl—I have your little note but it has put me so out of heart that I can't write any more just now.—You are a dear affectionate—gentle—feeling creature—My poor little Effie—Oh that I were but with you— I *do* think that your headache would be better if you could lay your head upon my breast.—Mine own,—I am so sad—Well— three months more, and then—I shall be near you at any rate with God's Blessing—I can't write any more—but I hope to have better news tomorrow—this has been a sad week. I have sent you—as this letter is not long enough—one of Roger's, and one of my friend Henry Acland's—You need not send them back—so that you keep them carefully.

'God be with you—dearest'

*   *   *

Denmark Hill
18 December 1847

'My Poor-dear Effie

'George's letter—received this morning before I went out— was not the best in the world to go out to breakfast upon—

however—I should have been worse if I had got none—It's no
use telling you how sorry I am—such things must be—but I
do wish you would put off having any illness till I can nurse
you—I do believe I shall make you nearly as well as you me—
and that's very well indeed—though I say it—it is very hard
that I can't be of any use to you, now; and very provoking that
I happened to be so long in writing this week, as you can't have
any letter till tomorrow—You see—on Monday I came up
from Folkestone and had no time to write all that evening—on
Tuesday I got your long letter—but was all day in town—and
interrupted on Wednesday till it was too late to write anything
worth sending. I will send you just a little line every day till
you are better—(only you know tomorrow no post leaves
London). I have two messages from my mother—which I must
deliver quickly lest I should forget. The first, that she wanted
you on Thursday excessively,—when Stavordale came, and I
was out—for she thought you would have done the honours
for her so delightfully—and so delightedly; The second that—
(I having hinted to my mother—as a little bit of foiblesse on
your part of which—somehow or another—I had been
possessed—that you were very fond of lace,) she would be very
much obliged to you if you would let her know by me, quickly
whether there is *any* kind of lace which you want, just now,
and which could be better got in London than in Perth—and
if so—to tell her the width that you would like it—and how
much. I hope by the time this letter reaches you—you will be
up—and able to tell me.

'—I thought it a pity that the ladies mentioned in Mr.
Rogers' note should lose their lives—and therefore *went;* Mr.
Rogers' protegees are usually young—and as pretty as he can
choose—so that I was sadly disappointed to find two old people
in ugly bonnets. They expressed great pleasure at meeting
me—I bowed—but as I didn't *know* who they were—and didn't
see anything about them to my taste—and as everything else
in the room was in excellent taste—except they and their
bonnets—(not excepting by-the-bye—my own waistcoat—in
particular, and appearance, in general)—I couldn't say anything about the pleasure being reciprocal. I should say however
that I was first in the room—and that Mr. Rogers looked very

well—very happy—and very kind—after a little chat about
Scotland (which I began to abuse—and did—a little, only
Rogers being deaf—didn't at first hear what I said—and when
he put his hand to his ear—I thought it a pity to say illnatured
things in such a confidential way—and so modified the mischief—until it was neither here nor there) he asked me
"whether he had ever inflicted his works on me"—I wasn't
imaginative enough—whatever Acland may say—to invent a
proper answer—and rather than say a commonplace—I said
simply—No—So he brought down the two volumes—Poems,
and Italy—proofs of the illustrated editions—and wrote my
name in both—"from his sincere friend the Author"—
Now—Effie—I have been intending among other books—for
a long time—to send you the "Poems"—and should have done
so soon—but as I have now two copies of them already—I think
it will be wiser to *buy* other books—(for we must be prudent
even in our presents—love) and when you come here—I will
give you my *present* copy—the one I have loved so much—and
learned so much from—you will not like it the less for that—
Only I cannot send you that just now—because it was *given*
me—by Mr. Telford—and must not therefore be sent out of
the house—But it must be yours—for of *all* the books that I
know—it is the most *entirely* fit for a Lady's constant companion—its grace—dignity—truth—sweetness—perfect and
high taste—stand altogether alone.

　'—Did you ever open—in my copy—if you did you must
remember—those sweet lines—

>　　Across the threshold led—
> And every tear kissed off as soon as shed,
> His house she enters—there to be a light
> Shining within, though all around were night,
> A guardian angel o'er his life presiding—
> Doubling his pleasures, and his cares dividing,
> Winning him back—when mingling in the throng,
> Back—from a world we love—alas—too long—
> To fireside happiness—to hours of ease—
> Blest with that charm—the *certainty* to please.
> How oft her eyes read his!—

'There is more—but as it speaks of a wife's *subjection*—I won't quote it—though it is very sweet—too—. Well—when I had received this gift—to me a very precious one—came the two dying ladies—I am afraid they were only doing it after the fashion of the Irish members on the floor of the House of Commons—I don't know anything about them—as I said before—except that one of them was somebody's daughter!

'Now that's frightfully tiresome—there's somebody come wanting me and I mayn't be able to write another word—if I get up again—I'll open my letter—but if not—I will write on Monday—that at any rate.

'Dearest—dearest love—Make George write me a bulletin *every day*—please—We will drink your *health* at dinner today.

'Ever—in much discomfort—

'Yours devotedly'

Ruskin was sixteen when he was first introduced to the poet Samuel Rogers by another poet Thomas Pringle who took the boy into the presence 'as a sacred Eleusinian initiation and Delphic pilgrimage'. Thus, with pomp and ceremony, began a firm and lasting friendship to which Effie Gray was admitted when she came to London.

Denmark Hill
19 December 1847

'My Dear—Dear—Effie

'I have been wearying so, for you—today. I always do on Sundays, but I have been up and down the house and in "my lady's chamber" literally—up in your old room—and poking about the head of the stairs, and trying to fancy that I am waiting for you—and that you are just coming out of your room and we were to go down arm in arm—as we used to do—(do you recollect my getting a scold—one day—for waiting for you—and being too late to say grace)—and then the idea of your being far away and ill came so pitifully upon me.—I trust I shall have better news tomorrow morning,—it was very tiresome that George's note came on Saturday—and how came he to put it off till he was "going out to dinner" so as not to be able to tell me anything?

F

'I don't know how I am to get over these four months at all. Even my mother is getting more impatient than she can well bear—and she begins telling me that Lent is neither here nor there! I wish it were *here* I am sure;—but it isn't—I know that well enough—and I am afraid it will be there—when I don't want it. But you say—my pet—that you would like to be alone with me a little longer—You know there's but one way of managing that—I should be very sorry if my affection for you were of a character which would in any wise render me less fit for any religious duty. I've a good mind to ask you to take me early in April—Will you?

'And yet—don't agitate this with yourself yet—I am a selfish—abominable—creature—(—all men are—I suppose— sometimes)—to torment you with all my feelings—vacillating as they are between this weary yearning for you—and a sort of half conscience—for my conscience does not speak clearly in this matter at all.

'How strange it will be—when I bring you into this house again—how differently placed with regard to us—From a sojourner—doubtful how long she ought—or how long she would care—to stay—become mistress of all—and such a beloved mistress too—For let me tell you, Effie, you haven't any idea how much you will have it your own way— You will find that you *may* stir the fire, indeed! *I* at least am not to call my self *myself* any more—so my mother says— She said the other night—When Effie comes, if *she* and *I* don't keep *you* in order: I shall wonder! we'll lead you such a life— if you don't do everything that is right!—No moderate expec- tations—at any rate—Then—I am to remember always— says my mother—that "what's *yours*, is *hers*, and what's *hers*, is her *own!*"—Everybody seems to expect as much from you— Lucy brought me in a flower the other day—which I wouldn't admire—there was an overblown camelia in it which I said was just like a great shuttlecock—Ay, said Lucy, I only wish *somebody* was here; *they* wouldn't let you say such things! I said, I wished somebody was here too—whether they let me say such things or not. But will it not be nice when we come up the steps arm in arm, and I give you into my mother's arms —and when she has held you a little—she will give you back

into mine—and I shall welcome you with such a long—long
kiss—and then we shall sit down for a wee bity in the library—
you in your old chair—then we will go to every room in the
house—No—the servants must all come to pay their respects
first—and you will see many a thankful, face,—love,—and
hear many a blessing—spoken lowly—and then we will go to
every room in the house—and when we go into your old one—
where we parted—we will kneel down together—shall not
we—We shall have something to thank our God for—and to
ask him for. So we will come down again—I don't know what
we shall do—what *I* shall do—for joy—(if all is well)—and
that evening—if it be fine—as it *must* be—I hope;—we will
have a walk in the acacia walk—where you said once—that
you saw "our paths were separate—you must go one way—
and I another"—and I said—Nay Effie—Who knows? I felt
then, that it could not be but that we should love each other—
I dared not say what I felt—but it seemed to me, the moment
I saw you—as if we were betrothed—and nothing could
separate us. Ainsi soit il!

'Monday morning—Thank God—I have your note—my
sweet I trust you did not hurt yourself in writing it—it was a
little too long to be written with a pink and white face and
upon beef tea. I have been looking at the pink and white
camelia to see if it will help me to fancy my poor little Effie—
but you must be much prettier—

'—And so I am to have a lecture about Confidence—Well—
I shall like it so much—But I must give you a little more text
for it first—I don't at all agree with you (!) that confidence
must be asked—not proffered—on the contrary I think it
should *never* be asked— It should be a relief to the person
giving it—a charge to the person receiving. The grace of it and
joy depends on its voluntariness—one should say—pray let me
speak to you and unbosom myself to you—not—on the other
hand—"Tell me what is the matter with you." There is a
chance of the imputation of curiosity in the latter case.—
Between friends—lovers—husbands and wives—parents and
children—nothing should ever be asked—It should be known
that the one is always ready to *hear*—and understood, that it is
both the pleasure and duty of the other to *tell* whatever is their

own to tell—In all these relations it must often happen that
things which cause us great concern must yet be kept secret,
because they are other people's—not ours—and this is another
reason why confidence should never be asked nor exacted. I am
ready to admit that a want of confidence between parent and
child is less dangerous—and in most cases, more unavoidable,
than between husband and wife but I think that the ideal of the
perfect parental relation is that in which the child both can and
does tell everything, of its *own*—in which—in all cases it
avails itself of the judgement, and rejoices in the sympathy of
its parents. That there should be a reciprocal [word missing]
would be *wrong*. The Parent ought not to have to seek his
child's advice—nor ought the child to be oppressed with the
Parents care—Besides—an old person ought to be able to
understand a young one *perfectly*—as a young one *ought not* to
be *able* to understand an old one—If the aged have made a
right use of their years—they must be incomprehensible in
some measure to the young. I never asked for my parent
confidence—What I know of their early life has not made me
wish to know—or think it necessary for me to know more—I
have no curiosity—and not much interest—less I believe than
I ought to have. The confidence on my part has been *nearly*
complete—and where it is not complete—it is either my fault
or theirs—mine for not liking to be blamed—theirs—for not
being able to sympathize with, or reason respecting, my condition and my objects. I understand what you say about
school—but I don't see what you *could have* to confide, then—
still I am ready to admit that—not having been in the habit of
being communicative—you might have felt no need of support
or of confidence last autumn—and I believe it is only selfishness
on my part which makes me wish you had told, not indeed *all*
that passed between us—for that I agree with you in thinking
should be sacred between us two—but something of what I had
said—and something—or all—of what you had *felt*. But it
wasn't "temporary insanity", was it, love? That's what I want
to know,—

'—Ah—cruel Effie—How I *bore* with your treatment of me
on Kinnoul I can't conceive—I really think I *must* be a good
creature. Not to take my arm—and I to walk on quietly and

bear it—I ought to have turned back at once and said I would go back to mama—and done it too, and told her plainly what was the matter. I did not get far in my account of the breakfast the other day—but all that is interesting I shall get told, bit by bit—I was just where the ladies came in—wasn't I—Of course—when they came in, the conversation turned upon youth and beauty directly—as being matters, I suppose—in which they hadn't the slightest personal interest.—Mr. Rogers who has a way of walking up and down across his fire, said that women were much too apt to take a man's opinion of himself— that they too often—therefore—fell in love with coxcombs— that if a man had only courage—and *walked* well, and would cross a chasm in a drawing-room when nobody else would venture—he possessed a great power with women—I thought —if that be so—I mustn't be so modest with Effie—I must try and hold up my head—next time—but really I do *not* think that *she* would have fallen in love with a coxcomb! Mr. R. then said that Will—mere force of will, would do a great deal—If a man is *determined* to get a woman—he generally may! Then— he instanced as an exception, the failure with Miss Coutts—of the gentleman—whom we are now waiting for—as he has come from Madrid to us, we *must* wait for him; did you ever hear Lady ——'s answer to him—when he was saying one day that "he wished Miss C. was poor" "That has been tried before, Mr. Milnes, without the smallest success."—A pause ensued—to break which, Rogers took up a book printed for private circulation which had been just sent him—of little canzonets—sonnets—etc—saying it was not bad—he read us one "to a discarded bouquet"—of which the first stanza I cannot recollect rightly—but the second

> But why make thee live on? Mistaken
> Such kindness, I own, with a sigh—
> The thing she has worn—and forsaken
> Has nothing to do—but to die—

was agreed on all hands to be pretty—and rightly expressive of the feelings of bouquets on such occasions—*My* bouquet was not discarded—you know—but received again into favour —and thus twice honoured—and ever since, beloved;—it would have been a weak and base bouquet to have thought of dying. Its colours are quite bright still—

'Mr. Milnes not coming—we gave him up—and went down to the breakfastroom where the two ladies being felicitously placed between Mr. Rogers and me—and occupied in sugaring their coffee to their liking—may be left till tomorrow.—for really I can't write more, today—except only my opinion that there *is* certainly a worse hand than mine in the world—and that's your Uncle Andrew's—with the additional disadvantage of being intolerably difficult to decipher—which mine is *not*. Can you make out the small sentence, for me—the half sheet— above Blacket place!—and if you can—you may as well tell Uncle not to write you Phemy. or Pheny—worse still—he might as well say Feeny—which is a kitten's name at once— Did you ever hear Mr. Harrison speak of his little six years old Octavia. He was calling to one of his Kittens—Here—Kitt— Kit—Kitten. It's no use calling "Kitten," said Octavia— indignantly, They stick themselves up for Cats!

'—Goodbye—I will send another line tomorrow—

'Ever—dearest love—Your own disconsolate

'J. Ruskin.

'Pray get better fast. Fasting very good—beeftea very nice for everybody—Love to Papa and Mama—and sisters—*not* to George—for having gone out to dinner when you were ill— He should have stopped at home and taken beeftea sympathetically. I shall,—always—I'll never dine when you don't. Kind regards to Uncle and Aunt,—and to Uncle A. when you can make him out—and are writing—'

*   *   *

Denmark Hill
22 December 1847

'My Dearest Love

'Io—Triumphe—I have found Mama's book. Is not that a sign of increased habits of order—that it is found and sent at last after thrice forgetting and three months search!

'—Being in love with you does me so much good—dearest—

I am really beginning—now that my heart has got into its place—to put everything else into its place. All that I shall *want* to put into her place, soon, will be You—and that's, ever beside me—

'We had such a noble sermon from Mr. Dale yesterday—it was St. Thomas's day—what a sweet thing it is to obey our church in remembering these holy apostles at set times! The memory of the just is indeed *blessed* not only by—but to, and in its work and power upon, all generations.—The sermon was naturally from the gospel of the day—the incredulity—but Mr. Dale set it in a light, to me, new, true and lovely. If you look back to some of my letters—you will find mention several times—and expression—too—of the *Incredulity* peculiar to *love*—the incapability of believing in its own joy or hope which is greater in proportion to the intensity of that joy. Mr. Dale first spoke of this—as—though not an excuse—yet in all probability a palliation in the eyes of his Master of St. Thomas's doubt—seeing that this apostle was as eminently distinguished by his *love* of his Master's Person, as by his disbelief of his resurrection. We do not enough recollect the manifestation of his character in the XI of John—in that when the other apostles plainly shrank—and endeavoured to dissuade our Lord from going into Judea—(v. 7.) it was St. Thomas who took the lead of all in his reckless and passionate devotion— "Let *us* also go—that we may *die* with him." while at the same time—in this very despair—and again in v. 5. of the 14th ch. he seems to have been behind the other disciples in his comprehension or acknowledgement of our Lord's Divinity. Join the operation of the intense affection and its *vehement* desire to be assured of the truth of what was more to it than life—and the feeble understanding of the Divinity of his master—and we see the entire nature of his Incredulity—and sympathize with the burst of faith and gladness in which it was cast away for ever. The rest of the sermon was on faith without sight—and its promised blessing, all most precious—I longed much to have you beside me—You said in answer to my long letter that you could not realize heaven. I believe that this is indeed the great obstacle with all of us. I believe the only way to combat it is to begin by endeavouring to realize the person

of Christ—and to desire to have been one of his disciples—to
have been with him on the earth—and who would not? I trust
you are now recovered, dearest; but I will go on sending a line
every day until you tell me you don't want any more—only it
cannot be more than a line.—You are a good girl to speak so
of my father and mother—though how you should think them
the kindest people you ever knew I can't understand—for
when you were here last—they *could* not be kind to you—they
were afraid for you—more for me—afraid to ask you to stay—
afraid to let us be together—much vexed with themselves—
angry with me—and a *little* with you—every way uncomfortable—my mother especially at first—my father at last—I
thought them thoroughly *un*kind—and I believe still that you
have a mistaken idea of them—and that whatever good you
may think of them—you will find that you get on with them
far better than you expect.—but of course there will be trials
now and then. But are you really *quite* sure that it is *quite true*
that you think them just now the kindest people you know?
Mind! I am to believe all you say—so take care. I am afraid it
is all up with the secret. Never mind—it will make you let me
come the sooner. It will ebb out through "best friends"—

'Bye-the-bye—you never told me whether that Lucrezia
Borgia air was different or not—I want to know—Is there any
music I can get for you here?'

*   *   *

Denmark Hill
3 January 1848

'My Dearest Effie,

'Yes—only *one* whole month between us now. I begin to
feel quite frightened, like Sindbad the Sailor when his ship
was drawing nearer and nearer to the loadstone mountain—I
hope you will not pull my bolts out—Effie—Love does such
things sometimes—. As you say—your hand might conceivably
be better; considered as an M.S. and notebook hand—and
though I am the last in the world who has any business to talk
about writing—yet, for that very reason, it may be in your
power to do me much good service by writing legibly. I don't
think Alison ever intentionally exaggerates, but he is

sometimes bombastic. "Patient determination prevailed over
enthusiastic valour"—is to be translated into—"The men
who would have run away, if they could, thought they had
better stand still—and the enemy, who came on at a great
rate—because they expected them to run away,—when they
found they didn't—ran away themselves." That is the usual
state of the case in all battles—and so with other forms of
historical narration. He is inaccurate very often—but I believe
quite as accurate as anybody else—who professes to give details
of affairs which couldn't be seen for smoke.

'But I never answered your yesterday's letter, about friends.
Seriously, my love—I will grudge you *no* good friends: and I
am really glad you have so affectionate a heart, but I must warn
you against admitting the advances of every one who "desires
your further acquaintance"—Hundreds of people who have
nothing to do but to amuse themselves—and can't do it—will
be glad of your cheerful society. and others—out of mere
idleness and curiosity—desire to know *me*—and to talk nonsense about art—or pass their heavy time over my pictures—
or sketches. Against their inroads nothing but the most *rude*
firmness protects me—and the people who cannot get at me
otherwise—will try to do so through you. I find myself so well
and happy when I am quiet, and so miserable in general
society that you will have to be very cautious as to the kind of
persons and number, whom you admit to terms of familiarity
—All this however we can talk over at our leisure—but in the
meantime—don't make your heart a lodging house for every
stray comer who will pay their twopence worth of fair speech
—else I shall have to come and cut the "twopenny rope"—
and let them down anything but easily. (You know in the
London old lodging houses the beds were hammocks—on
ropes which were let go every morning at 6.)—but rather
arrange your guests on the reformed lodging house principles
—about which you can ask your Uncle Andrew—and have
them in good order and give them fair entertainment—for
indeed—if you don't look to it—your heart will soon be a mere
caravanserai—or posada—where there is such a crowd, and it
is so hot, that it is better to sleep out o' doors—And you know
my love—that you said you liked to be called a Phœnix, but

you must remember that there was but *one* Phœnix at once—
whereas—if you bring your Friends upon me by Forty at a
time—I shall be compelled to liken you rather to a Crane—
who leads a Triangle with an illimitable base,—of Cranes
behind her—so—or perhaps I shall begin to think myself
Alibaba—with a multiplying mirror among the Forty Thieves
—or perhaps I shall be reminded rather of Milton's "locusts
warping on the eastern wind"—and shall come home some
day expecting something nice for dinner—and a quiet chat
across the table—and find six and twenty cousins or so in the
pantry—and everything eaten up, and shall be obliged to see if
I can live like Mr. Jingle, on a pair of boots and a silk umbrella
with an ivory handle! Or if I am reduced—as it seems likely—
to live in the Cupboard—for the sake of a quiet life—on the
top shelf;—after the Cousins have emptied the dishes—licked
the plates—and scraped the saucepans, you will—like old
Mother Hubbard—come to the Cupboard—to give poor
Johnny a *bone!*

'Well—I mustn't write any more nonsense—*today*—I
really beg your pardon exceedingly, my love—for this
unseemly scrawl—but I have been etching today, and am
resting my eyes while I write—by looking—not at my paper—
but at an imaginary Effie Gray—presiding over a sort of
Council of Trent of sagacious Friends.

'Goodbye—and remember—if we are not to be eaten up and
out of house and home, that we shall at least want a broomstick
like St. Dunstan's—that would cut into ever so many semi-
broomsticks—every one of which would sweep the house—
fetch a pail of water—or make a bed—without any aid or
supervision whatever—and then come and ask what was
wanted next.—

'I'm very glad Mama has got so nicely away—Tell me how
she enjoys herself—Be assured though, mine own, that—
whatever I may say—I will do all I can to make your *real*
friends welcome—and will love them and try to make them
love *me*.

'Love to George—and all—

'Yours ever devotedly—dearest

'J. Ruskin.'

Denmark Hill
19 January 1848

'Much did I enjoy my letter this morning—and to think that
I may hope for one tomorrow—and the day after that—and
next day! What a happy mortal I am—if it weren't for the six
weeks—But six weeks are a good deal, whatever you may say;
still, it doesn't sound quite *frightful*—as the five months did.
And so my dialogue is not like us?—I grant it—but who knows
what we may be in six years! I haven't the slightest idea what
will become of us—perhaps we shall get quite cool, and like
other people in that time—and may have quarrelled so often
that we shall do it as a matter of course—about everything—I
don't think the dialogue is like Mr. and Mrs. Carroll at all—in
the first place—you will find you are very goodnatured and all
right until I propose things quite unendurable—and in the
second place, I think I have *rather* the best of it—which poor
Mr. C. never had. And if I made Mrs. R. unlike you in being
somewhat foolish—I could not help it—because it is quite
impossible for me to *conceive* myself opposing you in anything
unless you were! ! There's a delightful estimate of myself for
you. I have been thinking a good deal over that hard question
of yours—whether I shall always love you as I do now—and I
still have but the same answer—it will depend upon yourself—
a wife has it in her power to make her husband love her more
and more daily, and so he, with her. and I do so thoroughly
intend to do everything that I *can* do, for your good and
happiness, that I do faithfully believe I shall gain your love
more and more as we live on—and I hope deserve it more and
more. and if you love *me* I am certain to continue to find all my
happiness in you. But I suppose it to be a melancholy and
undeniable fact that something of the romance of love must
pass away—something of its outer flush and bloom—I can
think of you or conceive you as old—50 or sixty—and fancy
myself a lover still—at 70—But to tell you the very truth—I
cannot look fairly in the face of the Great Fact that you must
one day—(God willing)—be *Forty*. It sounds very unpleasant
indeed—to be sure—I shall be 50—if I see that day,—and I
don't know what my views of things in general—and of you in
particular, may be by that time. And that's all the philosophy

I have—upon this great and interesting question—for indeed, I am not in possession of sufficient data to reason from.

'I don't regret our little quarrels, now; I think even at the time there was a kind of luxury in them—I don't know what it was—but I cannot help suspecting myself—now and then—of having in some slight degree, made matters worse for the sake of the delight of making friends again. Do you think we shall be able to quarrel in that sort of amateur fashion at Bowers Well. I'm afraid not—I don't think I could even *play* a quarrel—now. I am quite passive—in your power—you may do what you will with me—if you were to put me into Bowers *Well* and put the top on, I should think it was all right, and the kindest thing in the world. You said I was cross the other day—peut-etre—but in the first place I was more anxious than cross—and in the second place—I don't profess to be in a good humour when I am away from you—A little thing puts me out now—but when I once get near you—Ah. what will become of me. I shall have no more independent existence than your shadow has—I feel as if I should faint away for love of you—and become a mist or a smoke, like the Genie in the Arabian nights—and as if the best you could do with me would be to get me all folded and gathered into a little box—and put on your toilet-table—and let me out a little now and then—when I wouldn't be troublesome—

'Goodbye—Only about 35 more Goodbyes

'Yours ever devotedly'

*   *   *

Denmark Hill
23 February 1848

'My Dearest Love

'Your little queer note of this morning—though a very sweet and kind one, has again made me anxious, and my mother, to whom I read part of it, fears also that you may bring on illness by over labour or over excitement. It is quite natural that at present you should feel yourself losing something of your youthful spirit—and that the care—fear—and feeling by which you must be oppressed—of an acute and

varying—often contradictory kind, should leave you sometimes despondent—often outwearied and weak. I trust this will
all soon cease—and that the spring and healthy flow of spirit
will return—. There *is* a time indeed—when, when the
lustre of youth fades from the heart for ever—and the whole
world becomes one of reality instead of imagination—but this
did not take place with me till I was six or seven and twenty,
I hope it will not with you—till even later—as your mind is
altogether more healthily constituted than mine. But above
all things—do not begin thinking about whether you deserve
to be loved or not—nor encourage any of the morbid phases of
modesty and self depreciation—I have suffered much from such
feelings—because my heart is not large—and my vanity
extreme—while I have enough sense to know what I am, and
am not.—But you have too much affection—and too little
pride—ever to make your happiness depend on what is
thought of you by others,—except only by those whose love
you will always have—and *feel* that you have. But—my
dearest Effie—I do think that ever since you left us last
summer—you have been managing yourself *very* ill—and I
think it a little hard that your father and mother should
always lay all the blame on your writing to me.—Whether, as
at first—you desired to turn your thoughts away from subjects that had agitated you—or whether—as has been the case
since October, you wished to preserve a tranquil and healthful
state of mind in circumstances necessarily giving rise to
anxiety and excitement—in either case, your best conduct
would have been a return—as far as might be—to a school-
girl's life—of early hours—regular exercise—childish recre-
ation—and mental labour of a *dull* and *unexciting* character. I
believe whatever the disposition or habits may be—this would
be agreed on all hands—by the wisest and most experienced, to
be the safest plan—and that the excitement of society—or of
music—and far more,—anxiety as to things to be *done* and
planned, were in the last degree objectionable.—Now—you
know—in the mineral room—the last thing before you went
away—I mentioned French, Italian and Botany as subjects—
two of which it was necessary and the other expedient—that
you should learn—and I thought that you would endeavour to

occupy your mind—and—(forgive me the impertinence) to
please *me*—by giving some time each day to these healthful
and unexciting studies.

'Now, love, I know that it has not been possible for you to do
this—. I know you have had much to do—much to think of;
still—your Father and Mother might remember that since we
have been engaged—and of course—before that—you have
not—so far as I know—except the writing of this last piece of
French and the reading the Misanthrope—done anything for
me or with reference to my wishes—except only the writing of
your letters.

'Now even this last—I should not have permitted—as I grant
it not to be a healthy occupation—had not I felt—and your
father himself admitted—that this was one of the points of
your education which had been least regarded—I wished you to
be able—as every lady ought—to write easily and gracefully—
and I thought the writing to me likely to give you easier and
happier practice than you could have hereafter. If I had seen
appearances of labour, or effort—about your letters—I should
have checked them—But they have all been written easily and
most of them rapidly—nor is the amount of writing (considerable I grant)—greater than should have been written at
any rate as a mere exercise.

'That you had a large correspondence besides—has not been
my fault.—In my own case—I have written no longer each day
than I usually do—but I have ceased writing to my friends for
the present—offended some—for whose offence I do not care—
the good ones trust to my affection—and suppose there is
reason for my silence. *You ought* to have done the same.

'That you have had charge of an household—anxiety about
your mother's health, agitation respecting your lovers—has all
been unavoidable—but it has been most unfortunate—Had it
been possible to have sent you back to school, among a number
of companions of your own age—to have given you plenty to
do—nothing to think of;—a great deal of play—*thorough*
play—and sent you to bed at nine o'clock every evening,—you
would have had no feelings of age come upon you—nor any
nervousness—nor any despondency—though you had written
me a letter every day as long as your sash—.

'But this could not be—and you have been doing and suffering partly of necessity—and partly through thoughtlessness—just everything in the world that you should not—*except* in this *one* matter of my letters—Music is perhaps of all things the worst for you just now—Playing to your father in the evening—or practising what is *tiresome* in the day, does no harm—but to sit down and make yourself miserable by playing in the minor key is so utterly useless—so absurd,—so wrong; that if it were not that I am glad to find you not quite incapable of doing naughty things—I could find it in my heart to be quite angry—and I have no hesitation in replying to your final question—"Am I not a wicked creature"—that you certainly are a *naughty* one.

'I don't believe, myself, that the going to Edinburgh will do you much good—however—anything is better than the way you are going on now.—and as to my letters—as I allow that they *do* add to the sum of what is mischievous—I would rather that you did not write me (*sic*) while you are at Edinburgh—except only to tell me of your safe arrival and then perhaps one just before I come—I shall be less anxious if you don't write than if you do.

'I have been with my mother today as far as our Chalk Pit—for the first time since I was there with you—I was very happy—how miserable I should have been, without the prospect of being soon with you—and never parting with you—

'Goodbye—and *N.* for ever!

'Ever, dearest—your devoted lover'

*   *   *

Denmark Hill
28 February 1848

'My Dearest Love—

'I feel very much inclined to do today as you say schoolgirls do when they get letters from their loves, and think of nothing else all day. That is so delightful a letter because it is so happy. I am afraid, by the Saturday evening—or Sunday morning—your happy heart would be a little chilled by the news from

Paris[1]—it made me very sad—very wickedly sad—all Saturday evening—thinking we should perhaps and probably lose our Chamouni journey. However, with a little reflection and self-examination, I recovered myself—partly by thinking how much was still in our power at home—and that you, contented and cheerful always, would make Cumberland as joyous as Switzerland.—then also—I thought how selfish and wrong it was to feel only for myself in so dark a time for thousands: finally I began to consider that there were more chances for us than against us, still; that all my forebodings about Switzerland had only served to torment myself—and I came on a passage of Jeremy Taylor this morning very apposite. "Enjoy the present whatever it be, and be not solicitous for the future for if you take your foot from the present standing and thrust it forward toward tomorrow's event, it is like refusing to quench your present thirst by fearing you shall want drink next day—if it be well today, it is madness to make the present miserable by fearing it may be ill tomorrow—for it may be it shall not, and then to what purpose was this day's affliction—but if tomorrow you shall want—your sorrow will come fast enough, though you do not hasten it"—I intend to act upon this—which is what you like—common sense, and philosophy too—and to enjoy our meeting at Edinburgh—if God permit—just as much as if it were all right in France, and not to believe that we cannot go until—if so it be—we really are ready to go—and can't.—And if not, I daresay we shall be very happy somewhere at home—But I don't like to think or talk of Paris much—for the cutting down of the Boulevard trees and the sack of the Tuileries are sad things enough—already.

'I am delighted by your account of your dancing—but I should not be if I really thought it were to be your last dance at home. I hope to see you dance, just so—or more madly still—when I *am* in the corner to be asked whether you have done well. Mr. and Mrs. Duncan are delightful too;—but what fools we men are, when we once let mauvaise honte get the better of us—twenty times more slaves to opinion than women—I suppose all his enjoyment in dancing was destroyed by the idea of his doing what was "absurd."

[1] Revolution had broken out

'How seldom it is that one sees a woman awkward or un-- comfortable from false shame—Partly, to be sure—they have the law more in their own hands—and whatever they choose to do becomes right—and partly, such shame as they may feel, harmonizes with and is absorbed in their own natural modesty which is a grace to them; and so is carried off —but in a man it is a foreign element—destructive of his dignity and independence—he walks with his head up and his neck cramped, and his face red under the crushing weight of his mauvaise honte, like a mountebank carrying a donkey on his nose—but a woman does but droop a little deeper when she is a little ashamed of herself—even though it be foolish shame —and flush a little more brightly—and half recover herself under the sense that her very distress is becoming to her— (always supposing it is not affected—for that is worst of all— false shame is to be forgiven—but feigned shame is unpardonable and revolting). And then—and for the chief reason of all —I suppose women have really more open and less selfish hearts—and are able to admit their enjoyments more frankly therefore—and to forget themselves more entirely.

'Another reason suggests itself to me—but I am afraid to state it—first because it seems a flat contradiction in terms— and I cannot explain or reconcile it—and secondly because it is very shocking—But really it seems to me that as women are in some sort more modest than men—so in some sort they are more impudent! Do you think so?

'I am sorry you are so much offended with Dr. Brown—but you know as Dr. Johnson says—flattery always is pleasant in some degree because it at any rate shows that the flatterer thinks you worth flattering—worth his pains, though the mode in which he endeavours to ingratiate himself may say little for his opinion of your judgment—This is not so with flattery for a mere and palpable gain—like Mrs. Nickleby's "My dear— Captn—said you were the finest child he ever saw in his life—I remember it particularly, because he borrowed twenty pounds of your dear Papa directly afterwards," but Dr. Brown has no object in flattering me—except the mere desire of making himself agreeable.

'But what is it that you do not believe about him and his

G

wife—Do you not think a wife likes to hear her husband praised—and don't you think you will be pleased yourself when you hear letters in praise of me—or do you intend to set them *all* down as flattery, and to dislike them excessively? I had rather have you do that—than believe all of them,—and, by whomsoever I may be flattered—I hope it will never be by my wife.

'Apropos of mauvaise honte—I am afraid I shall be stared out of countenance when I am in person submitted to the Critical Observation of the envious Population of Perth. I have a great mind to bring my Florentine mask with me— what do you say to walking down George St with me in the shovel hat and black domino—I am prepared by your warning to be taken for a Jesuit in Edinburgh—it is only one step farther to a Hobgoblin in Perth. And so you are going to bargain for an unwitnessed meeting! Well, I should like it myself—but I am afraid you will not obtain your request and what is more, I think it is asking a great deal too much. You know such a meeting is not to be seen every day—and if I were Aunt or Uncle I should positively *insist* on being by—besides— I really don't think they will be at all in the way—I don't mind them a bit.

'I daresay you are quite right about school after all—*I* find work good for me just now because I am interested in it— and when I am busy upon architecture or mathematics I some-times very nearly forget all about you!—and retain merely a kind of pleasant sense of all's being right—whereas if I go into Society—or have any thing to manage or to do that is mechan-ical only, I get thinking about you and wishing for you and making myself ill—Besides—were your School friends in love, happily so, and Engaged—for there's all the difference—Still, I fancy home is the better place after all—I am sorry to change my opinion so weakly—but I was wrong—certainly—except only in supposing that you could have got interested in your work—and—indeed—that is not supposing more than a proper amount of sense and firmness.

'Distressed Love I know no cure for, but I think promised love ought to make people more industrious and happy—and not "fit for nothing all day".'

Denmark Hill
13 March 1848

'I am *very* sorry my wicked letter made you sad—and yet
selfishly glad I wrote it—and the naughty one before it too.—
since they have obtained for me two such lovely letters to
conclude the sweet series which I have of gentle and forgiving
and loving and rejoicing—and comforting expression of your
kind heart—many a kiss have I given to the letter of Saturday
—and a joyous evening I had. I could not get away—for we had
company, but I stole a moment at the fireside in the dining-
room, and saw the first page and those closing words—and if
you could but have felt my poor heart leaping for joy—But I
did not think the second letter so sad, neither;—I was nervous
and ill, certainly,—but you would not have had, if you had been
here—to enter the lists with me—and fight a l'outrance—no,
one little touch of the hand and whisper to the ear would have
put all right—. But I like your plan very much—as a general
one—and it will be much better than yielding to my mood—
except only when I really want to talk to you about what
distresses me—and to be a little pitied and adored—and then
gaiety alone would not do. But I do not think you will often see
me committing the sin of discontent—after I am with you. I
may sometimes be mortified or vexed with myself—but I
trust that my regrets of things quite past are now nearly at an
end. If people do right they will never be but cheerful, and I
do hope to be enabled to do right—not absolutely of course—
but in the main, right, hereafter. I am truly rejoiced to hear
you are so happy, my love: and—don't think me vain—I
suppose it to be because I am coming—. But you must not only
be a very happy creature—but a very clever creature—or the
old Judges would not give you whole hours of tete-a-tetes.
Lady Trevelyan is very kind—not that I was not sure that
everybody would love you and think well of you—still, her
saying that you were worthy of me is very delightful—
because, you know, it is a compliment—no—a testimony to us
both, to me more than to you, but it is very kind of her too;
and I know no one—of whom I know so little, of whose friendship I am so desirous for you.

'Thank you also again and again for the details about the

marriage—and I shall like to be surprised by your bridal dress better than if I knew it before, and I shall like something over silk better than silk alone, and a veil instead of the mere pendant head-dress—and the rest all very nice—only I shall not see it half while we are being married—nor in the morning at all,—not that I shall look like a ghost, I hope, nor desperate— still, I shall be thinking of what I am promising to you, and not of your dress—and of what I am receiving in you—and in your heart—and perhaps I shall hardly be able to look at you at all. But you shall put it on again for me in the evening—will you not? when I can look at you as long as I please—or at least until I dare not look any longer for fear I should die for joy.—and then—or when I get frightened less you should disappear like the white lady of Avenel—I will—oh—I don't know what— and to think only six weeks today—and at this time—God granting it—you will be mine altogether—it is too much. I cannot at all thank you—I shall never be able to thank you for all you have said to me, dearest—much less for all that you are going to be to me. But what a frightful place to stop at— Berwick—the very saddest and darkest town I ever— But then I had just parted from you, and that was perhaps the reason Edinburgh looked so ill—Bye-the-bye—my last letter could not have been so sad, for there was all that defence of my L's in it—of which you say nothing—but I suppose you thought it a sad defence—and of a piece with the rest.

'And now love—I have not another letter to write to you, I hope—for many a day to come—I wish this was a better letter—I have only time to say that I hope the next letter I write to my dearest Effie, how long time soever may intervene —will be more fond and kind—far, than any of these—and will have for its chief purpose to express my deep joy and gratitude, in and for the more than fulfilment of all my dearest hopes: and the possession of far more than ever I hoped— though I seem to hope—yes—and to believe of you every- thing that is pure and lovely, and as your own *Changeless* name signifies—of good report—and if there be any virtue and if there be any praise—I think of it as in you—Ever—my dearest —and for ever—Your faithful and entirely devoted lover— servant—and soon, God Grant—your own husband—''

Lady Trevelyan, wife of Sir Walter Trevelyan, was a life-long friend with whom he corresponded regularly. Ruskin's growing anxiety about spending the honeymoon abroad was caused by the rapidly deteriorating political situation in Italy, France and Austria. It was said of that year 1848 that men opened their newspapers wondering what revolution would have broken out and what king would have gone into exile. Europe was certainly no place for a honeymoon couple, or as Ruskin more picturesquely put it:

'I don't think a prison would do for us at all, my love—a cavern—or a desert island, are very well and a desirable family property—but a mere cell, with a sentinel before the door and nothing before the window but a flower pot or two— or even an entresol in a street at Verdun, with a permission to walk on parole—round the ramparts before dinner—commanding a prospect of a green moat with some frogs in it and perhaps a rat or two,—and a regiment of poplars beside a straight road and a windmill in the distance—would be perhaps something too sober a way of passing the honeymoon—the comb would have too much of the cell in it and too little of the sweet. No—I think rowing on Derwentwater—or exploring castles in North Wales would be a much more wise method of beginning our wedded life.'

Effie's letters—and she wrote nearly every day—though never reaching such heights of eloquence can never have caused Ruskin a moments doubt that he had completely won her heart.

Bowerswell
8 February 1848

'I told Papa the other day' she wrote in February 'that you said you never would be really jealous without cause and he says unfortunately jealous people always *find cause* which I think quite true but I hope at heart you are really not a jealous being, and the absurdity of your giving as a reason that my manner to you and other people was quite the same is really the most preposterous thing I ever heard. You must have been thinking of something else when you wrote that! but really

John I love you so much that I don't think much about *the* jealous part of you for I do not believe you will be at all so after we are married and I daresay you will allow me to ask anybody I like to take some pudding without behaving afterwards as madly as Mr. Munn.'

*   *   *

Bowerswell
10 February 1848

'I do not know how I can sufficiently thank you for your inestimable letter this morning so full of tenderness and affection almost too kind and good. You will quite spoil me, my love, it almost made me weep with joy to think myself so beloved not but that I was fully impressed with that before, but this morning's letter almost made me rejoice too much in thinking that so much happiness was permitted to me who am so unworthy of it. I am indeed happy beyond telling in thinking you love me so much and truly glad am I if by expressing my earnest desires for continued happiness on your part I added one moment of pleasure on your birthday to you I wish I could have added my thoughts more fully to my wishes for you and was much dissatisfied that my letter was so unexpressive of my feelings for had you been here much much more should I have said to what I wrote. You will indeed be a kind husband to me. Many trials we shall probably have but not from want of love on either part—that must be the greatest trial I think in married life finding that the only being perhaps in the world whose affection is necessary to you as a part of your being not loving and assisting you in all your joys and cares, leaving you with the utmost indifference when you are in trouble to get out of it the best way you can, and in Joy not partaking the feeling but perhaps trying to subdue it if not in a similar mood, this would be I think the summit of wretchedness and misery. You who are so kind as a son will be a perfect lover as a husband. What I meant by saying that we had much to find out in each other was not that I expected to find great faults in you, I think I know all that I have to expect, and I shall see your coat brushed and mend your gloves and

SOPHIE GRAY
A pencil drawing by Sir J. E. Millais, BT., P.R.A.

especially keep you from wearing white hats and in order to compromise the matter with you I shall promise never to wear an *excessively* Pink Bonnet which can be seen all over the Exhibition although I suppose you have not particular objection to one of a paler hue. Pink is a very favourite colour of mine but I will subdue the shade out of respect to your superior discernment in these matters.'

They were married by the Minister of Kinnoull in the small drawing-room at Bowerswell on 10 April 1848.

It was a gay scene. Effie's small sister, Sophie, and her young Jameson cousins distributed favours to the large assembly of friends and relations. The carriage drove away under a shower of satin shoes. A few worldly-wise elders were not quite happy. The bridegroom seemed to them rather a queer fellow and out of his proper element in such company, but Effie looked serenely happy, so perhaps their slight feeling of anxiety was unjustified.

CHAPTER V

Bewildering Honeymoon

THE honeymoon couple spent two nights at Aberfeldy before moving south to the Lake District. For Effie those first days together must have been a strange and alarming experience. She was not yet twenty and as she told her father six years later, when her proud reserve at last broke down, she knew 'little or nothing about the relations of married persons in the closest union on earth'. But, nevertheless, it must have been something of a shock to listen night after night to her husband's eloquent explanations for not consummating their marriage which ranged from his hatred of children to his eagerness to preserve her beauty seasoned with many references to the Scriptures. As soon as she recovered from her first surprise, she contested his religious arguments but 'he soon silenced me and I was not sufficiently aware to the position I was in'.

But he allayed her immediate perturbation by assuring her that he would consummate the marriage when she was twenty-five!

It was not till five years later, when his strange love had changed to persecution, that he told his wife that until he saw her body he imagined women were quite different and that the sight of her on their wedding night disgusted him.

Effie decided to bear her cross alone and until that last, despairing letter to her father, she never gave an inkling of the truth, though not disguising the growing hostility of the Ruskin family.

From Aberfeldy she wrote:—

Aberfeldy
11 April 1848

'John and I have just had tea after a delightful walk to the Falls of Moness, the water was in good quantity and they looked very beautiful. I asked our guide if she knew anything of the Campbells of Croftness, our old host and hostess at the time of the Queen's visit, and she told me that the old man is dead but the Countess is still there. These places about here strongly recall that pleasant trip to my mind and we are now sitting writing in the very room that we had that day to eat our expensive potatoes and *pye* as George would spell it. We had a beautiful ride today from Blair Athole to Tummel Bridge, the weather was lovely, the air like crystal and the sky as bright as bright could be. The pass looked grand even without the leaves on the trees which are a great loss. Loch Tummel was very fine and when we got to the Inn we were at with the Thomsons where we were so happy the woman recollected me directly and seemed highly amused at my coming back with a husband. She advised John to take Foss and come and live there. John and I superintended the cooking of dinner in the queer kitchen which consisted of Ham and eggs and Fine Potatoes with small trout. The country all along looked lovely but when we arrived at Kenmore we found the Inn repairing and we could not get in so that we were obliged to come on here and go back through Kenmore to Killin where we purpose being all tomorrow.

'We go to the Star in Glasgow on Friday and from Saturday all the next week our direction is Royal Oak—Keswick—Cumberland. John and I are as happy as two people can possibly be and he is exceedingly kind and thoughtful. Your concerns are the only thing wanting to make our happiness complete, but I hope you too may be made happier soon.'

This gave her parents a picture of connubial bliss and in her next letter she was priding herself on the success of her efforts to make John more sociable.

Tarbet Inn
13 April 1848

'We reached Killin yesterday at five having had a long ride. I was disappointed in the drive up Loch Tay, the clouds were black and thundery and the Loch looked black as Erebus and Ben Lawers clumsy, but Killin was beautiful as when we last saw it. We walked to Finlarig and were much amused with our Guide who afterwards took us into his cottage and treated us to cake, cheese, and whiskey—Tell Papa I love the Highlanders more than ever ! ! my admiration increases with each new specimen; John is quite amused with me talking to every one we meet and highly approves of the mode in which they are drawn out, he is coming on well in this new thing for him! He thought of sending for Peter McAlpin to see if he had any pearls or Cairngorms but they said he would have none at this season. We have not met a single creature |on the road or at any of the Inns since we left, and the people say we are the first this year excepting a newly married couple who are passing the Honeymoon here, but who have been invisible to us yet. We had a splendid drive today and John admired Glenfalloch and the head of the Loch more than any part of our tour. The rocks very very bold and grand, we went out on the Loch for an hour before dinner and John pulled the boat a considerable way up and down the Loch.'

Ruskin, too, was writing happy letters and shortly after their arrival at Keswick he wrote to his old friend, Miss Mitford:

'I am resting with my kind wife among these quiet hills. . . I am recovering trust and tranquillity. . . My wife looks forward to being presented to you—remembering what I told her amongst my first pleadings with her that, whatever faults she might discover in her husband, he could at least promise her friends for whom, she would have every cause to love and honour.'   (Friendships of Mary Russell Mitford.)

Effie's letters from Keswick give a good account of their life there. Perhaps she saw the shadow of coming events when John asked her to invite his father to join them whilst still on their honeymoon.

Keswick
16 April 1848

'We had a beautiful drive down Loch Lomond, the Primroses in quantities out on the banks. On reaching Glasgow we took a turn along the streets and went into Campbell's shop to see it, at half past six Mr. and Mrs. Richard Gray, Mr. Ruskin's old

friends, came to dine with us and we gave them a very good
dinner and Champagne. They were very kind and glad to see
John after ten years—next day at 11 we left by Railway and
had a long weary day of Railroad to Penrith, the passengers
got out at Carlisle to dine and I took a cup of tea, the Station is
exceedingly handsome and all appeared satisfied with what
they got. We had three gentlemen in our carriage, going to
London on business, who amused us with their various conversation. The country through which we passed after leaving
Glasgow was so ugly that I could not believe it my own
country and therefore I had not so much regret as I should
otherwise have had in leaving it. We dined at Penrith and
could not see anything remarkable excepting the ruins of the
Castle which had little beauty. The Pea-soup was bad and the
Fish good. We had a long ride of eighteen miles to Keswick
almost entirely in the dark. This is a pretty place but the day
is not good so I will say nothing about the Hills which, as far
as I can see, are merely good hills without crag or colour like
our Highlands, but I will tell you more about them when I get
up Skiddaw. But still everything looks very sweet. We went to
the one church this morning and had a good sermon, we were
rather late and had all the juveniles of the place staring us in
the Face. We are going again in the afternoon, we have very
comfortable warm rooms but it is as cold here as in Scotland.
Mr. Ruskin is at Liverpool, we have written to ask him to come
here and go home with us.'

*   *   *

Keswick
19 April 1848

'I had a sail yesterday on the Derwentwater which is small
but lovely. Today we had a delightful excursion to the top of
Cawsey Pike 2500 feet—on our white ponies with a guide and
George.[1] We had a ride of five miles before reaching the base
of the hill and then all the way to the top was rugged, barren
in the extreme, but the ponies went very well nearly all the

[1] Ruskin's valet

way but so steep was it that we had to come down on foot—we felt all over aches and bruises from the rough riding but the view was beautiful, so many hills one after the other and so near with such fantastic forms, but very stony and barren. We had a good luncheon of sandwiches and Rhubarb tart and George lay stretched at a little distance amply supplied from his pockets. We reached home at five in time for dinner.'

*   *   *

Keswick
22 April 1848

'Yesterday the clergyman Mr. Myers called on us, he is a very nice person he invited us to dine with him on Monday first and we are going, and also to call on his wife today who was unwell and not able to come yesterday—He is brother-in-law to Dr. Whewell, Master of Trinity, Cambridge, and it was curious John was just going to write to him a letter of thanks for his ministry during the week when he came in. We were rowing on the lake yesterday for two hours before dinner. We landed at one of the Islands which under the trees is quite carpeted with wood-anemones, primroses and strawberries—we brought home a very large bouquet of them. The country is beautiful now, and the hedges and trees in half leaf. We went up Skiddaw the day before yesterday I do not think I mentioned it, it is 3020 feet the highest hill I have ever been up, we saw Carlisle quite near and far into Scotland on one side across the Solway, and over the hill Helvellyn and others to Snowdon in Wales, coming back it was dreadfully cold but the ponies went admirably. I enclose a little note from the Countess to me which I will be obliged to you to send back.'

Mr. Ruskin was not able to join them, which must have been a relief to Effie, but was back at Denmark Hill before the end of April to receive the young couple whose honeymoon had been interrupted as John was eager to get to work on the proofs of a second edition of *Modern Painters*. They were to have rooms in the house—an arrangement that suited old

Mrs. Ruskin admirably but not one that usually commends itself to newly married couples.

Denmark Hill
28 April 1848

'Mrs. Ruskin is speaking to me every moment and I can scarcely write a word. After writing to George from Kendal we left on Wednesday at 11 and got to Preston where we dined, and to Birmingham in the evening. We got into the third Hotel we tried and hardly succeeded even there as the town was so full owing to a Concert of Mendelssohns music, and the numbers of strangers who had arrived for it. We left yesterday at 10 and arrived at Euston Square at three where we found Mr. Ruskin waiting with the carriage which he drove, very nice and handsome being all newly painted and lined, and Powell in new coat with Numerous capes, and hammercloth etc. in honor of our arrival. Mr. Ruskin greeted us most warmly and when we arrived at the gate of the garden the carriage stopped and the Gardener presented me with the most splendid bouquet of Geraniums, Orangeblossom, Heath of the most delicate kinds, Myrtles, cineraria, etc., all tied in ornamental Paper and with White Satin ribbon. When we came to the door the servants were all standing with Mrs. Ruskin to welcome us, the women looked so nice with their neat caps of white net and ribbon and green and stone colored mousselines up to the neck with their muslin aprons. Mrs. Ruskin had on a most splendid rich drab or pale brown satin with rich fringe on the front and a white blonde cap. She and Mr. Ruskin never saw John looking half so well and are quite delighted to see him so happy—and she bids me say how happy she is to have me here and she hopes now I will feel quite a daughter to her, but to go on—When we had dressed and gone into dinner a band of Germans came and played delightful music before the windows all time of dinner and it was a great treat. We spent the evening very happily. I played to Mr. Ruskin and Mrs. R spoke to John and me and made kind speeches. Mrs. R has given us the top of the house and very comfortable it is. Mr. Ruskin, John and I go tomorrow to the private view of the Academy where we shall see all the *nobs*.'

Effie continued her efforts to draw her husband out of his shell, which met with the approval of her father-in-law who wrote to Mr. Gray:

Denmark Hill
24 May 1848

'I am glad to see Effie gets John to go out a little. He has met with most of the first men for some years back but he is very indifferent to general Society and reluctantly acknowledges great attentions shown him and refuses one half—Seven years ago he refused to spend a month at the Duke of Leinster's— He has had many valuable Invitations and disregarded them— I got him to dine with Sir Stratford Canning with difficulty and to go to Sir Robt. Peel's House Opening—I only discovered by chance two years ago that Lord John Russell was one of his Party—I am glad to find his acquaintances, obtained merely by fair Talent and good Conduct, immediately took Phemy by the hand—John some months ago refused Mr. Blake of Portland Place's Invitation, but they both went on Saturday and met first-rate people and on Monday they dine at Lansdowne House— by invitation from Marquis and Marchioness of Lansdowne— but John would rather be in Switzerland—I hope they will contrive to be happy and take a due share of Society and solitude—Effie is much better calculated for society than he is—He is best in *print*.'

Effie's letters tell of a continual round of social affairs to which she persuaded John to accompany her though he no doubt grudged every minute spent away from *Modern Painters*.

Denmark Hill
29 April 1848

'On Saturday in the morning Mr. Ruskin reads Gibbon's Rome aloud to us for an hour and then John gave me a little bit of drawing to copy. At twelve we dressed. I put on my pale glacée silk White, lace bonnet, black Mantilla, pale gloves etc and John was also very well-dressed to go into town for the private view of the Water Colours. You know it is a great compliment getting these tickets and you only meet there the

artists themselves and the nobility, we stayed till five and
standing all that time and being introduced to so many tired
us all very much. The Pictures were beautiful, but I was
engaged in speaking to so many that I merely had a glimpse of
them. Mr. Ruskin took me on his arm and John went into other
parts of the room which was much crowded. We saw the three
Dukes and Duchesses of Sutherland and Argyll and Northumberland, the Ladies were not particularly well dressed, but
they were in Mourning—the two first had on black watered
silk with White Glacée silk scarfs and white broad fringe and
White silk bonnets trimmed with black and white blonde. The
D of Northumberland is like a good-natured farmer, the Lady
a merry looking little body with the sweetest voice I ever heard.
I was introduced to so many people that I almost forget them
but the names of some of the artists you will know. Copley
Fielding, Stanfield, David Roberts, Landseer, Taylor, Cox,
Prout; and they all complimented John on his improved looks.
Then Mr. Milman the Poet, which is a capital introduction,
and above all Rogers who spoke to us and asked us to breakfast
on Wednesday first which will be a great treat. He must be a
wonderful man for his age is 84, and he looks in such delicate
health. With him were Mr. and Mrs. and Miss Blake, friends
of John, who have immense property in Hertfordshire and have
a high position in society and very enthusiastic about painting.
Then Calderidge, the 2nd Master of Eton, who asked us to
Windsor to visit him. Lord Ravensworth's sons, the Liddles,
who are great admirers of John, one of them amused me
exceedingly, being a dashing looking young man and in this age
of Nonchalance displaying the greatest energy in speaking to
everyone from the Duchess of Sutherland down to the picture
dealer at the table and seemed lost in admiration between his
Lord Charles feet and exquisite gloves which he kept drawing
off and on with the same energy he displayed in conversation.
Mr. Ruskin and I had the greatest fun watching him, he is
coming here one day I believe. Mr. Ruskin was in the highest
spirits and said during dinner when we came home that it was
the first time he had ever come away without buying a picture,
but he did not want any now he had the living picture etc.
John congratulated me on what he terms my *grande succes* on

my first appearance in public. I am sure you will relieve me from all charge of affectation in telling these compliments of myself but it is only to show you how entirely pleased Mr. & Mrs. R. are with John's wife, which I know will gratify you and which I am most thankful for.'

*   *   *

Denmark Hill
3 May 1848

'This has been a very busy day. We drove into town to break-fast with Rogers, we found him in his drawing room with Mr. Mrs. and Miss Blake and a Mr. Burgess, the room covered with articles of vertu of the rarest kind and pictures such as are not to be found elsewhere. He showed us some clever drawings and then one of Sir T. Laurence, the first drawing he ever did of a young girl, a mere sketch, then a portfolio of very rare letters some to himself from Fox, Burke, Sheridan, and others of Washington, Franklin, John Dryden, Duke of Marlborough, Alexander Pope, etc. etc. We then went to breakfast which was the most perfect thing I ever saw. There was a splendid bouquet of real flowers on the table, then the preserved fruits and rolls were in different cut glass dishes and two men-servants handed the Coffee and tea. Mr. Rogers occupied himself in cutting the crusts of the outside of the rolls for me as he said the inside was for Royal birds who flew from the Palace to him to be fed. When we rose from breakfast he told us about all the paintings which are perfect gems. As you know he has a Giotto and there is not another in England. He showed me a sideboard carved which Chantry had done for him 45 years ago, when he was a poor workman with an apron and when he himself did not know him. In looking over a book of prints I said something and he patted me on the cheek and said I had a fine taste. We came away at twelve and John thought we would leave our card on Mr. Turner. We knocked for some time before anyone came. At last he opened the door himself and let us in. He was so kind and took us into his room without a fire and bare and miserly, but he ran and brought out his wine and biscuits and we all drank each other's health, and then he took us up to his gallery where we saw *such* pictures. I would pawn all I had for the *"Old Temeraire"* but he has been offered £1000 and we won't have it, A Steamer drawing a wreck through calm water and such a sunset as you never see in any pictures but his own.'

*   *   *

Denmark Hill
7 May 1848

'On Friday we had a small party, Mr. John Cockburn of Edinburgh, Mr. Newton who is more agreeable than ever and was more common sense than usual. His description of the defence of the British Museum on the day of the Chartist Meeting was the most absurd thing I have heard for long. The government had quite forgotten to send more than three days provision which they ate up in one day and were very drunk, the rest most of them were blind and lame with a number of spectacles.'

The last of these three letters was written on her birthday, amongst her presents was a sonnet from W. H. Harrison.

THE BRIDE'S BIRTHDAY

Two themes for gratulation have we here—
Thy birthday and thy bridal, Effie dear!
Dearer than e'er thou wert; for thou art blent
With my friend's destinies—a being sent
    To shed sweet light upon his darkest hour
For such will come—ay, hours of care and sadness
What are Life's warp and woof but gloom and gladness
    A mingling of the sunshine and the shower?
But thou wilt walk beside him in the might
And wealth of thine affection—making light
Life's heaviest burthens with thy priceless love.
And he will guard thee as his cherished Dove
Of Peace, and make his heart of hearts thy shrine—
God's Grace be with thee Effie and with thine.

7 May 1848.   Wm. Hy Harrison.

The social round continued until the middle of June.

H

Denmark Hill
10 May 1848

'We are going tomorrow night to see Jenny Lind in Die
Regiment's Tochter; John asked me whether I would go
twice to the stalls or once to the boxes as it would be all the
same. I said twice to the stalls, but Mr. Ruskin thinks it
rather infra dig to go there so he went and took a box in the
grand tier opposite to the Queen, in order, I suppose, that we
may be properly seen. But he said, as he took us, he liked the
box better but if John and I want to go again we can do the
other. He has offered Mrs. R. the handsomest cloak in London
if she will go but she wont, so I suppose Mr. Newton will or
else Mr. Richmond.

'On Monday we dined at Lady Davy's, she invited a very
select party to meet us—Mr. Lockhart, Hallam the historian of
the Middle Ages, Dr. Hook of Leeds, Lady Frances Hope, the
Marquis and Marchioness of Lansdowne and Miss Burdett
Coutts, John and I—every thing was in first rate style and I
was much amused and enjoyed all I saw. Four men in livery
were on the stairs and at the door. I had some agreeable small
talk with Lady Lansdowne and Miss Coutts, both extremely
agreeable, then dinner was announced and we all went down.
John took Miss Coutts and the Marquis took me. In going down
the gentlemen had little black shovel hats which they gave to
the footmen on entering the diningroom. Dr. Hook said grace
and then we had dinner which was most substantial. 1st two
soups, 2 Turbot and oyster patties, 3 then a leg of mutton and
chicken and tongue, entremets, Champagne & Seltzer Water
with ice broken handed round to put in your tumblers, very
luxurious on a hot day, 4 Jelly and Plovers eggs put round like
a little castle the eggs being turrets. Duckling and asparagus
most splendid, which the Fair Ladies ate with their fingers in
a most scientific manner. Lord L. talked to me all time of
dinner, a nice old man and so clean and neat in his dress. He
told me how much he hated Railways and talked a good deal
about France and was very clever and interesting. For dessert
by the way we had a splendid Pine, Ices and preserves, the
table cloth being kept on. Then we went to the drawingroom and
the Ladies chatted together and we got on very nicely—I

daresay Mama will like to know their dress and appearance. The Marchioness is rather a stout woman and tall, above or about 50, beautiful soft eyes, fine features and small hands with no rings but the marriage one, her hair braided flat and a blonde cap with pink flowers, a stone silk dress with two broad flounces Ruched and a Brussells lace cape and scarf, very kind manners and lively and handsome—I liked her extremely, Miss Coutts had on a pale green satin with a lace scarf. She is very tall and the finest features possible and an immense quantity of black hair beautifully dressed with a bunch of roses on one side and fine diamonds, her face is disfigured however by redness over it like Mrs. Bolding, but I did not find it disagreeable and she is the sweetest creature I have seen for a long time—I talked a great deal to her and she seemed so gentle and amiable in her opinions.

'Lady F. Hope was a very stout young woman with her eyes half shut and a white barege dress with 6 rows of broad blue fringe on the skirt and body, a black lace shawl, and headdress with quantities of ornaments. At ten some others came in —Lord and Lady Lyttelton, the former a stupid looking but very clever young man, the Lady very untidy rather pretty trollopy looking person. Miss Lyttelton very plain looking, squints but a nice person I spoke to her about music, she played twice she has a fine touch and plays very nicely. Lord and Lady Murray were there and I thought her playing infinitely superior, she asked me to introduce John to her, we talked a good deal about Edinburgh and Scotland. I have just got a card from Sir Walter and Lady James for dinner on Monday next. I have not seen either of them but here, that is not necessary if they know your names or have heard of you. The mode of introduction here would alarm you, Papa. The parties introduced if Ladies make a stiff slow curtsey and then the elder speaks, if gentlemen a very low bow with hat in hand. They mutter something about "Happy to have the Honor" etc. etc. Every new arrival at Lady D's, although they all know each other, made a most formal bow and after a minutes pause entered into a rattle of talk very amusing. I had met the Hon. R. Cavendish before, Lady D. did not know it and she introduced us. He did the same Muttering Had the Honor

etc etc and then he set me laughing for a quarter of an hour—
he is something in style like Mr. Liddle.'

*   *   *

Denmark Hill,
20 May 1848

'John, Mr. Ruskin and I are going today to see Mr. Windus's
pictures and, as we are going at eleven, I write a few lines to
tell you of our party on Saturday at the Blakes, which was very
distinguished. They have a very large house in Portland Place
finely furnished. As we sat down to dinner at eight the company were as follows, Miss Blake at the head of the table, then
the Marquis of Lansdowne, myself, the Bishop of Norwich who
took me down, then John, Sir James Wigram, the Vice Chanr.
Mrs. Stanley wife of the Bishop, Mr. Blake, Lady Morley, Mr.
Blake junr; Miss Stanley, Mr. Blake M.P.—another Lady of
Rank whose name I did not hear and the Marquis of Northampton completed the party. I was most agreeably situated, the
Marquis made me a pretty speech upon the honor and pleasure
etc etc of being next me again, and the Bishop is like Lord
Cockburn in appearance, as quick as a needle and exceedingly
clever. I never heard such stories as he told me. He and John
got into a long and learned discussion upon the migratory
habits of seagulls, and I listened with great interest to Lord
Northampton's and Lord Lansdowne's stories of the French
just now. Some were most laughable and kept us all in fits of
laughter and as they were all told in French they had great
point. The dinner was very fine and a great deal of French
Cookery about it, we had green peas and all the other rarities
of the season.—We went upstairs and Lady Morley, who is
distinguished by her loud talking and incessant wit, kept us
laughing by her odd remarks for half an hour until the
gentlemen came up. Her description of the homeopathic
system was the most amusing thing I have heard. One of the
principal medicines, she says, is called *Caffia*, consisting of one
grain of coffee pounded, soaked in water, then purified, then
boiled, then put into a phial corked and leathered, with
Poison put on it, but she made it much more ridiculous and

said more about it—When the gentlemen came up Miss Blake showed us her paintings which are wonderful for an amateur—I saw nothing like them in the Water colour Exhibition.'

*　　*　　*

Denmark Hill
24 May 1848

'We are going tomorrow night to Covent Garden Opera to see Grisi in Norma & Alboni in one scene of the Cenerentola, Mr. Newton is going with us to our box. I had a card last night from the Marchioness for us to dine at Lansdowne House on Monday first at 8 o'clock, we are going and I think I shall enjoy it very much and we shall likely meet some interesting people. It is exceedingly kind and shows the estimation John is held in as that society otherwise is so difficult of access. But I take some credit to myself for John met them often before and never was asked till now. I got a note from Sir Walter yesterday telling me he would send the order and today it has come signed by Col. Berkeley Drummond of the Scots F. Guards to admit us inside the square of troops in the Horse Guards. I think we shall have to leave town next week for Dover or some place but it depends on our engagements. I am happier every day with John for he really is the kindest creature in the world and he is so pleased with me, he says he thinks we are quite a model couple and we don't do at all badly together; we are really always so happy to do what the other wants that I do not think we shall ever quarrel. He is particular with me and takes a great deal of trouble in teaching and hearing me things and Mr. Ruskin is also I think very fond of me and so is Mrs. Ruskin.'

*　　*　　*

Denmark Hill
28 May 1848

'That night we had a delightful box in Covent Garden and saw Grisi in Norma which was very splendid. Costa trains the band so beautifully, the house was very full. The ballet was very poor and there were an immense number of children in it

with baskets of flowers in which it disgusted Mr. Newton so
much that he said he should have liked a murder of the Inno-
cents. I had immense fun listening to John & him, for both
are so clever and so entirely opposite in their wit. Mr. Newton
has come out in an entirely new character. He is now lecturing
in the British Institution on Greek Art and he says all the
pretty women in London come to hear him, consequently an
entire change has taken place in His outer man and he is
now perfectly dressed and has his hair arranged in Massive
curls over his head (in imitation I think of the antique) and
bears in his hand a crush hat etc etc. Norma was splendidly
acted by Grisi but I still prefer Jenny Lind.

'Next morning John, Mr. Ruskin and I went to the Horse
Guards where we saw a fine Review of cavalry and Infantry.
The staff was very brilliant. I saw Henry Oliphant there and
while I was speaking to him a charge of horse came on the
wrong side and separated us—the Troops and music filed off to
St. James to serenade the Queen. John & I got into the carriage
and drove round to the Palace as fast as we could, we went
into the Square and heard some Splendid airs, we then went
about our business and, coming through Bond Street at one,
there was such a mass of carriages with the people going to the
drawingroom that we walked all the way down to see them.
All London seemed in the same state and it was delightful to
see the evident marks of so much loyalty. The houses were all
preparing for an illumination in the West end. The ladies all
looked very much alike but the gentlemen were in greater
variety and the most part were in uniform. The Town looked
beautiful at night I heard and Lansdowne House was particularly brilliant.'

*   *   *

Denmark Hill
1 June 1848

'Now you will like to hear of our dinner on Monday which I
enjoyed very much indeed. We drove at eight to Lansdowne
House, which I should think is one of the largest in London,
in Berkeley Square but enclosed from the Square by high walls
and a green in front. When we got to the door there were five

men in fawn and scarlet with powdered hair to receive us, the
sixth was in plain clothes, and led us into the drawingroom.
The Hall is large and extremely plain but very handsome all
the floor being inlaid black and white Marble with some fine
antiques round it. We then went through the reception room
into the drawingroom which was very splendid and of
immense size, the wall all painted in compartments and on the
roof and hung with very fine old pictures with antique frames,
one a very fine picture of Rembrandt by himself was lighted
by lamps from the sides. One side of the room was an immense
Divan with a mirror the same size behind it which went back
into the wall, and gave great size to the room. Lord Lansdowne
received us most kindly and made an apology for Lady L.
whose nephew had died in the morning and she had gone out
of town, but his daughter in law, Lady Shelburne, was there
and his son L. Shelburne. He then introduced us to them.
Lady S. is very pretty about 23 with very white and pink
cheeks and black hair and eyes, she had on a black net dress
with 3 flounces edged with satin, the skirt an immense size,
a beautiful necklace of large pearls and handsome bracelets one
of the fashionable shape in gold and stones. She is Lord S's
second wife and has two children, and he so young, about
26, with a black imperial, rather goodlooking. I don't know
who she is but you will for she said she used to live at Tully-
allan, & Meikleour belonged to her mother. Lady Davy was
there, and Sir Harry Vaughan something,—a Frenchman of
rank whose name I did not hear and Mr. and Mrs. Sartoris, she
is one of the Kembles and niece to Mrs. Siddons, a very clever
woman John said, for he sat by her. I did not admire her, she
was so fat and covered with old point Lace. We waited for the
Earl and Countess of Eglinton a long time but they never came,
so we went into dinner, Lord Shelburne took me and Lord
Lansdowne asked me to sit by him so that I was between the
father and son. The diningroom was very handsome with
niches all round with real antiques of Apollo, Mercury,
Jupiter etc., and lying on a thing like a tomb at the end of the
room was a sleeping Venus, one of Canova's last works. The
dinner was very beautiful and the finest I ever saw. The
Dessert was exquisite of fresh Grapes, peaches, nectarines,

Melon, and strawberries and very fine wines iced, two beautiful frosted silver wine coolers and gold candelabra. I had a great deal of amusement and lively discussion at dinner with Lord Shelburne for we did not agree on a single subject so that we had plenty of conversation. Lady S. and the two gentlemen talked French all dinner time. Lord Lansdowne had the bill of fare beside him and he took it up every now and then and asked me what I would have; we went into the drawingroom had tea and coffee, the gentlemen came in, we had some agreeable chit chat and then came away.'

Ruskin had made friends with Charles Newton at Oxford and referred to him in *The Queen of the Air* as 'a sure and unwearied kind guide, always near me since we were at College together'. His name occurs frequently in Effie's letters.

Early in July Ruskin took his wife to Oxford for Commemoration. Effie's first letter which she began at Reading, where they stopped a night, gives an account of the last party they attended in London, a big 'rout' at Lansdowne House, and her next letters describe the continual round of festivities.

Bear Inn, Reading
1 July 1848

'Now I will give you a short account of the party. John called on Lady Davy in the afternoon to ask her what time we should go, she said nobody ever went before half past ten; we were very near in St. Georges Hotel, Albemarle Street, so that we left there at that hour and found Police stationed at the ends of all the streets leading into Berkeley Square to make the line of Carriages go all one way. We reached the house without interruption and found at the door a large Awning for the people to enter under by. I went first into a side-room where there were a number of neat maidservants who took the Ladies things and gave them tickets for them; we then passed through five or six most brilliantly lighted rooms with all the furniture taken out excepting some chairs at the side till we reached the grand Salon, which is accounted the finest room in London and was filled with a dense mass of between six and seven hundred people. I saw the room very well about two hours afterwards when it became very warm and the people all

left it nearly and crowded the other rooms. It was very
splendid when empty, being illuminated by a transparency
from above and clusters of wax lights under which were
numbers of antiques placed in the niches with beautiful
flowering plants in large china pots under them. But to return
—we were more than half an hour getting up the room to Lady
Lansdowne and on our way met a number of people we knew
and spoke for a little to Mr. & Mrs. Lyell, Lady Morley, Mr.
& Miss Blake, the Bishop of Norwich's family, Mr. Milman,
Mr. Danby Seymour, his mother and sisters, Lady Davy and a
number more. At last with difficulty we reached Lady
Lansdowne who was in mourning of black watered silk and
white blonde cap and pearl ornaments. She looked tired, we
made our courtesys to each other and she thanked us for
coming very much and said how disappointed she was at being
from home when we were last there, we then parted as she
had to welcome more. Sitting next the wall, near her, sat The
Grand Duchess of Saxe Weimar and the two Princesses her
daughters who were as ugly tedious looking young Ladies as
you would ever wish to see; the Poor things looked very
Uncomfortable sitting doing nothing beside their mother and
not speaking and laughing like the rest. They were dressed in
deep mourning with large jet ornaments on their necks and
white flowers with long tendrils hanging from them. The
Duke and Duchess of Cambridge arrived, she quiet and he like
the public Auctioneer. Mr. Newton said he would do well for
the National Assembly of France just now. After a while Lady
Lansdowne saw them away and I suppose went to bed herself.
Countess Shelburne was going about a great deal and looking
extremely pretty in Pink watered silk & white lace with roses
in one side of her black hair and loops of hair on the other. I
hear she writes long letters to her friends about me and the
Earl says he wishes he knew some other people that I do, for he
would like to dine with me once a week—so Lady Davy told
John. Rather amusing! is it not. I did not meet Lord Lansdowne
or his son all night for the crowd was so great and we did not
try. I at last in one of the rooms passed the little Countess who
was sitting chatting French, she ran up to me and said "Oh! I
am so glad to see you again", and then she & I went to the

Sofa and she sat on the edge of it again. I said to her, "Whats the use of making yourself uncomfortable?" She laughed and said—"That's very true"—and came round and sat amongst the cushions. I said, "Do you not wish yourself in bed". She said "Oh yes! that I do and I shall go whenever I can". Then I left her to go through the rooms with Mr. Newton who showed me Mrs. Norton, Lady Dufferin, Viscountess Palmerston, the Turkish Minister, Lady Brougham, Sir William Molesworth, and all the Lords and Ladies you can think of. The Ladies were splendidly dressed in all kinds of dresses and Diamonds, especially the young Lady Dunmore who is very handsome. I heard one Lady say she could not go to the Spitalfields Ball because she was too poor in these hard times but she would go to the French Play as she could get there for nothing. She was dressed in a magnificient dress of pale blue Velvet a Pearl net work on her hair and diamond loops in her sleeves! Another Lady had on a pale primrose satin with black Lace flounces and velvet bows all about it with diamonds inside. Tell Mrs. Duncan that I saw Lady Morgan who is very little and rather deformed, painted up to the eyes, white Net streamers from each side of her head, a very bad expression, a dark glace silk dress with a black and white net dress over it. Mr. Newton to whom she spoke says she is an odious woman for she is always telling him he is clever and he cannot bear that. Mrs. Phipps, Mrs. McLean's sister, was there but I did not think her so handsome as the other, she was in white lace with large bouquets of roses. My own dress came in time and is very beautiful, 4 skirts of white tarlatane sewed at the edge with a wreath of flowers in white floss silk with double berthe to match and it looks like silver at night over white glace silk with large bouquets of pale green gauze ribbon and a wreath of green different kinds of leaves in my hair.

'And then we came away from the party at one o'clock and next day, yesterday, being very tired we came down here to Reading and last night we took tea at Miss Mitford's who is a dear old lady and lives three miles from here. She has a beautiful garden from which she gave me a bouquet, she is very fond of John and being very poor her house is a little cottage with wee rooms something like Miss Burrels. She is

now 60 and is energetic and literary still and, I think?, very
romantic. We had a beautiful drive home. We are going to
Oxford this afternoon from whence I will send this letter on
Monday. *Oxford.* On Saturday night we were at a large party
at Dr. Daubeny's Professor of Chemistry, Agriculture and
Botany. He gave us a lecture in the lectureroom on *Enclosures.*
We afterwards went into his house where we had fine music
and scientific pleasures such as looking at the circulation
through a living Frog in a microscope and the lungs of a
serpent. The Gardens looked beautiful, also the Greenhouses
and hothouses filled with exquisite flowers and foreign trees—
We are overwhelmed with Invitations and we were to have
taken our dinner at a large party today at the Master of Pem-
broke's, Dr. Jeune, and ditto in the evening at the Deaness of
Christ Church (Mrs. Gaisford), but John has a cough and I
want to be fresh for the Concert tomorrow which is the
"Creation" and if I go to two parties tonight I will be tired.'

* * *

Broad Street, Oxford
4 July 1848

'This week has been one continual round of festivities and
every two people meeting on the street exchange invitations
Mr. Gordon says. On Tuesday we went to hear Haydn's
Creation in the Theatre which I enjoyed very much. The
place was crowded and it was very hot: John thinks all that
music detestable and goodhumouredly read a book the whole
time being very glad I enjoyed myself. Yesterday was the
Commemoration in the Theatre and we went in at ten o'clock,
the Ladies being all separated from the gentlemen had a very
gay appearance, and the place was crammed full. Then above
was the underGraduates gallery and, after the rest of the
Theatre was full, all the young men, the doors being opened,
rushed in and filled the place just like savages. Then they
called out names and shouted or hissed as the person was
popular or not, first the Queen and Royal family, then Guizot
—tremendous cheering, then Dr. Pusey followed by Jenny
Lind, then the Ladies in white gowns, ditto in Pink bonnets

and ditto in black which met with no approval, then "the men that got thePrizes" followed by the "men that didn't get them", then Mr. Gladstone, who had come to have his degree, was cheered and hissed for seven minutes till both parties were quite exhausted. The Organ then played God save the Queen when every person joined which was very impressive. Then the Chancellor Dr. Plumtre conferred the degrees on Baron Hugel, Mr. Gladstone, Mr. Hallam, Mr. Cotton etc. the last is Mrs. Acland's father and was staying here. I daiesay ɪaɪa will know his name, he was or is governor of the bank of Ergland and a great promoter of all good schemes in the country and always interesting himself greatly in Church extersion. Then Sir Thomas Dyke Acland a wonderful man in arother way, so energetic and so amusing, he lives at Killerton a fine ɪlace in Devonshire and both he and Mr. Cotton were most liberal in their invitations for us to come and visit them. Sir Thomas has promised to show me some Perth worthies ɼainted on the back of a screen if I come, and I strongly suspect from description that the redoubtable Baillie Luke is amongst the number.

'I was introduced the other day to a couple who were calling here—Mr. and Lady Anna Gore Langton—I daresay you will recollect her trying to elope last year and when in the middle of the ceremony the Duke of Buckingham her father coming in and catching them. She is a very lively person & very plain, he a perfect stick and not a word to say. I daresay as he has plenty of money, that was the attraction. I heard the Latin poem read and then came out. I saw Jane Holland there looking very stout and Mr. and Mrs. Foley and Frank Holland. In the evening we went to tea in Exeter College Gardens and it was a lovely sight, all the tea parties sitting under the trees and a fine band of music. When it got darker the garden was illuminated the same as at Taymouth, and the lights placed so as to throw the light on the old buildings. We went afterwards into the large Hall to hear some Glees and then came home. This morning we went to Christ Church Hall to breakfast, about 50 sat down at Mr. Hills invitation and enjoyed a very nice meal with fine fruit afterwards. This afternoon we are to dine in Exeter College Hall and there is to be music afterwards.

The heat is something intense and the Ladies are all dressed in thin Tarlatane dresses, Lace bonnets and pale glace silk Mantillas.'

*   *   *

Broad Street, Oxford
10 July 1848

'Mr. Marriott spent the day with us and he and John had long discussions on Divinity. Dr. and Mrs. Acland are I think Puseyites, and so is Lady Trevelyan and not Roman Catholic, but I should think she went much farther than our friends. You need not be afraid of us turning Puseyite for I see nothing like it and John is always arguing against it, at least he was yesterday which was the first time the subject was mentioned.'

Meanwhile Ruskin's fertile mind was occupied with a new project, a book on architecture, and he and Effie left Oxford for 'a pilgrimage to the English Shrines'. (Preface to the first edition of *The Seven Lamps*) with Salisbury as their first stop.

If Effie had any hopes that she and John would resume their interrupted honeymoon she was soon disillusioned when Mr. and Mrs. Ruskin announced their intention of accompanying them—not, as Ruskin's biographer remarks, the wisest arrangement in the world, one may think.

John, too, had no time to pay attention to his wife as he worked at taking measurements from morning to night which even his proud father found rather trying. 'My son', he wrote to Harrison, 'occupies himself with the architecture of the cathedral, a lovely edifice, but I find it very slow.'

John soon caught a cold and the fuss his mother made caused Effie much amusement, though she would doubtless have preferred to have looked after him herself.

White Hart Inn, Salisbury
20 July 1848

'John's cold is not away yet but it is not so bad as he had with us and I think it would go away with care if Mr. and Mrs. Ruskin would only let him alone. They are telling him 20 times a day that it is very slight and only nervous which I

think it is, at the same time they talk constantly to him about
what he ought to do, and in the morning Mrs. Ruskin begins
with "don't sit near these towels John they're damp" and in
the forenoon "John you must not read these papers till they
are dried", and in this steaming weather George has to take all
his clothes to the kitchen fire to air them and does not let him
go out after dinner. We dine at half past four and from five to
seven it is as warm as the hottest part of the day. John follows
scarcely any of the directions and it would amuse me, all this,
if I did not see that it makes John notwithstanding quite
nervous, and whenever they ask him how he is he begins to
cough, then John coughs for a little and Mr. R. says "that
cough is not going away, I wish you would take care", and
when I never speak of it I never hear him cough once; his
pulse and general health are perfectly good. While I am writing
John is out of the room and Mr. and Mrs. R. are concocting all
sorts of remedies, Mrs. R. is proposing *tea-papers* for his chest
—they are most kind but I think all this does him harm.'

   The tea-papers did not come up to Mrs. Ruskin's expectations
and a few days later all the Ruskins were ill and they decided
to abandon the pilgrimage and return to Denmark Hill.

                              White Hart Inn, Salisbury
                                      27 July 1848

'John I am sorry to say,' wrote Effie, 'has been in bed since
Monday night but he is much better and I think excepting a
little cough now he is much better; he finds himself very
comfortable in bed, reading, being read to, and amused in
various ways. And I think he feels little trouble and a rest from
his work more than lying there for illness, but I think it will
do him good, the only thing I am fearful of is its weakening
him, but whenever the house is ready at Denmarkhill we are
going home which we all think is the best plan. I think I am
the only person who is enjoying the place and in good
health, for Mrs. Ruskin has really a very bad cold and Mr.
Ruskin rather worse than usual of his stomach complaints. I
sit in my bedroom which John now has to himself with him till
one o'clock sewing and talking or reading a novel for a while

aloud, then drawing and reading French to myself; at one Anne goes out and walks behind me for two or three hours, I generally get far ahead and then stop till she comes up. Mr. Ruskin is so very particular about me and always sends George or Anne when I go in the Town.'

At that date it was not thought proper for young married women to go out unescorted.

Effie told her parents that she was enjoying herself but, as appears in her last letter to Mrs. Ruskin, she did not share John's amusement that Mr. Ruskin believed he was occupying a separate room because of recent intimate relations with his wife.

'Whilst we were at Salisbury when you caused me to be put in another room on account of an illness, which he told me his father supposed to arise from his recent connection with me, he used to laugh and say his father was imagining things very different to what they were'.

On return to Denmark Hill John was 'laid up by his mother in pillows and coverlets' and occupied himself planning a tour in Normandy which resulted in the writing, immediately afterwards, of *The Seven Lamps of Architecture*.

CHAPTER VI

The Seven Lamps of Architecture

EARLY in August Ruskin's father accompanied his son and Effie as far as Boulogne, where he saw them off by rail to Abbeville.

John was in a fever to make the most of his time and for the next six weeks he was at work from six in the morning till late at night, measuring, note-taking and sketching.

It was no time for frivolity, and both his young wife and his servant George assisted him with notes and tracings. Effie was keenly interested in everything she saw and no doubt preserved John's health by persuading him to break away from his work for a walk in the evening. From Abbeville Ruskin wrote to his father:

'It is most fortunate that I have come here, straight from Salisbury—not even bluntirg at Winchester the severe memory of that Gothic; for, much as I admired Abbeville porch before, it comes uj on me now in such luscious richness,— so full, so fantastic—so exquisitely picturesque that I seem never to have seen it before—. . . there is not a street without fatal marks of restoration, and in twenty years it is plain that not a vestige of Abbeville, or indeed of any old French town, will be left . . . I seem born to conceive what I cannot execute, recommend what I cannot obtain, and mourn over what I cannot save.'   (Cook)

Some extracts from Effie's letters written from Abbeville give a picture of their activities:

Abbeville
9 August 1848

'We went on board the steamer at three and though it was a lovely day I went down stairs and, the Ladies Cabin being full, I went into the General Cabin and laid down all my length with a gentleman ditto at each end, and so on all round, with one or two on the floor; in about ten minutes all the Ladies were ill, and when two or three heavy lurches came in the middle of the Channel the whole assembly rose en masse from

EFFIE GRAY IN 1853
A pencil drawing, signed by John Ruskin and herself

their reclining position dreadfully sick. I was very ill about eight times and Mr. Ruskin coming down once said it was like a scene of the plague or something. The Stewards however were very attentive and brought me some nice eau de cologne which revived me a little. But the worst was a German or Frenchman, whose moustache Imperial and beard nearly covered his face, being besides a very large man, he was in a dreadful state and moaned and groaned and roared terribly. However at half past five we landed and were ushered into a custom house where our passports were looked at by some soldiers dressed in green, and after that we took a Fly and went to the Hotel des Bains, Boulogne where John and Mr. Ruskin immediately broke into raptures at being again in France and the inferiority of England, which amused me very much.

'I walked about the town yesterday morning and I was very much impressed with the *Character* everything had, the faces of the people, their smooth hair and picturesque caps, with scarlet petticoats and yellow or red garters. They were unloading cannon from the ships in the Harbour. They say this morning that the French have declared war with Austria and gone over the Alps but we have not seen a paper yet. John is out sketching the Cathedral, St. Wogram, from a cafe opposite. As it is so wet and has been raining for ten days we came here to the Hotel de L'Europe which is a splendid place in a large court with nobody in it but ourselves. Mr. Ruskin left us at Boulogne to go home; the railway was delightfully comfortable and the carriages much more comfortable and better fitted up than any I have seen in England and better as to punctuality but no passengers scarcely; the poor people here say the revolution has ruined them and they wanted nobody but Louis Philippe and it is only these villains in Paris who caused all the misfortunes.'

*   *   *

Abbeville
14 August 1848

'John is quite in his element here and very happy. There has only been one arrival since we came of an English family going to Italy, they have a very large carriage and are six with four

I

servants; they are just setting off with four horses, two cages full of canary birds, and a fat sick dog in a basket. John goes out immediately after breakfast and draws till dinner time at half past one. I work and read in French for an hour or two, Dumas' Monte Christo; these Novels of the time are the best books for learning you Modern French. I have read half of the first volume but I do not think nearly so much of him as De Balzac, about the same difference as between James and Sir Walter Scott, but Dumas is fertile in invention and interesting. In the evenings we take a walk into the country which I enjoy very much, the long lines of trees are so picturesque and the masses of poplars. Yesterday being Sunday I went to Mass at ten o'clock in the magnificent Cathedral of St. Wilfran, the whole front is covered with the most elaborate flamboyant tracery and the niches are still filled with statues. I was very much confounded with the mixture of the grand and the ridiculous in the whole scene; we were a little late and, on entering, the priests were chanting in a very sonorous voice and all the people kneeling and muttering with their lips and at the door the Verger was chasing a dog out with a besom in the most absurd style. In the Services, which were very well attended, I did not observe more than six men in the morning and none in the evening. I asked the waiter the reason; he shrugged his shoulders and said "Ce n'est pas l'habitude". The men were all at their shop doors smoking long pipes, all the shops being open and the families sitting round the doors with groups amongst them of the 4th Cavalry with their helmets and long plumes; all were very quiet and happy. A little child in a white muslin frock and black velvet spencer was dancing on high stilts to a man playing a trumpet, the company of horsemanship 20 in number rode past with a band playing a fine march and announced that this was their last day of performance. You may imagine my astonishment accustomed to the quiet of a Scotch Sabbath.'

From Lisieux Ruskin wrote:

'You never saw anything yet in France so lovely as this Normandy—just fancy vallies like rich bits of Italy, tufted with elm, poplar, willow, and Spanish chestnut, set between round sweeping grouse hills of purple heather, as bare as Schehallion. I think Effie makes the heather grow under her feet.'

And from Rouen:

'I still feel this place Unseen; this is partly, however, owing to my slowness in taking in; I cannot grasp it; every time I walk into the Square it is new to me. Still I verily believe that I now know more about it than any English architect, and than most French, and I have improved in my drawing in these three months considerably.   (Cook)

Effie wrote from Rouen:

Rouen

17 August 1848

'We went and saw the Chateau which is almost in the town and was very melancholy. There is an immense collection of pictures of no merit excepting as interesting historical portraits, all the Condés, Montmorencies, D'Artois, I should think in French history, and none, either ladies or gentlemen, remarkable for beauty. One room is fitted up with Pictures of the Queen's visit but the Ladies dresses look shockingly vulgar although only six or four years ago. The floors are of beautiful inlaid wood of different colours and some fine Gobelin Tapestry. The government still keep it in great order. The Hotel was very disagreeable and redolent of French smells in every variety. Next morning we went to Dieppe which we merely passed through, got into the Railway and came here through the most lovely country of wooded hills and vales. I had no conception France was so lovely, we have nothing in Scotland or England like the multitudes of trees planted as they are here. We are in the Hotel D'Albion, very comfortable and a nice Piano.

'John is perfectly frantic with the spirit of restoration here and at other places, the men actually before our eyes knocking down the time worn black with age pinnacles and sticking up in their place new stone ones to be carved at some future time; you could not conceive they could be such idiots and worse if you did not see it. John is going to have some Daguerreotypes taken of the Churches as long as they are standing; it is valuable as they are destroying them so fast. John says he is

quite happy in seeing I enjoy myself so much, and if it was not
for my gentle mediation he would certainly do something
desperate and get put in prison for knocking some of the work-
men off the scaffolding, but that I always keep him in good
humour and he does not know what he should do without me.'

Though Effie told her mother that she was keeping John in
good humour she can hardly have failed to notice that he was
now suffering from depression probably brought on by tired-
ness after his tremendous exertions. At Lisieux he had written
to his father:

'If one were to calculate averageable life at eighty years, with a
doubtful evening after that time, and suppose this represented
by a day of sixteen hours from six morning till ten night, I am
now at *Noon*, you at *six* in the evening—with both of us the
day is far spent—I never think my day is worth much after
twelve o'clock. And yet I fear—forgive me if I am wrong—
that neither of us have either chosen our master or begun our
work.'

(Library Edition Vol. XXXVI Letters Vol. I)

From Rouen he used the unusual medium of a birthday
letter to Effie's brother, George, to reveal his inner discontent.

Rouen
1 October 1848

'You are still at an age when birthdays are not subjects of
regret, though they may be sources of resolution. By the time
that you are my age, I trust you will be better than I am—and
have been more useful in your generation—my last ten years
have passed like a fable—many of their days very happy, but
I begin to find now the pain of looking back upon happiness
which has been profitless. Your sister read to me your mother's
account of your long walk from Blair Athol, it reminded me of
many such happy wanderings of my own—now so far forgotten that I remember of them only that they *were* happy—
while I cannot recover their details with distinctness enough to
enjoy them again—Their only effect has been that of deadening my powers of present enjoyment. A life more laboriously

spent is probably one far more gladdening in the retrospect—
the animal spirit of the youth is given to him that he may not
sink under its irksomeness—while it quickens his powers of
after enjoyment of the reserved pleasures of more advanced age.

'I write this in the feeling that there must be moments when
the letters you receive or hear from your sister describing what
she has seen—must sometimes give you rather pain than
pleasure—you will not envy her or me—but you must nevertheless sometimes think it strange and hard that while you are
at your desk day after day—we are wandering in perpetual
liberty.

'I am not one of those who maintain that each position in
life has an equal—though different kind of happiness—I
believe the amount enjoyed to be enormously different—but
that in the retrospect of the most fortunate there is probably a
bitterness which would be well exchanged for the exaltation
over duty done under a severe lot,—without taking into
account what of course—is cast out of all account in every care
or thought that we take about this world—that there will be a
much more sure balance of accounts hereafter.'

From Rouen they went to Falaise and thence to Mortain,
Coutances, Bayeux, and to Rouen for a second visit. Effie kept
her parents well posted with their doings and the following
extracts from her long descriptive letters continue the story of
the tour.

Falaise
27 August 1848

'We left Rouen on Wednesday at seven in the morning in a
Diligence. John had taken the Coupée for himself so we were
very comfortable and saw the six grey horses prancing in front
in very fine style. The country was perfectly beautiful and like
our richest Highland scenery with the rich cultivation of the
South at the bottom of the little Hills. We passed the old
Abbey of Bec from whence came two of the early Archbishops
of Canterbury, Anselm and Lanfranc, whose tombs I saw when
there. The Abbey, now turned into a mill, raised its tower far
above the wood in which it was embedded; at the foot a heath-
covered hill. We reached Lisieux skirting almost the whole way

the forest of Monvery, an immense tract of tree country in which William the Conqueror was hunting when he learned the death of Edward the Confessor, before invading England. It was pouring rain when we reached at three and as we could do nothing we dined in the very uncomfortable Inn and felt extremely cold. The people did not seem accustomed to strangers and we could get nothing we wanted. There were some interesting old wooden houses in the town and the Churches were fine, at least one was. Here they gave us the cheese of the country and how the people eat it is a marvel to me for it is small, made of cream and kept until it is in the last stage of decay with the most disgusting smell possible. Next day we left in the diligence for this place at three. The diligences go very slow when they have only two horses and although the distance was only thirty miles we did not reach the Hotel de France till nearly nine o'clock. The country was most beautiful and the sky heavenly till it got dark. We passed several Chateaux near the road and a fine one at St. Jo, a curious little village which belongs to an Englishman. John and I always go to mass in the morning when there is no Protestant Church, and he reads the service when we return and again in the evening; we take our bibles for the hour the mass lasts and read while the prayers are going on and listen to the Sermon, when it comes, for it is generally a very good one, but today the service was the worst I have seen and I was quite astonished with the horrid set of Priests who were more dirty than you can conceive, but the Organ was very fine and burst two or three times into a few noble chords of martial Music from I think some of the Italian Operas.'

*   *   *

Mortain, Normandie
3 September 1848

'We left Falaise on Thursday at 8 in the morning and arrived at Vire at three in the afternoon, a very long ride and our Conductor stopped I should think about a score of times on the road to speak to his acquaintances and first to breakfast and then dine quite at his ease. We were in the open coupe but the country was exquisite and the heather fine, we passed Condé sur Noireau where there was a Fair but it seemed an uninteresting place, but the situation beautiful, close to the Valley Corbeaux where are a long double line of high rocks; at Vire we remained the day, the Inn dirty and uncomfortable the town so so, and seemingly especially under the direction of the Virgin, for there were several statues of her on the Houses in stone niches with in French under them "*Marie protège la ville*". There was a Norman Castle here but only a fine ruin remains and charming walks round it with long rows of quaintly cut trees, and the river running below. The people seemed all very busy and at Vire most of the army clothing is made, we saw some curious old wooden houses, and a great many old women spining, as in Scotland, and a number of the other women sitting at their doors making a coarse kind of Valenciennes lace for caps. The women there and here wear a different sort of cap, it is of sewed net over a blue calico frame with broad plaits of the net sticking far off the face and out all round. The Inn here is detestable, we have to pass through a kitchen worse than the one at the Bridge of Tummel to get to our bedrooms. In John's dressingroom we sit and have our meals, but the floor of my room is so dirty that if any part of my clothes touch it they are covered with dirt directly and our washing basins are little, so small in fact that every time I wash I send the water over in streams on the table, they have no cups and our breakfast and tea are taken in bowls nearly as large as the basins. The Abbey Blanche is about a mile out of town, formerly a convent but now a Seminary for young men and boys. The people here appear to be quite another race and much more religious. This morning at eight the Church, which we see into across the Street being raised on a mound, was filled with hundreds of men and some women, the former in blouses of blue and glazed hats, at prayers all down on the bare stone on their knees and when we went to mass at ten the Church was again quite full and it is very large. I was pleased with the service and it was more sensible than what I have yet seen. I looked over an old woman and found many of the prayers very beautiful and almost exactly like the English prayers but some others were very different. We have returned and John, having read the

Morning Service, has gone out to walk till dinnertime. I walk
with him from four till seven in the evening but the heat just
now is too powerful for me or I should think for anyone but
John, he could stand any heat I think and like it for it is like
Italy. We go on Tuesday morning to Avranches for a week to
allow John time for some sketches of St. Michel.'

*   *   *

Mont St. Michel
9 September 1848

'Avranches is considered one of the handsomest towns in
Normandy but we found it very stupid and uninteresting
excepting the beautiful view across the rich plain to the sea and
Mont St. Michel standing far off; next morning we got an open
Cabriolet and started for the Mount—12 miles although
looking only about five. The country became, as we approached,
only sand and tamarisk trees and, instead of Mont St. Michel
being in the sea as we expected, it rose hugely and grandly out
of a desert of sand, the same for many miles round a dead flat
without a single speck on its surface. We drove five miles
across and arriving found, contrary to all expectation, a very
nice clean little Inn where we took up our abode. We found
that the sea does surround the Mount once a week some feet
in depth but owing to the deep flat for so many miles a few feet
of tide covers the whole of this desert of sand; you will know
the position of it on the map, and I have asked John to draw a
little sketch of it which I think he has done very well; there is
the fine Gothic Church at the top, then the Castle now holding
500 prisoners, and then the little town between the Houses.
There are some who have little gardens with vines and ripe
grapes hanging all over the rocks. Round the fort is an immense
thick wall thirty or forty feet high with large towers at
intervals. We went through the Castle, which is immensely
strong but it was melancholy to the mind. Instead of seeing the
noble Knights of Malta and St. Michel in the splendid Hall des
Chevaliers and the Holy monks in the still perfect cloisters you
meet files of prisoners with their green jackets and yellow
trousers and hideous countenances, and although the end of the

church is kept as a chapel for them they all dine in the nave at long wooden tables, with the kitchen in one of the side Chapels. It was melancholy enough and strange; I was glad to get out, but as you may well conceive from the land it has a very fine appearance and is 400 feet high and the rock is red Granite.

'We leave on Monday for Coutances and then to Bayeux. We once intended going to Dol and Dinan in Brittany but we think that remaining some time at Caen and Rouen on our way back will bring us not sooner home than the first week of October, and I think we should not be longer out of our house than that if we go to Switzerland next year. John and I tried to walk as far as the sea this evening but the sand deceives one so that you walk and walk and seem not a bit farther off the Mount, so we gave it up and returning sat down on the rocks and played a game a little like Bowls putting a stone for a mark and having a number of others to try who could throw nearest the mark. Now we have come in to have our delicious Café au lait which we shall have served as soon as the cows come from the country opposite where they feed all day to be milked.'

*　　　*　　　*

St. Lo
17 September 1848

'John is taking a fine sketch of the Facade of the Cathedral; he sits in a wool comber's shop, not a very healthy or clean place. I go down occasionally and find him beside three women who comb the wool ready for spinning; they told me it was very unhealthy and it certainly was very dirty work for their aprons were covered quite black with the oil coming out of the wool. The womens caps here are very fine with long lappets hanging down to the waist edged with the finest broad Valenciennes lace. It must surely be very cheap but at Caen where 20,000 women and children make it I am going to buy some if I fancy it. I sit in the sun in the forenoon when John is sketching and draw and work by myself. John makes many lamentations, being obliged to leave me for as he says such long dull hours and also after dinner, but I am quite happy and I go for him at five and enjoy my walk till teatime very much. John is looking very strong and well and so am I, and so is George if one may judge by the rumours of extraordinary breakfasts and dinners he sometimes gives us hints of having taken, and I often see him when he goes out with me quietly munching a pear or some walnuts.'

Though Effie reported that John was well and strong, his output of energy was tremendous and neither can have been sorry when the time came to return home.

They had acquired a house of their own at 31 Park Street, Grosvenor Square, and between November 1848 and April 1849 he wrote *The Seven Lamps of Architecture* which was described by a reviewer as 'a hymn in architectural loveliness' and made a great sensation in literary circles. Effie, happily free from her husband's parents, was busy getting her house in order. Whilst the young couple were abroad Mr. Ruskin and Mr. Gray were exchanging a series of slightly acrid letters on the subject of Effie's brother's future. Mr. Gray wanted Mr. Ruskin to help George to obtain employment in a Colonial Broker's Office but Mr. Ruskin refused and amongst the reasons he advanced was that George, as a clerk, would be an embarrassment to his son and Effie, who could not admit him into their house and society. This, very naturally, infuriated Mr. Gray.

If Mr. Gray was a reader of *Punch*, then publishing Thackeray's famous 'Snob' papers, he will have been aware that 'it was impossible in the condition of society not to be sometimes a snob', but he must have been surprised to find his old friend was a prince of snobs from the following letter:

> Denmark Hill
> 1 August 1848

'The allusion to the Society my Son and your Daughter might move in might convey an impression of very absurd and very inordinate ambition—and the exclusiveness attached to it in relation to George might seem heartless and unkind but the facts are these. I happened to make my Son a Gentleman Commoner at Ch. Church Oxford—partly to increase the comforts of a youth in delicate Health—partly to see during

my own Life how he would stand such an Ordeal—partly from
the vanity of showing I would give my Son the best quality of
Education I could get for Money and lastly because the Dean of
Ch. church said I ought to do so. He conducted himself well—
he was resolute in moderation; he was at once introduced to the
highest men by two young noblemen whom he had met on his
Travels—he showed Talent and got the prize for English
Verse. He was invited to the Duke of Leinster's and many
places he refused to go to—I have not named to any one, what
Company he has kept since leaving College—but I was
gratified to find him admitted to Tables of Ministers, Ambas-
sadors and Bishops—but I was aware this arose from his having
shown some knowledge in the fine Arts a subject chiefly
interesting to the higher Classes—How little he valued high
Tables may be gathered from the fact that, not from him, but
by mere chance I heard, that one of a Select Dinner Party of
eight of which he was one, was Lord John Russell—John cares
nothing at all about high people. He is not a Tuft hunter and
values people only for Intellect and worth and associates only
with people who have tastes like his own. He detests crowds and
London Seasons, but the Men whose Intellects he desires to
come in contact with, are only to be found in distinguished
Circles or Coteries and hence he will be found in high Society
just so far as it is necessary. I deem this long History due to
George, that he may comprehend my hinting the probability
of a divided Society. It is not George alone, but Mrs. Ruskin
and my self are equally excluded. John has brought Lords to
our Table but we are very marked in regarding them as John's
Visitors and when Sir Wr. and Lady James last breakfasted
here John and Effie presided and neither Mrs. R nor I ever
appeared. I have got them their House in Park St. to be among
their own Set—when they like to put up with Wine Merchants
or Colonial Brokers they may dine here now and then—but I
hope there is no undue pride in my desiring the young Couple
to retain some hold of good Society. My son's inclination is
rather the recluse—and there is always danger of a Recluse
getting rusty and Society shaking him off as rapidly as it took
him on—whether by his Book, or tastes I cannot tell—but
there a very kind interest taken in him and Effie gains golden

Opinions. In a Letter I have just sent him from Lord Eastnor
—are these words—"I heard of your Marriage last month
quite accidentally from Lady Stratford Canning at Constantinople—" I think it rather pleasant than otherwise both to you
and me to have our Children spoken of by such persons.'

Effie strongly disapproved of Mr. Ruskin's attempts to draw
them into the quarrel about her brother's future.

Rouen
10 October 1848

'Mr. Ruskin' she wrote to her father 'did send us one of
your letters and what he had written, I thought it quite
unnecessary and entirely disapprove of the whole system of
sending letters about . . . I assure you that we never sent any of
your letters to Mr. Ruskin nor did I ever let John do so. . .'

and in another letter

Gisors
17 October 1848

'John was writing to his father only saying that George's
intentions were all good, so I hope this will be the last said
upon an unpleasant subject which corresponding upon has
done no good, but it ought to end in each party thinking no
wrong is intended on either side and I think you ought to
excuse Mr. R's suspicious character when you consider the
claims he has upon him every day from his relations, most
teasing for him who has given so much and makes him look on
the worst side, but be sure no ill was intended so there let the
subject drop.'

When, some years later, the Ruskins were concocting their
own version of John's married life they remembered this
storm in a teacup but conveniently forgot Effie's determination
not to be embroiled and that she championed Mr. Ruskin.

CHAPTER VII

Doctors All

MR. RUSKIN must have been much gratified at the young couple's social activities during their first winter in London.

Though John grudged every minute from *The Seven Lamps*, he found time to take his wife to parties where she made many new friends and thoroughly enjoyed herself:

> 31 Park Street, Grosvenor Square
> 16 November 1848

'I have had a number of visitors all of whom I have missed, but calling again have. seen them—Mr and Mrs Milman—he is Prebend of Westminster and the Poet of that name—lives in a superb house of Inigo Jones's building inside Westminster. Lady Chantrey, the sculptor's widow, I have not seen yet but she is a very hospitable kind person. Mr. and Mrs. William Gray, cousin or something to Lord Gray, Mr. Eastlake, the Thomsons Welbeck St., George's horror and mine at least Mrs. T. is, I suppose they want to know John but they won't, although they know me. All the other people are out of town but the Flemings called and, as they have done so, I shall call the first day I can for I find that the distances here preclude the possibility of people being more intimate than they like. We sat an hour the other day with Lady Davy who entertained us with most interesting and instructing conversation, a great deal about the Queen and Court, from the Court to the State and Church, Louis Philippe and his sons who she has an immense contempt for etc etc, quite wonderful. John had a delightful letter from Mr. Newton from Rome—what a mind he has! I never read or heard a more powerful criticism upon the antiques of Italy and upon Rome itself, he is a Greek living in our days with his whole mind devoted to its art, I quite long for his coming back, it will be such a treat. Mr. Tom Richmond I suppose was so pleased that he asked John as a favor to be allowed to paint me, he is a portrait-painter by profession.

John's drawing of me is a very pretty drawing but the lower part of the face not the least like me so that he is going to begin another tomorrow and keep the other to practise upon, but I hope he will succeed and please Papa.'

*　　　*　　　*

31 Park Street
21 November 1848

'Mr. and Mrs. Richmond drank tea with us last night, they are very refined excellent people and enjoyed themselves very much, I gave them roasted snipes for supper which Mr. Telford sent us. John's friend Lord Eastnor comes on Friday evening. I expect to be very much entertained as he is quite an original, very clever and has just come from Turkey. He is Earl Somers' son and has lived from one country to another for many years, coming home to see his Father every year and then vanishing again after two or three months. John is much taken up about the state of the world at present and he said to him the other day in a very serious tone, ''Well! Eastnor, what are you going to do in the middle of all this uncertainty and commotion?'' ''Oh!'' he said, ''I am going into Devonshire!'' The tone was so absurd that it quite upset John's gravity and made him roar with laughing. I did not see him but John was saying, talking of France, that the morals of the people were so bad that they were enough to bring it about, Lord E. said ''Why they are not half so bad as the Swiss or Germans''. John was astonished. ''Why'', he said, ''the single circumstance of husbands and wives separating for the least difference in character or opinion is bad enough, but to give you an instance a friend of mine dined lately with a party of six at Berlin *who were all married to each other*.''

*　　　*　　　*

31 Park Street
2 December 1848

'Did I tell you that John had been so good as to get two tickets to hear the ''Elijah'' in Exeter Hall on the 15th where Jenny

Lind sings the first part; it will be a very grand affair and it is for the purpose of aiding the Mendelssohn scholarships at Leipsic founded by the great master. I am to have plenty of visitors today for George has just come to say that Sir Robert H. Inglis is down stairs—I do not know him so I shall wait until John comes up for me. Mr. Gordon from Oxford dines with us today. Besides all these Mr. Evan Nepean, the Clergyman of the district, was here. Sir R. Inglis is very agreeable, appears very religious and clever; as John says, we are getting into the thick of it and to crown all who should we meet the other day coming from calling on me but Mrs. Thomson and three daughters. I could not but introduce John so that today comes an invitation for Friday the 8th. John wants to go, strange to say, and now I must conclude and hoping to see you in the course of 5 weeks or so.'

*   *   *

31 Park Street
2 December 1848

'I dined last night at Sir Robert Inglis's. Lady Inglis is a nice little old Lady very kind and agreeable. The party was a large one of 20 persons but very quiet and enjoyable and everything as to dinner, pictures and rooms very first rate. In the dining-room is a very fine picture of Wilberforce (who was a great friend of Sir Robert) by Sir Thomas Lawrence and at the bottom of the room two equally fine by Richmond of Thomas Babington Macaulay and Mr. Hallam the Historian. There was some very fine Greek wine at dinner from Chios and Samos, which Lord Glenelg wanted me to take some of with him, but I said the name was so delicious that I was content with the sound of that without the taste. Sir Robert went out with a lady, when dinner was announced, calling behind him the names of the gentlemen who were to take the appointed Ladies and follow in the order named, which is an excellent plan as at some of these dinners, when you don't know the names of people who are some times very particular about their place, and step down before a very ugly Duchess without ever knowing what you have done, but this prevents mistakes although rather laughable. However I was appropriated to the Lord Chief Baron and we marched down stairs in great form, he giving his immense hat to the footman at the bottom. We went to the top of the table and on my other hand was Lord Glenelg, a delightful person not young but with quite white hair. The Lord Chief Baron, whose own name I don't know, was very imposing, very pompous and very gravely amusing. He began telling me of his luck in sporting, he had never, he said, but twice and that was at Drayton with Sir R. Peel shot without a license. I quietly intimated that he might have been taken up for poaching. He said "Ah! true, but I afterwards paid for some years for a license though I never shot, but when they became ten per cent dearer I did not take out any more." Mr. T. B. Macaulay sat opposite and he is quite a Lion at present from his very clever History from James II down that everyone is reading just now. I never heard such a man at conversation, he goes from St. Chrysostom's sermon at Antioch to the people not to pick each other's pockets in Church to M. Thiers speeches twenty years ago, gives them word for word, then back again to Greek Mausoleums 4 Centuries B.C., gives you all the names of the people who built them contemporary with the battle of Salamis, then to Seringapatam streets and mud houses and going at such a pace, quite wonderful. It was quite worth going to see alone and I owed the pleasure to Lord Glenelg who, knowing I had not seen him before, said he would bring him out which he did most excellently.'

Sir Robert Inglis, was M.P. for Oxford University, and a trustee of the British Museum; Lord Glenelg, now retired from public life, had had a distinguished career as M.P., Irish Secretary, President of the Board of Trade and Treasurer of the Navy; Mrs. Eastlake, whose husband became President of the Royal Academy, was destined to play an important part in Effie Gray's life, as it was she who became her confidante and support during the periods of her greatest trials.

The party going came to an end after Effie and John, both far from well, were compelled to attend a series of Christmas parties at Denmark Hill.

Denmark Hill
4 January 1849

'You may fancy how dull and weak I feel when I tell you I have not tasted meat for a week and during that time only tea, and beef-tea and today nothing at all. I asked leave to remain in my room today which John and I thought the best thing, but I was not allowed, and again today, as almost every day this week, company six o'clock dinner and not in bed till between twelve and one. It is against all common sense to suppose that either John or I can be well with such a total change of life from our early hours and moderate habits, and at present my appetite is quite gone. If I had been at home and managed myself I do not think such would have been the case but it can't be helped with these people in the house, and nobody can understand I suppose why I am dull. I hope to see you next week when two days and quiet at home will I hope make me quite better before you come, which will make me still better. John's cold in the head is very bad and Dr. Grant entirely disapproves of all that Dr. Richardson had been giving me so one does not know what to say when Doctors differ!'

After the parties Effie became seriously ill. The two doctors that were called in quarrelled over her case, and the unfortunate patient took 'more and more messes' in order to satisfy the doctors and Mrs. Ruskin, but with no avail.

John, exhausted after his tremendous concentration on his book, yearned for a complete change of scene and decided to go to Switzerland with his parents in the spring, and there accumulate material for a third and fourth volume of *Modern Painters*.

Effie was not well enough to accompany them, and for more than one reason was glad to go to her old home when the Ruskins left for the Continent.

The London doctors, whose 'messes' she had uncomplainingly drunk, had entirely misunderstood her condition, and she had not been at Bowerswell long before her mother and the family doctor discovered that she was suffering from a nervous ailment. There is, too, a passage in one of John's letters written

K

from Switzerland which shows that Effie was already beginning to tire of the continual intrusion of her in-laws.

'I often hear my mother or father saying "poor child—if she *could* but have thrown herself openly upon us, and trusted in us, and felt that we desired only her happiness and would make her ours, how happy she might have been; and how happy she might have made us all".'

Though Mrs. Ruskin must have been overjoyed at recovering possession of her son for a few months, John's strange love for Effie was, as yet, unabated. From Paris he wrote:

Paris
24 April 1849

'I expect a line from my dearest love tomorrow at Sens; Do you know, pet, it seems almost a dream to me that we have been married: I look forward to meeting you; and to your *next* bridal night; and to the time when I shall again draw your dress from your snowy shoulders: and lean my cheek upon them, as if you were still my betrothed only; and I had never held you in my arms.

'God bless you, my dearest.'

From Dijon:

Dijon
27 April 1849

'You will be wondering much mine own—of my seeming neglect of you, these several days back—but I was really ashamed to make any more apologies to you: and I could do nothing *but* make apologies: you know I told you how I had been plagued with my plates: well—I stopped at Folkstone chiefly that I might take great pains with the last I had to finish—that it might redeem all faults in the others. I sent this plate away on the Friday evening; and on the Saturday evening I got down the proof of it. It was absolutely good for *nothing*: I had over laboured it, and it was as black as a cinder: I could not bear to put off our journey, so I took a plate with me; and set to work at Boulogne on Monday: the only clear *day*light I had; that was the reason I did not write to you—Tuesday we were all day on railroad: and we have come about 280 miles over bad roads from Paris here: I had but bits and scraps of time in the morning and evening: and I have but half an hour ago sent off in a flat little box, the new plate to Cornhill: It ought to be there on Tuesday and if the book *can* be out on your birthday, in spite of this delay, it shall be. The new plate cannot I think be very much out of the way, though it may be harsh and scratchy; and very different from what it would have been if I had had more time: However—I am now quite clear of the whole affair: and though I have been much annoyed these last few days; I have not suffered, my eyes feel quite strong and I look forward to a glorious campaign of sketching among the Alps. I will really write you some decent letters now, though you must put up with this shabby one tonight: as we start early tomorrow and I have quantities of litter to put away. Good night, my dearest, dearest bride.'

From Geneva on 1 May:

Geneva
1 May 1849

'I believe this will reach you before your birthday, and my next, though it shall be sent as soon as I can write it from Chambery may not until after your birthday: so I must trust my fondest wishes and dearest love to this one: and my hopes that we may never be separated any more on that day: I went this morning to Mr. Bautier to buy you a bracelet, which shall be sent as soon as may be: when you want a *set* of Geneva ornaments you must come with me to buy them, I cannot trust my own taste.

'I do not like to write you letters about our doings here— lest it should grieve you that you are not with us: and I cannot write about the Alps or express my feelings to you, because really I do love these places so much that I would only distress you by showing how hopeless it was ever to wean me from them.'

From Chambery:

Chambery
2 May 1849

' Darling Love,

'We have had rather a fatiguing drive today: reaching however this our *farthest point* at ½ past five when I may now turn and look back to my dearest wifie, and wish her many happy returns of her birthday, and one happy return of her husband in due time. But I am afraid my pet that you could not have managed to travel with us at the place we have come, at all. Let me see: Monday, up at six, off at ½ past 8,—days rest at Boulogne. Tuesday, up at ½ past five, off at eight, for Paris get there at four. Wednesday up at six, off at eight, get to Sens at six—evening—Thursday, off at ½ past eight, eleven hours to Mont Bard. Friday, off at 10, seven hours to Dijon. Saturday, off at eight, 10 hours to Champagnole. Monday off at ½ past eight, nine hours to Geneva—one whole day at Geneva, off today at eight 9½ hours here. I find I can't write tonight—too sleepy.

' 3rd May—It is a lovely day—all the peaks of the mountains as clear as crystal, and I have got a cluster of gentians, cut up with their turf yesterday which I am going to make observations upon for my next book. I like my plates better than I thought I did, when I look at them quietly I think they will rather make a sensation. A thousand loves and fond wishes.'

*   *   *

Chambery
3 May 1849

' We were shown over the house by a lively monk; I had a bit of an argument with him on the propriety of his shutting himself up with his brethren in such a place and letting the world fall into all manner of mischief—but having a dampish great coat on—and fearing to dry it upon me, could not have it out, but had decidedly the best of it. While we were up at the Chartreuse my mother was making herself as comfortable as

she could in the country inn below—she partly succeeded; and
the people were mighty obsequious in a disagreeable way: the
bill very much like our friends at Honfleur. One of the serious
items in it was a little bottle of the Elixire de la Chartreuse—a
kind of liqueur distilled by the monks—very like the strongest
whisky with sugar candy in it: a very satisfactory compound,
said to be good for all kinds of complaints: especially for that of
over sobriety. I have therefore brought a whole bottle of it for
my wifie; enclosed in another bottle of pine wood, and sealed
by the monks.

'I had nearly forgotten to ask you, love, whether it would
be very irksome to you as you read Sismondi to note *every
word* that bears in the remotest degree on the interests or
history of Venice? as I want to get at all the facts of Venetian
history as shortly as I can, when I come home. Note every *man*
who is a Venetian, wherever he appears: and make references
to the places distinctly in a little note book kept for the purpose.
It will be a great assistance to me if you can do this.'

In a letter to his friend, George Richmond, Ruskin thus
describes his encounter with the monk.

'By-the-bye, I have been to the Grande Chartreuse too—got
wet going up, and couldn't finish an argument I got into with
one of the monks, on the impropriety of his staying up there
and doing nothing. He compared himself to Moses discomfiting
Amalek by holding up his hands. I begged him to observe that
Moses only came to that when he was too old to do anything
else. I think I should have got the better of him, if it hadn't
been for the weather.'   (*Præterita*)

A few days later Ruskin was annoyed at hearing from his
wife that comments were being made on them going separate
ways, and he replied.

Geneva
10 May 1849

'Your friend Miss Boswell must be a nice clever creature; but
it seems to me that she has a good deal more cleverness than

judgment or discretion, or she would understand the very
simple truth, that it was not *I* who had left *you*, but *you* who
had left *me*—Certainly I never wanted you to leave London,
but you could not be happy unless you went to Perth: and
away you went: much more to the astonishment of *my* friends
in London, than my departure for Switzerland can be to the
surprise of yours in Scotland: I wonder whether they think
that a husband is a kind of thing who is to be fastened to his
wife's waist with her pincushion, and to be taken about with
her wherever she chooses to go. However, my love, never mind
what they say or think; I shall always be glad when you can go
with me, and always take you with me wherever I think it safe
for your health that you should go; when it is not, you must be
prepared to part with me for a month or two, as I must either
follow my present pursuits with the same zeal that I have
hitherto followed them: or go into the church.

'Do not vex yourself because the Raffaelle drawing puzzles
you—you happen just to have pitched upon the most difficult
one of the whole set—because the closest in line: the one of
Jacob and Rachel—of the finding of Moses, or of the blessing
of Jacob would have been easy in comparison: but rather give
the thing up than plague yourself about it: remember there is
a great difference between pride and resolution: I think in
general that not to give up a thing because we "*will* not be
beaten" has more of bulldog-ism in it than of sense: There are
times when we "Must not be beaten": as the Duke said at
Waterloo: but there are other times when we ought to be
beaten, when the victory is useless: as it would be in this case
if it cost too much: I should recommend—and would have
done so at first, had I had time to write anything, that you
should only copy from these pictures a feature here and there—
a hand, foot—head—arm—bit of drapery—or of foliage—
taking the easiest—that is to say that which has fewest lines,
the first—Do not however think your time lost over the
Abraham, as your hand will gain steadiness with every line
you draw.'

From Chamonix, where the party arrived on 14 May, he
sent Effie an amusing comment on the visitors' book.

Chamonix
14 May 1849

'I was amazed in looking over the travellers book at the Montanvert to see the enormous number that pass there, usually in a year—and not less surprised at the vast averages of fools that compose the numbers. There is hardly a single person who writes his name there who does not commit himself—I think the air of the ice—or the looking down for the first time from a great height at the valley, turns their heads—for the world could not go on if there were so little wit in it: the chief thing seen in them all is intense vanity: desire of distinction at any price and for anything mixed with various forms of other vulgarity: and it is very droll to see the self-complacency manifested by people in their vague ideas that they have done something more wonderful than any of the two—three—or four thousand who have perhaps preceded them in the same year. I have half a mind to see if Couttet will lend me one of his books, to publish it—it would serve the people very right—One or two sensible entries are refreshing: one quiet one among a quantity of balderdash pleased me:

William Stokes. Manufacturer. Sheffield.

I doubt not he enjoyed and probably felt the thing as much as any of them. I will make some extracts in my next letter from the travellers book *here*. They may amuse you.'

Ruskin's biographer, Cook, says that the month spent at Chamonix was among the most fruitful times in his life. With his faithful guide, Couttet, he spent long days on the glaciers and in the valleys, observing and sketching for his new book. Meanwhile letters from Bowerswell were holding out no promise of his wife's complete restoration of health, so he and his father thought it was time for them to suggest remedies.
    John wrote:

Vevay
27 May 1849

'It seems to me in the first place that your chief complaint is a nervous weakness preventing you from taking exercise enough to bring on perspiration—you would faint before you would perspire—you will not I think get out of this but by forced exercise to the utmost of your strength every day—until you are able to take enough to put you into a heat—and then you will get well fast enough if you take it regularly.'

His father wrote to Mr. Gray.

Vevay
4 June 1849

'It is impossible for Baths to effect any change on the functions of the Skin—instanter—Some regular course of Diet—Baths—and Exercise will require to be persevered in for some time. A pleasing division of pursuits pursued with Interest will be medicinal.'

All this advice about a case the father did not understand and the son understood, but kept his knowledge to himself, must have irritated Effie's parents who, since their daughter's experience in London, had a poor opinion of the Ruskins' ability to deal with illness.

In June, Mr. Ruskin wrote another of his long verbose letters to Mr. Gray deploring the estrangement between his family and Effie, but evidently entirely unsuspicious of the cause of her nervous ailment.

Vevay
June 1849

'I address you again to repeat the expression of my sincere regret at the continuance of our daughter's bad state of health and further to inform you of the trouble we are all in from not knowing what should be done, if anything can be done on our part to bring about an amendment. It is evident to me that my son also suffers from not being able to make out what his wife's entire feelings and wishes are. . .

'I excuse her in not being able to sympathise in many of his local attachments, they come from early association, and from peculiar pursuits. Ninety women out of a hundred would soon tire of this place and would prefer what I have heard Effie say, she would, the flying over a desert on horseback, but I would expect from her great good sense and talent that she would see that her ambition, of which she has too much mind not to have good share, would be little gratified by her husband abandoning the haunt, where his genius finds food and occupation, to seek for stirring adventures, which might end in more mishap than profit. I am quite aware that his pursuits to ordinary people may appear absurd, but Effie is not one of these ordinary people. . .

'If I might take the liberty of prescribing for her own comfort and amendment, I should urge an effort to be made to sacrifice everything to duty, to become interested and delighted in what her husband may be accomplishing by a short absence and to find a satisfaction in causing him no unnecessary anxiety that his faculties may be in full force for the purposes to which they are devoted. . .'

From Chamonix John went on a tour alone which included Mont Blanc, Martigny, Zermatt and then returned to Chamonix.

Though now thirty, he was still in thrall to his parents, and he had difficulty in obtaining 'leave of absence' (as his biographer calls it) from his parents, but not without alarm on their part on account of his illness at Courmayeur.

Shortly before he started on this tour he wrote two strange letters, one to his wife, and the other to her father.

The one to Effie was written on 24 June, in reply to one from her in which, after Dr. Simpson had diagnosed one cause of her nervous ailment, she said how much she would like to have a family.

Chamonix
24 June 1849

'I have been thinking of you a great deal in my walks today, as of course I always do when I am not busy, but when I am measuring or drawing mountains, I forget myself—and my wife both; if I did not I could not stop so long away from her: for I begin to wonder whether I am married at all, and to think of all my happy hours, and soft slumber in my dearest lady's arms, as a dream. I got a letter on Friday; that in which you tell me you are better—thank God; and that you would like a little Alice[1] of our own. So should I; a little Effie, at least. Only I wish they weren't so small at first that one hardly knows what one has got hold of.'

Ten days later he wrote a long letter to her father in which he propounded for the first time that Effie was suffering from incipient madness, which was to become, in due course, his disgraceful excuse for not consummating the marriage.

Chamonix
5 July 1849

'Having heard the late correspondence between you and my father I think it well that you should know from myself my feelings respecting Effie's illness as this knowledge may more straitly direct your influence over her. I have no fault to find with her; if I had it would not be to her father that I should complain: I am simply sorry for the suffering she has under-gone and desirous that you should understand in what way your advice may prevent its recurrence. If she had not been seriously ill I *should* have had fault to find with her: but the state of her feelings I ascribe, now, simply to bodily weakness; that is to say—and this is a serious and distressing admission—to a nervous disease affecting the brain.

'I do not know when the complaint first showed itself: but the first that I saw of it was at Oxford after our journey to Dover: it showed itself then, as it does now, in tears and depression: being probably a more acute manifestation, in consequence of fatigue and excitement, of disease under which she had long been labouring. I have my own opinion as to its principal cause—but it does not bear on matter in hand. I was not however, at the time, at all prepared to allow all I should have done for her state of health—and in consequence—when, some week or so afterwards, she for the first time showed causeless petulance towards my mother, I reproved her when we were alone. The matter in question was indeed one of very grave importance—being a wish on my mother's part that I should take a blue pill when I went to bed—the first case as far

[1] Alice Gray born 29 March 1845

ALICE GRAY
A pencil drawing by Sir J. E. Millais, BT., P.R.A.

as I remember of "interference" on her part since our marriage. It was however also the first time that Effie had heard herself blamed: and the effect upon her otherwise excited feelings was permanent—and disposed her—as I think, to look with jealousy upon my mother's influence over me. I was at this time very sufficiently vexed, for my own part—at not being able to get abroad—as well as labouring under severe cough—so that I was not able to cheer Effie or support her, just at the period when she began first to feel her changed position and lament her lost home. It was a sad time for her therefore altogether—and the mental and bodily illness were continually increased. No further unpleasantness however took place between her and my mother and we got abroad at last.

'I had hoped that this would put us all to rights: but whether I overfatigued her in seeing Cathedrals—or whether we drank too much coffee at night—her illness continued to increase.

'So she returned worse than she went and I am still in entire ignorance that there was anything particularly the matter with her.

'The depression gained on her daily—and at last my mother, having done all she could to make her happy in vain, was, I suppose, partly piqued and partly like myself—disposed to try more serious reason with her. Finding her one day in tears when she ought to have been dressing for dinner, she gave her a scold—which had she not been ill she would have deserved. Poor Effie dressed and came down—looking very miserable. I had seen her look so too often to take particular notice of it—and besides thought my mother right. Unluckily Dr. Grant was with us—and seeing Effie look ready to faint thought she must want his advice. I being thoroughly puzzled about the whole affair, thought so too and poor Effie, like a good girl as she is—took—to please me—what Dr. Grant would have her—weakened herself more—sank under the influenza—and frightened me at last very sufficiently—and heaven only knows now when she will forgive my mother. So far as I know then—these are the causes—and this was the progress—of her illness—and of the change of feeling towards my parents. You know—better than I—what is likely now to benefit her—but I look forward with confidence to her restoration of health by simple physical means—and I am delighted to hear of the shower bath and the riding and the milk instead of tea—and the quiet. When I have her to manage again, I hope to do it better—and not to reason with—nor blame a physical weakness—which the course of time will, I doubt not, entirely cure. In all this, however, you will perceive that I look upon the thing as a purely medical question—not a moral one.

'If Effie had in *sound mind* been annoyed by the contemptible trifles which have annoyed her: if she had cast back from her the kindness and affection with which my parents received her and refused to do her duty to them under any circumstances whatever but those of an illness bordering in many of its features on incipient insanity, I should not now have written you this letter respecting her.'

He then takes up Mr. Gray's oft repeated suggestion that his parents should leave the young couple alone and defends in long, flowery passages, the right of parents to interfere, and continues. . .

'I hope to see her outgrow with her girl's frocks that contemptible dread of interference and petulant resistance of authority which begins in pride and is nourished in folly and ends in pain. Restiveness I am accustomed to regard as unpromising character even in horses and asses.'

The letter ends with more long passages about Effie's reserve which is a 'simple bad habit', and concludes with permission to show the letter to Effie or 'read it to the whole world'.

To have written such a letter a few days after giving his wife fresh hope that he was at least not averse to terminating their unnatural relations would have convicted an ordinary man of gross duplicity. But then no ordinary man, married for fifteen months to a young and very intelligent wife, would have resorted to levelling such a horrible accusation against her in order to divert attention from the real cause of illness, which he alone knew. And only a very extraordinary man would ascribe the failure of his married life to a blue pill!

Though he makes so much of the blue pill, too much coffee

and inexplicable weakness, he makes the strange admission that he believes he knows that principal cause, but it does not bear on the matter. It would be interesting to know what was in his mind when he wrote those lines.

Mrs. Gray summed up this astonishing letter on the envelope: 'Remarkable letter from J. Ruskin in which he artfully puts down his then so-called wife's unhappiness to everything but the real cause which he himself only knew'.

During the coming years Effie often presented a gay, carefree exterior to the world; the world little knew how often she sat in her room, forlorn and in tears.

At the end of August, he returned home to find Effie in better health, but London held no attraction for him. Whilst in Switzerland a new book had been occupying his mind, and he was burning to start for Venice as soon as possible. He gave Effie a fortnight to get ready, and then they left together to spend the winter in Venice in order to obtain material for the *Stones of Venice*.

CHAPTER VIII

Stones of Venice

EARLY in October 1849, the Ruskins started for Venice accompanied by Effie's friend, Charlotte Ker. For Ruskin, Venice would mean unremitting work, and as it would be improper for his wife to go out alone, he gladly fell in with the plan of providing her with a companion.

On the way they stopped at Chamonix so that Effie could see his beloved Alps and Alpine scenery. Effie was entranced with all she saw, except the peasants, and she had some strange experiences when travelling from one place to another.

> Chamonix
> 21 October 1849

'The Valois, with the Rhone winding through and enormous rocky mountains on each side, would make a splendid kingdom if the Government and people were what they ought to be, but, alas, they do nothing. The Rhone overflows its banks, although that could easily be remedied, every year, and this year the people have had no harvest and the villages full of stagnant water and the smells proceeding therefrom perfectly awful. At Viege we saw idiots and goitres in plenty and could hardly get postillions to bring us here—a stage and a half. The proper postillion was rushing about as fast as his drunkenness would allow him in his Sunday clothes for he had just buried his mother. John would not have him and the Postmaster took his place. We had not gone twenty yards before the Postmaster met one of his postillions on the road and asked him to take his place. In dismounting he was so drunk that he pulled the saddle round and lay on the ground with one foot in the stirrup, unable, so fat was he, to move till George assisted him. The drunken contentment with which he lay amused John especially. But that was not all. The new postillion was as tipsy as his master and on taking his place executed the same feat with sounds in German and French of anything but a melodious character.'

Drunken postillions were not the only danger to travellers in those days, and John accepted his guide Couttet's offer to accompany them to Venice as protection against robbers, but cancelled the arrangement when he was assured that a guard would be provided from one town to the next.

On arrival at Venice they established themselves at the Hotel Danieli, and for the next five months John worked at a feverish pace measuring, drawing and making voluminous notes for his new book. After these months of heavy toil he wrote to a friend:

'I went through so much hard, dry, mechanical, toil there, that I quite lost before I left it, the charm of the place ... I have got all the right feeling back now, however; and hope to write a word or two about Venice yet, when I have got the mouldings well out of my head—and the mud. For the fact is, with reverence be it spoken, that whereas Rogers says "There is a glorious city in the Sea", a truthful person must say "There is a glorious city in the Mud". It is startling at first to say so, but it goes well enough with marble, "Oh Queen of Marble and Mud".' (Cook)

There could be no time for frivolities or taking his wife about.

Albery's Reale
29 December 1849

'He has shut himself up in a room', she wrote to a friend 'his dressing room it is, and there he has breakfasted alone and, I suppose, intends to remain during the day knowing he cannot be disturbed by us, as he has heated his stove to such a degree that when I went to see what had become of him I could not remain a moment in the place, although he considerately hoped I would stay if I liked.'

But Effie fortunately had Charlotte to go out with, and, already infected with her husband's enthusiasm for lovely things, she and Charlotte explored every corner of Venice and wrote home vivid accounts of the pictures, the buildings and the people they met.

Their principal guide and mentor was a Mr. Rawdon Brown, who had arrived in Venice in 1833 to discover the tomb of Mowbray, Shakespeare's 'Banished Norfolk', and had stayed ever since. Ruskin found him an invaluable helper when collecting material for his books.

A lasting friendship sprang up between Effie and Rawdon Brown, with whom she corresponded regularly when away from Venice, partly on John's account to obtain his opinion—his knowledge of the antiquities of Venice being unique—and partly on her own account, as she had found in him a real friend and wise counsellor. Effie and Charlotte found it very necessary to have a man with them when out walking.

Danieli's Hotel
20 December 1849

'Mr. Blumenthal often walks with us after three o'clock when his business is over, and we are much the better for him for the Italians do not in the least mind what they do or say to you, for I suppose their own ladies are not over and above well conducted and they suppose us the same. They pass me and say "dear creature" and lots of things like that and throw bouquets at me.'

The months passed happily for Effie, she was in better health than she had been for a long time, she had found many good friends in Venice, and in all her letters to her parents there is only one passage that refers to her more intimate relations with her husband.

'I daresay now his health is better he will also feel more amiable and as I, too, am stronger I hope we shall be better friends. For all I care his parents may have John as much with them as they please for I could hardly see less of him than I do at present with his work, and I think it is much better if we follow our different occupations and never interfere with one another and are always happy, but I shall take care to let them be as little as possible together for they had far too much time for grumbling about nothing before.'

Whilst John was absorbed in his work and Effie enjoying a winter in Venice, Denmark Hill and Bowerswell were once more in a state of strained relations, and this time for a more important reason than young George Gray's future.

An anonymous letter had fanned into flames the Ruskins' smouldering resentment at their failure to enchain Effie and their fear of losing their domination over their son.

In October Mr. Ruskin wrote to Mr. Gray:

London
20 October 1849

'As I dislike all reserve I deem it my duty to name to you the having received an anonymous letter—not of any great importance and apparently from some inferior person—yet such things are very strange and not a little painful. It is a card with words in print formed by cutting letters and words out of books. The words are:

"There was no need for pretending bad health
Miss Ker laid plans with flattering lips.
You see we shall keep him from the advice
of his Mother and all shall be well.
What a separation.
Father let me warn you, be separated no
more from your only son, your affectionate
son—he dearly loved his Father and Mother
I beseech you look after his health."

I do not mean to trouble John or Effie about this but I should be glad if you could throw any light upon it. I am sorry to trouble you but I think it is due to you to inform you of such a thing.'

Mr. Gray's reply suggesting that anonymous letters should be put in the waste-paper basket, and that the parents should not interfere with the young couple, only added fuel to the fire.

London
29 October 1849

'I observe the way you treat anonymous communications. I have not had my own magnanimity much tried in this way, the letter being the second only ever addressed to me, the first

L

having been a very innocent request to cut my trees overhanging the road, which interfered with the anonymous
writer's umbrella when he carried it high above his head. I
should not however utterly disregard every anonymous letter
or even all gossip. The world is bad enough but in a great deal
that it says there may be particles of truth. There required
no anonymous letter to suggest to Mrs. Ruskin and me that
there seemed to be an amazing effort made to withdraw our
son as much as possible from the influence and society of his
parents. It was not the imagining this but the clear perception
of it which gave Mrs. Ruskin and myself uneasiness. Was it
likely we should feel otherwise than hurt at seeing a creature
who came to us so readily and, as often as we asked her,
professing considerable attachment to us and appearing happy
with us, at once change on becoming our daughter-in-law and
evince a repugnance both to ourselves and to our house so
marked that the French people who were here and who saw
Effie, in place of staying to help Mrs. Ruskin with her visitors,
hurry my son away from the house, gave expression to their
sympathy by declaring they would become our children themselves. It is singular that whilst you were fancying a want of
proper feeling in John we were fearing the like in Effie, and as
I speak to her as I write to you I told her the last day she was
here that I almost feared she had taken my son to please
somebody else because she left him so easily. I knew John's
attachment was unshaken, but he had firmness of character
enough not to become the altered man towards his parents
which it was sought to make him—towards that mother
especially to whom, under God, he was all that he now or
ever will be. I know Effie's power and acknowledge her
talents. My son may with her become a more social being,
better man of the world, and with all I trust a very happy
man, but with all deference to Effie and to all she can ever
bring about my son, I feel that he may lose as much as he
may gain by his total withdrawal, if it shall prove so, from
maternal influence and authority. Let him turn out as fine a
character as he may, he will not surpass or even be that single
hearted and simple being he was when he left his mother's
side. To her teaching, to her influence alone do I ascribe the

impression he has made on the public mind. It is not that his books are so superior but that they are different because his character is different from that of any other writer. With these convictions as to the part his mother had in forming his character you may suppose that your advice to us not at all to interfere any longer with the young couple was hardly agreeable or palatable—that to propitiate your daughter as yet a child who cannot yet be expected to comprehend the higher points of her husband's character, nor of his writings, if she has ever read them, the Voice of that parent was to be silenced, whose nurture and admonition had made him all that he ever will be noticed far above ordinary scribblers of books. I am very sorry to cause you a moment's pain but I do not think you are yet fully aware how much Mrs. Ruskin's feelings and mine have been wounded nor wherein our expectations have been disappointed.'

Mr. Gray was certainly left in no doubt that Mrs. Ruskin intended to fight hard to regain and retain her dominance over her son, but he was at a loss to know how to reply to this strange letter. Effie's mother, incensed by the latter and having seen for herself the atmosphere in which her daughter had been living in London, now took up the cudgels on her behalf and wrote to Mr. Ruskin.

> Bowerswell
> November 1849

'I take up my pen to endeavour to restore peace between you and my daughter, although I feel it almost a hopeless task, as I went over the same ground with you in London, apparently without doing any good. You complain of Effie's altered manner towards you after her marriage to what she was before. It does not the least surprise me for we found her very much changed. You say she did not remain to assist Mrs. Ruskin with the visitors but hurried John away home and that your visitors noticed it, neither does this surprise me as I have seen her here quite unfit to keep up appearance of being able either to entertain or be entertained from real illness.'

After some further comments on the 'melancholy' with which Effie's relations spoke of her changed appearance she continued:

'I do not wonder that you felt the change of her manner as you were at that time ignorant that there was anything the matter with her.

'You insinuate that Effie enticed John away from the influence of her parents. I assure you there has been no enticement required or no effort made. It was very obvious that John was delighted to find that Effie could go and Effie was delighted to be able to go, and as for Miss Ker she was never more surprised in her life than when she was asked to go —she could not believe they were in earnest. Therefore do not let these vile insinuations bear in on you. Much has done to pollute our minds by hints and insinuation upon John's remaining away so long with his parents from his wife, but we looked on them as false friends and as people who did not understand John's character. I think nothing will shake his affection for you both, nor I am sure would Effie wish it, but she at the same time would like to be treated with the respect due to a wife and not to be treated like a child—indeed she has never been accustomed to it as it has always been acknowledged she had sense and judgment beyond her years, which has commanded respect wherever she went.'

This letter restored peaceful relations and, as John on return from Venice spent most of his time at Denmark Hill, Mrs. Ruskin was satisfied that the battle was going in her favour.

John was now a famous man and interest in his relations with his wife extended far beyond the family circle. Mrs. Gray's brother, the Sheriff, whose letters were always heavily interlarded with quotations from the scriptures, reported that the Edinburgh gossips were busy with the young couple.

15 Heriot Row, Edinburgh
6 December 1849

'She is right to keep these Austrian officers at a distance. They are a bad set and will stare as much at them as they choose. But they must be far gone if that gives them any pleasure. It would be of much advantage to them if they could meet with some quiet good English families especially of a religious character. There is much in all they see and even innocent objects of pleasure to draw the heart away from serious thought or the highest aims and objects of our being . . . I am sorry to say that I have had some trouble in defending Mr. Ruskin from the attacks that are made on him on account of his strange behaviour to Effie last summer. Many of his admirers here are quite vexed and disappointed about it and find a difficulty in reconciling reports with their impressions of John's writings.'

John and Effie, probably unaware of the public interest in them, left Venice in March and after short stays at Valence, Vienne, Lyons and Bourges arrived back at their Park Street house in the middle of April and in time for the London season.

CHAPTER IX

Rank and Fashion

On return to Park Street, the lives of the young Ruskins entered a new phase. Effie's hopes of winning John from his parents were soon shattered.

31 Park Street
April 1850

'I daresay' she wrote to Rawdon Brown 'in a short time I shall get settled and by myself for John is going to be even busier than he was in Venice. He says he will sometimes go out with me in the evening, but every morning after breakfast he is going to Denmark Hill to write and remain the whole day till six when he will return to dine with me. I endeavoured to point out to him that he might shut himself up in his study here and then I might see him sometimes during the day, but he says he has no light in town nor his Turners and that I will soon find acquaintances and can take care of myself (which I think you rather doubt).'

She knew now that she was fighting a losing battle but she made the best of things and managed to persuade John to take her out sometimes to evening parties, which he cordially disliked.

'Horrible party last night' he wrote to his mother 'stiff—large—dull—strange-run-against everybody—know-nobody sort of party. Naval people. Young lady claims acquaintance with me. I know as much about her as Queen Pomare! Talk. Get away as soon as I can—and ask who she is—Lady Charlotte Elliott—as wise as I was before. Introduced to a black man with chin in collar. Black man condescending—I abuse several things to black man, chiefly the House of Lords. Black man says he lives in it—asks where I live—I don't want to tell him—obliged. Go away and ask who black man is. Mr. Shaw-Lefevre—as wise as I was before. Introduced to a young lady—young lady asks if I like drawing—go away and ask who she is—Lady

Something Conyngham. Keep away with back to the wall and look at watch. Get away at last—very sulky this morning—Hope my father's better—dearest love to you both.'   (Cook)

He was right in his surmise that Effie would soon make acquaintances. Her beauty and intelligence won her many friends amongst the leading hostesses of the day and at the height of the season she was attending as many as three parties in a day. She met all the rank and fashion, and at the frequent dinners at Denmark Hill and at afternoon parties she also met all the leaders in the literary and artistic world.

One day it was Thackeray who 'but for his broken nose would be a handsome man'; the next day Sullivan who 'as conductor at the Opera House is a perfect sight in himself'; the next day G. F. Watts who is, she thinks, 'the great man of our age in painting but yet unknown as he has lived so much in Italy' and she is often at Mr. Carlyle's, the historian, whose works 'John admires so much'.

In May she was presented at Court. John sent a full description of the event to his father:

'I got through excellently well, and I believe did what was right—and I thought that Prince Albert put something like markedness into his bow, but that may be his general manner. The Queen looked much younger and prettier than I expected —very like her pictures, even like those which are thought to flatter most—but I only saw her profile—I could not see the front face as I knelt to her, at least without upturning of the eyes, which I thought would be unseemly—and there were but two or three seconds allowed for the whole affair. After waiting an hour and three quarters I think they really might allow people a quarter of a minute each and time off. The Queen gave her hand very generously, but looked bored; poor thing, well she might be, with about a quarter of a square mile of people to bow to. At one place there was the most awkward crush I ever saw in my life. The floor was covered with the ruins of ladies dresses, torn lace and fallen flowers; but Effie was luckily out of it and got through unscathed, and heard people saying "What a beautiful dress" just as she got up to the Queen.'   (Cook)

Effie gives another picture of a Court in those days:

31 Park Street
21 June 1850

'We then entered the reception room where was a dense crowd
of waving plumes and diamonds crushed as close as they could
pack. I was fortunate in getting a seat which if I had not I am
sure I would have fainted. Several ladies did and one went into
dreadful hysteria and screamed and laughed like a lunatic. She
was carried out. We stayed in this broiling but amusing
condition for two hours, the heat was dreadful but I was close
to the door and saw all coming in. The diamonds were
splendid and in greater quantity than I ever imagined. I was
close to the Nepaulese and thought they looked nothing beside
the noble forms and bright uniforms of the English. At length
the doors opened and we slowly were wedged forward to the
Tapestry room. Passing this door was dreadful for the Officers
crossed their long spears and only let a certain number pass. I
got no damage but I saw lace lying on the floor . . . The Queen
looked immensely stout and red but very calm. I kissed her
hand which was fat and red too and made a reverence to the
Prince and Duke of Kent and then somebody threw my train
over my arm again.'

It seems strange that the experience of years had not yet
taught the Court officials how to organize a Court and it is not
surprising that débutantes often arrived at the Palace in a
state of abject fear.

John appears here in a new light. He cared nothing for
Society and meeting its leaders, which must have been a great
disappointment to his father, but he is delighted that Prince
Albert put 'markedness' into his bow to him.

It was inevitable that Effie should attract admirers and she
wrote very amusingly about the elder ones who she skilfully
kept at arms' length. She avoided 'hurting the London convenances' and, though callers sometimes stayed so long that
they obviously hoped to be asked to stay to dinner, she rigidly
observed her rule not to dine alone with a man, and 'would go
nowhere without a proper invitation'. One of her descriptions
of a party will give a picture of her life.

31 Park Street
18 June 1850

'And then to Lady Westminster's breakfast. John who hates all such things left immediately, but I found plenty of friends and, being particularly under Mrs. Eastlake, staid until Lady Davy who knows everybody got tired and we left with the rest of the company. After six the crowd of carriages was quite a sight, the three streets leading to Grosvenor House and the Square were perfectly full. Six saloons, including the splendid Picture gallery, were filled with the elite of London including the Nepaulese, the Duke of Wellington and all the beauty and talent of the year . . . I assure you the iced strawberries and cream and peaches were most refreshing in the perfumed air of so many ladies in lace and glace silk and men in lemon kids . . . The Marchioness is a very pretty young looking woman, her daughter the Duchess of Northumberland is much older looking than her. Lady Westminster was draped in embroidered white muslin over blue silk, a white jacket lined to correspond, a point lace cap trimmed with blue satin ribbon mixed with diamonds and turquoises and most splendid pearls on her neck. Two grown up daughters, pretty but the heavy cheeks of the Grosvenors, also dressed in white without bonnets were walking about. All the rest of the company had bonnets and no walking dress but very gay . . . Lady Seymour came in with two grown up daughters wearing gypsy hats with streamers hanging down behind frightfully ugly, but rather pretty girls, she not much style but sweet eyes. Lady Jocelyn, Lady Dufferin and the Duchess of Roxburgh looked handsome. Lord Gough was there, Prescott the historian etc . . . I had just time to swallow a mouthful of dinner and go to the Opera.'

In July London Society was disturbed and much divided about the Prince Consort's plan for a great exhibition in Hyde Park.

31 Park Street
2 July 1850

'I have been forced to give up riding owing to the heat' she wrote to Rawdon Brown 'but I shall continue it again whenever I can with comfort if I am not shut out of Rotten Row by the

Buildings to be erected for the Exposition next year. I wonder what Lord Clarendon would have said to such desecration. However Prince Albert's scheme is so unpopular that it may yet be removed to some other place and some of the most beautiful trees in the park saved from the hatchet for a few more years, but it was to be decided in the House last night. London was in rather an excited state for two or three days. Sir Robert Peel was near killed two days ago and is still in great danger . . . The Queen also had rather a narrow escape the other night in coming from the Duke of Cambridge's who has been very ill. A man rushed from the crowd and struck her on the head with a stick, the skin of her forehead was a little injured but she appeared afterwards at the Opera and was most enthusiastically received.'

Sir Robert Peel and the Duke of Cambridge died a few days later and London Social Life came to an end; 'everyone is either on their way or going to Italy or Germany' wrote Effie on 12 July.

But all this gaiety was not making Effie a happy woman and John, though so seldom with his wife, was not getting on so fast as he hoped with his book.

To Rawdon Brown Effie wrote after the season ended.

31 Park Street

'London society appears to me to be badly composed, everybody suffering for everybody else and nobody consequently happy. I am much better out of it. People are very kind to me wherever I go and make me out to be a much better person that I am and spoil me but I would much rather be at Venice. I would much rather look at the calm melancholy beauty of Grand Canal from your windows and in sight of the Foscari than the crowded salons of Grosvenor House where the other day I tried to look at Pictures and Nepaulese Princes and diamonds from out of a sea of the most dense of the Fair and highborn of the land, where indeed the heat, the crowd, the silk, and the lace took away from all idea of individuality, and I ceased to think those pretty who are the beauties of the present day, and I was not sure whether I was myself or somebody else all the time. John of course ran away at once.'

Poor Effie. All the glamour of London society, all her opportunities of meeting and talking with celebrities, could not compensate for the unnatural life with her husband, and, to add to her unhappiness, she had been told by two doctors that she would be in much better general health if she had a baby. She had only been able to reply that her husband had a profound dislike to children.

The end of the season gave Effie an opportunity of spending a few weeks at Bowerswell and she expected to find London very dull and empty when she returned. But she found it

31 Park Street
30 October 1850

'quite the reverse and I am going out a good deal and have engagements of different kinds. John will be obliged to go about with me when the season comes round. I think it better to enjoy myself and leave him to his book now which every interruption retards considerably. He has given me a general order to refuse all invitations for him and go out everywhere I like which I am very happy to do. It is a great amusement to me after being a good deal alone all day to go out in the evening and hear what is doing. John thinks it very good for me so long as he is not disturbed or bored.'

So she dines one evening with Mr. Ford 'whose Handbook on Spain is amusing'; the next evening with Lady Emily Dundas at the Admiralty; and a few days later is wondering if she will have the courage to dine with the Houston Stewarts, also at the Admiralty, to meet three Cabinet Ministers, Lord Minto, Fox-Maule and Sir Francis Baring.

The dinner proved not at all frightening; she sat between Sir Charles Adam and Sir James Gordon and was delighted with the 'kindly feeling all these old sailors seem to have for one another'.

At another party, which gave her less pleasure, she thought Thackeray 'loud and vulgar and fond of good living', Cockburn, the Solicitor-General, 'a brilliant clever man', and Panizzi, the Librarian of the British Museum, a 'clever, free thinking, Roman Catholic', and all 'more liberal in their opinions than

was edifying'. There was also Mr. Morris, *The Times* leader
writer who was 'even worse' and held forth on the iniquities
of the Papists.

So far Effie's strict observance of the 'convenances' had
disappointed the gossips who found it hard to believe that a
beautiful and attractive young woman, living so much alone,
was still resisting the advances of her many admirers, but in
January she met Clare Ford at a dinner party and his attentions
to her soon set tongues wagging.

Her brother, George, who was very shrewd and had stayed
with her in London two or three times, was now convinced
that the Ruskin family, by leaving Effie almost entirely to her
own resources, were hoping that she would compromise
herself, but she, as yet, had no such suspicions.

She was not particularly attracted by Clare Ford when they
first met.

'On Saturday two Guardsmen Clare Ford and Minnie's lover
Captain Tyrwhitt take the girls and me to the Lyceum to see
a new burlesque, the former youth is exactly like Lord
Dupplin without his discontented expression, full of life and a
most excellent opinion of himself which I think is not to be
wondered at, as his head is not very steady and women spoil
him by flattery.'

He was undoubtedly greatly attracted by Effie but not for
the reason attributed by gossip. In February she wrote to her
mother.

31 Park Street
February 1851

'Clare has taken it into his head that I am the only just woman
ever he met, which idea, in the meantime, without any nonsense, is doing him so much good that his family privately
thank me. The fact is that every woman he has been with has
spoilt him and he has run into every sort of vice and is still so
young that he is not hardened but disgusted, and as I endeavoured to show him the folly of making himself miserable when
he could find happiness scattered like Manna all over the world,
he is particularly obliged to me for saying every thing disagreeable to him, keeping him from spending his money, drinking

Brandy with his coffee and smoking till three in the morning. He never sleeps as you may suppose and he gets up and writes to me on the fallen Nature of Man and his weakness and etc, most strange productions with all his Father's genius in them totally without application, and imagination running away with reason. I have nearly persuaded him to go and live by himself in Switzerland with a servant and get into regular hours and a healthy tone of mind. John helped me to write a long letter to him. By the bye John has finished such a clever Pamphlet on the Church which I am sure you will like—it is so Protestant. It is "Notes on the Management of the Sheepfold" or something like that, it will be published the 1st of March.'

Clare's efforts to come to more intimate terms received short shrift and after one rebuff he flung away and told her she would one day die of propriety.

Some months later she was able to give a satisfactory report of her reforming effort:

31 Park Street
19 July 1851

'Clare is going on very nicely, he has been very industrious during the month he passed at Exeter and now he is back in town he goes on with his work at home. I do not see him at all whilst I am by myself. Cecilia thinks he will draw well if he perseveres. She calls this house of mine "The Reform Club".'

Cecilia Northcote was a daughter of Sir Stafford Northcote and sister of the first Earl of Iddesleigh and was often with Effie at Park Street.

Clare Ford was appointed attaché to the Legation of Naples in 1852 and eventually became British Ambassador at Madrid, Constantinople and Rome. He died in 1899.

She was very fond of Lord Lansdowne and tried to persuade him to buy a Sir Joshua Reynolds which came into the market, but he replied that all his money was going to his tenants who would starve without his support. He was helping them to emigrate as fast as possible but was at the moment supporting 2,000 people.

In February Effie responded to suggestions made by her friends and decided to give a weekly evening party so that she could return hospitality, and the 'lions' at her first party were Thackeray, Dickens, Bunsen (the Ambassador), Milman (Dean of St. Paul's) and some of the leaders in the fashionable world.

Her circle of friends steadily increased and she met all the famous men of the day at parties.

At Sir Walter James's, Gladstone took her into dinner.

31 Park Street
28 February 1851

'He and Lord Hardinge had a wonderful debate about the Roman Catholics. Lord Hardinge's sentiments did him the greatest honor and he spoke with the greatest temper and judgement. He ended by saying "I hold that man the best Christian and the truest patriot who would check every advance of a religion so dangerous and so destructive to every country I have visited . . ." Mr. Gladstone very cleverly defended the Roman Catholics, denying their religion, but saying, since the Emancipation Bill passed, that as things were now they should have their titles but that Lord John should never have allowed the thing to have gone on, and mentioned as curious that the Duke of Newcastle, Lord Aberdeen, Sidney Herbert, all in different places, and himself at Naples watching the progress of the Question these last two or three months without any means of correspondence had all separately made up their minds not to legislate.'

At the Countess de Salis's gay party there were

31 Park Street
29 April 1851

'lots of fashionables amongst others the Duke of Wellington looking extremely good humoured and well and flirting away tremendously with two Miss Hattons who make such a noise and are so lively that I suppose he hears all they say which is something. He is always talking to them and laughing and shaking their hands so that the people have made a pun on him saying Why is the Duke the rudest man in London? Because he always comes into a room with his Hat on. I saw and spoke with another military hero, Sir Charles Napier. He was very lively and said he quarrelled with everybody and now he had the Court of Directors to fight with, that it was the nature of the animal to quarrel, and that he was only comfortable when he was in the middles of his enemies.'

Another day she is discussing with Carlyle John's pamphlet *Notes on the Construction of Sheepfold*, which had created a considerable stir, and finds him delighted with it and the hits at the Puseyites, and that evening meets the Herschels, Dr. Whewell, the Master of Trinity, and Cobden who has a 'most disagreeable mean face'.

During April much of her time was spent sitting for her portraits by G. F. Watts and George Richmond.

She though Richmond's picture a 'most lovely piece of oil painting and much prettier than me. I look like a graceful doll', and much preferred Watts' masterly drawing. Her friend, Charlotte Ker, bought the Richmond portrait.

The great event of the season was the opening of the Exhibition in Hyde Park and Effie was thankful that she had two male escorts, Lord Glenelg and Mr. Newton, as the organization was not much better than at the Court. But once inside she was thrilled with all she saw and had 'never seen the Queen look so happy and so well as she walked the whole round smiling and bowing to everyone and talking to the Duchess of Sutherland who held her bouquet and fan'.

Meanwhile John had completed the first volume of the *Stones of Venice*, which was published in March, and during April he and Effie paid two visits. The first was to Farnley, where their host was Mr. F. H. Fawkes, the son of Turner's friends, and where Ruskin wished to study the art treasures. Ruskin afterwards described Farnley as

'a perfectly unique place. There is nothing like it anywhere; a place where a great genius had been loved and appreciated, who did all his best work for that place, where it is treasured up like a monument in a shrine.'

Effie was much amused at Mr. Fawkes's description of his efforts to keep the railway from crossing his property by

chasing the surveyors off his fields and, when they endeavoured
to work on the high road, placing himself on his pony between
the two men who were levelling and reading the paper, and
when they then tried the ditches ordering them again off his
property.

At the Master's Lodge at Trinity College Cambridge, which
was their next visit, John was in his element as he was able to
discuss archæology with the Master, Whewell, and Professor
Willis, both leading authorities on the subject. Effie liked
Cambridge and compared it favourably with Oxford:

Trinity Lodge, Cambridge
8 April 1851

'There is a reality and simplicity and an earnestness of life
about the people here that I did not see at Oxford. There is
hardly any Puseyism here. Dr. Whewell says there is an
excellent feeling amongst the Young men, much better than
used to be and they were very violent about the Papal
aggressions.'

The repeated references in letters of that period to the
Puseyites and religious questions seem strange today but at
that period passions were running high.

John had left Venice intending to return for a second winter
as he still had much work to do for the completion of the
Stones of Venice, and in August he and Effie started for Italy
accompanied by the Revd. D. Moore, the clergyman at
Denmark Hill, and his wife. They stopped for a time in
Switzerland where at the Hospice of St. Bernard 'Effie made
the monks play and sing not Gregorian chants merely, but
very merry and unclerical tunes.'

Effie's account was more highly flavoured than her husband's.

'We saw a couple of children's funerals. I never saw anything
so dreadful, the little coffins where the children lay were
covered over with Wedding cake finery and little boys as
bearers. A fat Priest led the way with the Cross and was
followed by a quantity of Cretins and horrid looking men and
women, all looking as happy and goodnatured as could be and

laughing like anything. They were in all manner of costumes from coarse red cloth to brown. We thought how horrid it looked to be chaperoned to one's grave by Cretins of Anste . . . By the time we had reached the snow level near the Convent it was bitterly cold. The monk received us very kindly and soon after we had souper, milk, macaroni, salt fish, fritters and very bad wine. We all agreed the establishment was going to the dogs. The place was filthily dirty, so were the dogs, and the smell was like a kennel. We got fleas and I was starved with cold. The monks were delighted to get me to play the most unclerical tunes on the piano and said they would be glad if we would dance for in fact it was Liberty Hall and we could do what we liked.'

Just before leaving Effie received a letter from her mother who had been disturbed by gossip about her daughter and her reply illustrates the difficulties of her life in London.

Casa Metzler, Venice

'My Dear Mama I received your things on Saturday night . . . Thank you also very much for your letter of advice. I assure you I value very much all the advice I get and act upon it. What you say is perfectly true and I am so peculiarly situated as a married woman that, being left much alone and most men thinking that I live quite alone, I am more exposed to their attentions. But I assure you—I never allow such people to enter the house and stop every thing of the kind which might be hurtful to my reputation and I would not for the sake of improving any person destroy or injure the only fortune I possess viz—a good name—which if you inquired here amongst the people calculated to know you would find that I had never been spoken about with anyone. If I was, the most respectable women in London would certainly not give me their daughters to Chaperone and although you think me unsuspicious I am quite quick enough to see observe or hear if anyone thought lightly of my conduct. I know quite well that George has been gossiping to you about Clare, as Furnival did to him. I soon got to the bottom of that and the result was

M

nothing at all excepting that John was very angry with Mr.
Furnival for putting such ideas into George's head, merely
thinking him jealous of Clare, whom he does not know and
cannot endure. As for Clare I have shut him out and will not
let any one in whilst John is away but Mr. Brown. Clare goes
abroad this week. What can I do more—I shall be quite as
particular with Paulizza and never will encourage anything in
my conduct but the most perfect propriety, but if you think
differently always write to me.'

Paulizza was a Venetian acquaintance who had been very
pressing in his attentions, but Effie, who quite liked him,
thought him rather futile and harmless and laughed a lot at
him.

During Effie's last three months in London something of
much greater importance to her life than this gossip had
occurred. Her husband had become the Champion of the Pre-
Raphaelites, of whom John Everett Millais was leader and one
of the founders.

In July Millais wrote:

'I have dined and taken breakfast with Ruskin and we are such
good friends that he wishes me to accompany him to Switzerland this summer . . . We are as yet singularly at variance in
our opinions upon Art. One of our differences is about Turner.
He believes that I shall be converted on further acquaintance
with his works, and I that he will gradually slacken in his
admiration.'

This story of two men of genius and a beautiful woman
might have taken a different course if Millais had accepted the
invitation.

How that invitation came to be sent is explained in the next
chapter.

CHAPTER X

Enter the Pre-Raphaelites

So much has been written about the genesis, purpose and achievements of the Pre-Raphaelite Brotherhood that it is only necessary here to give in outline the story of a movement that created such a great sensation in art history and was on everybody's tongue and in every newspaper of the day. This outline is necessary because without it the story of Ruskin, Millais, and Effie Gray cannot be fully understood.

The story begins with Holman Hunt seeing Millais for the first time at the prize-giving at the Royal Academy in 1838 and, like all who were present, watching with amazement a small boy of nine walking up to receive the gold medal. The two boys made friends and for the next two or three years spent much time together discussing their work and the art of the day.

The outcome of these discussions was a sense of dissatisfaction with the conventionality and pedantry of art as displayed in the paintings of the day, and determination to leave the beaten track and strike out a new line for themselves. They decided to take Nature as their only guide and inspiration and to go back to earlier artists than Raphael for examples of sound and satisfactory work.

D. G. Rossetti, a pupil of Holman Hunt's, soon joined them and it was he who coined the title Pre-Raphaelite Brotherhood. A little later William Rossetti, Woolner, F. G. Stephens and James Collinson became members of the P-R.B. as it was now called.

Millais himself summed up their purpose as 'The Pre-Raphaelites had but one idea—to present on canvas what they saw in Nature'.

The distinguishing characteristics of the Brotherhood were expounded in an excellent article in *The Artist* fifty years ago.

'The three chief members of the Pre-Raphaelite Brotherhood —Rossetti, Millais and Holman Hunt—were men of personalities and endowments that were striking in the extreme— born makers of epochs, men who, whatever the vocation that they had elected to follow, would undoubtedly have left shaping traces of their individualities upon it. And, to set themselves in triple harness, they were a trio of a singular diversity of aims and gifts; one might add destinies. Quite extraordinary was the dissimilarity between the kinds of success attained by each of them. Millais trod swiftly and straightly the path of popular approbation and academic honours, culminating in the highest dignity that the Royal Academy has to bestow. Rossetti and Holman Hunt, after the first, held themselves completely aloof from the Academy and all its works. . . Millais was gifted with a sense of sight of crystalline clearness to which Nature made a perpetual and brilliant appeal; he had a hand that, even in childhood, was singularly skilful to record the impressions of the eye. And his hand had been severely trained, first by the prescribed academic methods, and later by the minutely elaborate labour of his Pre-Raphaelite work, until it set down facts almost with the facility with which the eye perceived them.'

Millais's first big work bearing the P-R.B. signature was 'Lorenzo and Isabella'. It was painted when he was twenty and when it was exhibited at the Royal Academy in 1849 aroused a storm of adverse criticism.

The art critics were divided in their opinion, some gave the picture their qualified approval, some remained silent but the general public thought that it was a prime joke, only surpassed in absurdity by Holman Hunt's 'Rienzi' exhibited at the same time.

'Christ in the House of His Parents', exhibited the next year, created an even greater storm, and if Mulready and Maclise had not taken a firm line with their fellow members of the Royal Academy Council it would not have been hung.

Blackwood's Magazine said:

'We can hardly imagine anything more ugly, graceless and unpleasant than Mr. Millais's picture of "Christ in the Carpenter's Shop"! Such a collection of splay feet, puffed joints and misshapen limbs was assuredly never before made within so small a compass. We have great difficulty in believing

SIR J. E. MILLAIS, BT., P.R.A.
From an engraving of the self-portrait in the Uffizzi Gallery

the report that this unpleasing and atrociously affected picture
has found a purchaser at a high price.'

A leading literary journal, whose art critic was a Royal
Academician, delivered this broadside:

'Mr. Millais in his picture without a name, which represents a
holy family in the interior of a carpenter's shop, has been most
successful in the least dignified features of his presentment, and
in giving to the higher forms, characters, and meanings a
circumstancial art—language from which we recoil with
loathing and disgust. There are many to whom his work will
seem a pictorial blasphemy.'

Charles Dickens, who in later years was a great admirer of
Millais's works, wrote in *Household Words* that the picture
was 'mean, revolting, and repulsive' and *The Times* art critic
searched his vocabulary for adequate words of opprobrium.

If Millais had been granted a peep into the future how
surprised and gratified he would have been to see his picture
for which he received £150 changing hands for over £10,000,
and how bewildering he would have found some of the
pictures that were attracting public attention.

The critics were belabouring him for painting Nature as he
saw it; what, he would wonder, were they writing now.
Perhaps the successors of those who were trying to kill the
P-R.B. with their pens had more imagination.

The spate of adverse criticism, which might have daunted
lesser men, did nothing to quench the burning zeal of the
young crusaders and Millais painted three pictures for the 1851
Academy—'The Woodman's Daughter', 'Mariana', and the
'Return of the Dove'—which caused another storm of abuse.
The Times led the way in a violent article, declaring that such
work 'deserved no quarter at the hands of the public'. Holman
Hunt, whose picture 'Valentine and Sylvia' had the same re-
ceptions as Millais's pictures, recorded that in the art school a
professor referred to their works in such terms that the wavering
students resorted to the very extreme course of hissing them.

There were, however, many whose opinion Millais valued
who saw what the critics failed to see.

George Meredith wrote:

Weybridge, Surrey

'I called on you this morning to tell you what great delight your paintings have given me. For, as I live in the country, I could not wait for an introduction to you, which I should otherwise have desired.

'I left at your residence a book of my own just published, if you will oblige me by accepting it as a testimony of the admiration in which I hold your genius.

'In "Mariana" you have, as I understand, greatly conceived a great poet; in the "Woodman's daughter" wonderfully embellished a small one. Both are exquisite.'

Thackeray, too, preferred his own judgement:

13 Young Street, Kensington

'A friend of mine, Mr. Arden, of Cavendish Square, wants very much to make your acquaintance and to give you a commission for a picture. Are you free to take one, and to see Mr. Arden. You must know you have some partisans about the town, and one of them had a mischievous pleasure the other night in praising your pictures at the table of a gentleman who is supposed to be the Times critic.'

It was Mr. Arden who bought 'The Order of Release'.

And now the P-R.B. had found a Champion, and a very redoubtable one, in John Ruskin who was universally accepted as the final authority in matters of Art.

Ruskin has sometimes been credited with being the inspirer of the Pre-Raphaelites, but he had not been impressed with 'Christ in the House of His Parents' which he said later he had 'passed disdainfully' and had been forced by a friend to look for its merits, nor had he any personal knowledge of the members of the Brotherhood until the next year.

It was Millais who, highly indignant at the hue and cry, sought his friend Coventry Patmore and begged him to ask Ruskin to take up the cudgels on behalf of the P-R.B. Ruskin, after studying the pictures anew, turned all his big guns on the critics in two famous articles in *The Times*.

His intervention was described as 'thunder out of a clear sky'.

In *Modern Painters* he wrote:

'Their works are, in finish of drawing and in splendour of colour, the best in the Royal Academy, and I have great hope that they may become the foundations of a more earnest and able school of Art than we have seen for centuries.'

Two years later his enthusiasm was still unabated and in a lecture he said:

'I thank God that the Pre-Raphaelites are young, and that strength is still with them, and life, with all the war of it, still in front of them.'

Ruskin went further than championing the P-R.B. with his powerful pen, and offered to buy the 'Return of the Dove' unaware that it had already found a purchaser.

His championship was the turning point in the fortunes of the P-R.B. Millais and Holman Hunt sent him a warmly worded letter of thanks when his letters appeared in *The Times* and, next day, Ruskin and Effie drove to the studio where the two artists worked and carried Millais off to their house, where he stayed a week.

Effie makes no mention of this visit in her letters, but Ruskin tells us that

'Millais's exuberant interest in human experience, as well as his child-like impulsiveness in conversation, made him in a few days like an intimate of many years duration',

and the invitation to Millais to accompany him to Switzerland, already mentioned, followed shortly afterwards.

No doubt he would have liked to have gone abroad with his new-found friends, but he had planned out his work for the autumn and winter, and whilst Ruskin and Effie were busy getting into their house at Venice, he was already at work on two of his greatest pictures, 'Ophelia' and 'The Huguenot'.

With these two pictures he at last conquered the public. But the chorus of fault-finding by carping critics was not yet stilled, and no paper, except *Punch* and *The Spectator*, showed the slightest glimmering of comprehension of the beauty of the pictures.

Mr. Ruskin, after his first visit to the Royal Academy next year, wrote to Millais:

Denmark Hill

4 May 1852

'I came home last night with only Ophelia in my mind and wrote to my son nearly as follows. Nothing can be truer to Shakespear than Mr. Millais' Ophelia and there is a refinement in the whole figure—in the floating and sustaining dress—such as I never saw before expressed on canvas. In her most lovely countenance there is an Innocence disturbed by Insanity and a sort of Enjoyment strangely blended with lineament of woe. There seems depicted, moreover, a growing wonder and fear on Ophelia just awakening to a sense of her situation. I should be surprised at the Times had I not observed that the public press cannot afford to be wrong. The same Times critic says Maclise has quite accomplished what the P.R. only attempt. I quote this to my son adding my own notion as follows—Maclise has a monstrous Alfred in Gunthrum's tent full of the same copper figures that perform everything for him in every country, in every age, and in every grade of society, high or low, civil or military.'

John, too, was delighted with the pictures, but not so uncritical as his father:

5 August 1852

'You know—I suppose—that the shadows in the Ophelia and Huguenot are all chilled and want varnishing or something—they spoil the pictures terribly—I think both exquisite. I hailed the conversion of Punch with great delight. When you do paint nature why the mischief should you not paint pure nature and not that rascally wirefenced garden-rolled-nursery-maid's paradise. Of course you cannot expect me to tell you all I thought of Ophelia and Huguenot in a note. I have only one quarrel with you—that you will mottle your flesh as if it was brick wall seen through a diminishing glass—or worsted work. I believe your hands and faces could be verily imitated—all but the drawing of the mouths and eyes—with small stitches of coloured worsted. The expression is glorious.'

Edward Lear, who always called Millais 'Uncle John' and his brother William 'Uncle William', expressed the same view on painting Nature in his usual humorous style:

65 Oxford Terrace, Hyde Park

'If all the landscapes at the Exhibition are better than that of my Uncle William which they have rejected—all I can say is—it *must* be a good exhibition indeed. I suppose it was because the tree was green and not asphaltum colour that they turned it out. But, after all, you must reflect, uncle, that trees are not green—at least they ought not to be green—they are gray i.e. black and white, and many are of a slimy rich brown. This you may not have observed, but to show you that I speak correctly—there is only need to refer you to the pictures which you will undoubtedly see hung up. Your own idea—and that of Daddy Hunt, Anthony and others—that grass is of a green colour is most ridiculous and reprehensible—and you should leave it off as soon as you can.'

We must now leave Millais on the banks of the Ewell, near Kingston, where he had found the background for 'Ophelia', and where for the next six months Charles Collins, William Millais, and Holman Hunt, at work on the 'Light of the World', were his companions, and return to the Ruskins.

CHAPTER XI

Venetian Interlude

HER second winter in Venice was, perhaps, the happiest period of Effie's first marriage, and the marriage, though so unnatural, might never have moved to its tragic climax if the old Ruskins had died that winter.

She was delighted with the rooms they had taken at the Casa Metzler, which were a great improvement on the rooms they had previously occupied at the hotel, but, unfortunately, had relied on John to obtain a grate.

Casa Metzler
October 1851

'A most important piece of furniture for the winter will turn out a failure. John said he would buy the grate which Mr. Brown recommended, and it has come, and such a thing! It proves that talents have been wisely distributed and that a man who can write the Seven Lamps is not fit to choose a fire grate. It is so small one could nearly put it in one's pocket, and John confesses he bought it for old iron and it only cost 5/–'

Venice, then under Austrian domination, was a centre of fashionable and military society, and invitations to parties were soon pouring in to the Casa Metzler.

England was very unpopular, thanks to her foreign policy, but individual English men and women were welcomed into society.

Casa Metzler
8 February 1852

'The Austrians', wrote Effie in February, 'are crowing over us finely just now at the brilliant figure England is making of herself after her paltry, mean foreign policy these last three or four years, and now she is without a foreign friend with the Caffir War, the French panic, the impertinence of the Rou- manians, and last, not least, a Cabinet full of old women to

trouble her, and she will find out perhaps at some cost what
Lord Palmerston has in store for her. The feeling is so strong
against the English and their position on the continent. It is a
very different thing to what it was. Before, the English were
all My Lords and their word was law and every respect was
paid to them before any other nation. Now we are all considered traders and if politeness is shown it is only to individual
merit.'

This distrust of the British Government did not deter
English people who wished to spend the winter in Venice, and
Effie was delighted to hear that the Dean of St. Paul's and
Mrs. Milman, the Cheyneys, Thackeray, and many of her
London friends would soon be coming out.

Her long letters to her mother describe a continual round
of gaiety and talks with many interesting people. Several talks
with the aged Marmont, one of Napoleon's Marshals who was
wounded at Salamanca; a party in honour of the Infanta of
Spain, who afterwards 'commanded' her to tea; tea with the
Archduke Albert; a memorable performance at the theatre
when Rachel appeared though now only a 'pale shadow'; gala
nights at the Opera; a great to-do when the Emperor, described
by Ruskin as a 'well-made youth, with rather a thin, ugly,
not unpleasant face', paid an official visit; and gaieties at
Verona where the famous Marshal Radetsky, then in his
eighty-seventh year, had his head-quarters, and where she was,
according to her husband, 'allowed by everyone to be—reine
du bal'.

All these exciting events might have been bitter-sweet to
Effie if John had shut himself up in his room as he did during
their first visit. But now he was for a short time a changed
man, and not only took some pride in Effie's success in society,
but accompanied her often to parties.

He wrote to his father: 'I have not much of interest to
communicate to you of my own adventures, but Effie sometimes sees a little of what is going on in the world. Venice is
more beautiful than ever and I am most thankful to be able to
finish or retouch my descriptions on the spot', but Effie's
letters tell a different story.

'I am rather tired today as I was up late last night, John and I
having taken it into our heads that we would mask and have
some fun as these last days of carnival a good many have
appeared in the evenings. We hired a couple of dominoes, black
with black masks and white gloves, and reached the square
about ten. I laughed so that I could scarcely go on and John,
who was as grave as possible, did the thing capitally. We found
quantities of masks in dominoes and fancy costumes of all
kinds parading about and entering the Cafés to throw bonbons.
Plenty of men spoke to me but what they said I dont know, I
replied by uttering the usual cries of the other masks and
shaking hands with one or two. We wandered about till half
past eleven when John wanted to take me to the Masked Ball
which used to be attended by everyone in Venice, but this
year as I heard of no one going I went home and sent John first
to see if I could go. He soon came back and said it would not
do for the music was bad and the dancing worse.'

'After dinner John and I went out to see if it would get
gayer as it got dark but the mob not the masks seem to have
increased and I was glad to return home. John calls me Mrs.
Scratch—he is so tired of hearing my pen scrape across the
paper and back. '

'John and I had a little walk on the square yesterday as he
wanted to see the Grand Duchess whom he admired at a
distance. He was much disappointed when he got nearer and
said as an Austrian said to me the other day, "Il faut être bien
indulgente aux Grande Duchesses". We had not far to go
before we found her as she walks up and down amongst the
people with her husband who is dressed in common Austrian
uniform by her desire, she being very young and far too
striking for this season. Fancy a beautiful pale pink glacé silk
dress, full skirt, with a black velvet Polka surrounded with
sable, and black lace and pink satin bonnet for walking in the
street in the middle of January! John wants me to be presented
but I dislike all Russians and I dont like the trouble of

arranging to go. I would much rather go to the Duchess De
Berry and the Cts de Chambord when they come. I was out
last night at Madame Esterhazy's where I talked with Marmont whose two arms looked perfectly sound and well.'

'John has just come in and says I am beautifully dressed and
he hopes somebody will call on me to see me, which interruption however I would gladly dispense with as then I will get
my letter written to you.'

'I am much better for having been at Verona and John
proposes going again soon for he finds he can write so much
better when he returns with a fresh eye—he writes much
more vigorously.'

It was John who was eager to accept an invitation to Verona,
as he wished Effie to meet the famous Marshal Radetsky. The
visit was a great success:

Verona
February 1852

'We arrived at Verona tired and hungry. Counts Festick and
Webner came into the carriage and John, knowing they would
talk the whole way, went into another part to study. I took
refuge in my work but they were so anxious to show me all the
places where they had bivouaced during the war, what bridges
they had blown up, and where they had slept months in the
open, that I could not be dumb altogether. Arriving at the
station we found Count T waiting to receive us with a formal
invitation from the Marshal for us. So you see he lost no time
in doing everything that was polite, and then added that we
had better come as soon as possible as the Marshal was so
punctual and liked everyone there at the hour invited. Our
old rooms at the Torri were occupied but they gave us very
good rooms at the back. John was very displeased as he likes to
look at all the beautiful monuments in front. They said the
other room in front had been kept for Count W——. I went
and told him that with his permission I would order his bed to
be carried out as I knew he didn't care in the least for any

monuments in Verona. . . . The Marshal inhabits the same Palace which Napoleon had and it is very richly and beautifully furnished without any pretensions to effect or show.

'The pictures and china and furniture all good, the latter of dark crimson velvet in some rooms and green and gold damask in the others, very handsome. The Ball room white and gold with a gallery above for the musicians and lighted by candelabra from the roof and innumerable wax lights, filled with hundreds of men in every Austrian uniform of Cavalry and Infantry, looked exceedingly brilliant. On entering, the stairs all lined with crimson cloth and orange trees and plants at each side. In the Ball room Count T presented me to Radetsky who looked very glad to see me and taking my hand turned round and presented me to the Archduke Ferdinand, which I believe was a very distinguished honor. He then took me the length of the ball room to the Countess Radetsky who also received me very kindly. I talked with her till Count Festick came with some half a dozen of his children, as he calls his officers, and I was soon dancing away with people of all nations.'

John's proud reference to his wife as 'reine du bal' was no exaggeration, and that she caused much heartburning among the impressionable young officers is evident from a letter she wrote on return to Venice.

Casa Metzler

'George told his master that he had heard that a duel had been fought at Verona about me and an officer killed. I laughed at the thing as perfectly absurd. It is a point of honor amongst Austrians never to speak about affairs of that kind and probably everyone knew but me. But it appears that Diller (one of Radetsky's aides-de-camp) had some words in the ball room with another officer about dancing with me—who the other man was I dont know—but they lost their tempers, went out next evening, and Diller got a very severe sabre wound all down the arm and cannot appear in the Marshal's presence until his arm is quite well. Did you ever know anything so foolish. These young men think as little of duelling as they do of smoking a cigar.'

In January John heard with great pleasure that Turner had appointed him one of his executors.

Casa Metzler
January 1852

'John is very pleased at having been made one of Turner's executors and to find that the pictures and gallery are all left to the nation so that they will not be dispersed. Some are anxious for him to write Turner's Life but he thinks not, and I dissuade him from it as what is known of Turner would not be profitable to any lady, and he has left no rules for painting or any memorial that would be any good but his great gift to the country. The sooner they make a Myth of him the better. John is busy at his drawings and books, writing beautiful descriptions. My music is my greatest amusement. I consider I have gained a great victory in converting my Italian master to Mendelssohn.'

Effie was up in arms when she heard that Turner had left nothing to John.

'One of the things that distresses me perhaps most is hearing them (*the old Ruskins*) railing against people behind their backs and then letting themselves be loaded with flattery by the Artistic canaille, by whom they are surrounded. I am quite of Mr. Cheyney's opinion that of all canaille they are the lowest with very few exceptions. Considering all that John did both personally and in his works for Turner and Prout, never to leave him a stroke of their pencil is to me wonderful. The letters that man Prout used to write John were quite disgusting with flattery.'

It is evident from the above letters that John and Effie were for the first time as happy together as they could be in the circumstances, and if there had been no letter post to England the future course of their lives might have been very different. But they had only been in Venice a few days when Effie heard from her father that Mr. Ruskin was at his old game of making sly suggestions about her.

Casa Metzler
10 October 1851

'I am not overpleased', she wrote in October, 'with Mr. Ruskin for writing to you that I am more domestic here than in London. It is not his saying this but his underhand manner I dislike. He always says something or other when I am far away which he never said or hinted at when I was at home. What going out I had in London was during May, June and July. What does he make of the 13 months before, during which time John was always with them and I sat at home alone many and many a day from morning till night and even during last season. They are strange people and I am free to confess I do not get fonder of them as I get older, although we get on better. I suppose you know they are coming to Switzerland in the Spring and John is to travel with them wherever they like. I never heard a word of it until it was all settled and the letters between John and his father are sometimes de trop what between sentimentalism and duplicity on Mr. Ruskin's side abusing everybody who stays with them and yet keeping them, and on John's side an obedience and making an excuse for everything he does and everybody he sees here as if he was doing harm—for fear the old people should think he leans too much to what I say.'

The old people were not content to widen the rift by letters to Effie's parents; they were determined to manage John's life, however far away he might be.

'Mr. Ruskin writes to him in this comforting manner at which I could not help taking a good laugh the other day "Mama is glad to hear you have a good appetite for all your meals, she says it is a proof, you have no disease in your constitution" (comforting that, isn't it) then follows rules à la Mrs. Ruskin for all the things he is to eat from breakfast till tea and when his stomach is out of order another diet and so on . . . he is always much better when away from their over care and attention which, as he is naturally extremely nervous, makes him ill by such constant enquiry, but by habit he is so infatuated that when with them they make him do anything they like.'

In December the state of comparative peace that had endured between Denmark Hill and Bowerswell since the anonymous letter was once again broken by the Ruskins.

London
15 December 1851

'I have a very agreeable correspondence with my son', wrote
Mr. Ruskin, 'with the exception of a few letters on the subject
of finance, having taken the liberty of telling them that they
much mistake their own character if the gentleman fancies
himself economical or the lady fancies herself a manager. They
have, like the soldier who spent half a crown out of sixpence a
day, spent £1,670 out of £1,074 per annum, for besides a large
sum taken from publishers for my son's books being all gone—
they have overdrawn above £1,000. My son says they were
unable to be in the circle they were at less and I confess I sent
them there. They have many virtues and their faults may be
ascribed more to their parents than themselves, and it is curious
coincidence that every fault on one side may be found a similar
defect on the other. My son is too fond of pictures and Effie is
too fond of dress. . . . As I told my son, it makes little difference
to me whether I die a thousand pounds richer or poorer but I
should like to see them exercise some control over their
expenditure. I would not inflict these details on you but that I
think you and Mrs. Gray might do a little towards restraining
Effie in uncalled for expenditure. You may ask me what I
mean and to produce evidence or instances of this tendency—
amongst others I might adduce the Swiss maid, the travelling
with so many boxes, carrying side saddles and hiring horses in
Geneva where a princess would be satisfied to take a mule.'

He ends with the information that John has promised to mend
his ways, and assurances that he only wishes the young couple
to be happy, and that he always carries in his pocket-book two
pieces of letters from Mr. Gray ready to prove that he had not
on an earlier occasion accused him of using words he had not
used.

Mr. Ruskin at least had the grace to admit that it was he
who had urged them to take a house in Park Street and to make

N

their way into the best society, but his letter was calculated to rouse Mr. Gray, who knew much better than the Ruskins, the kind of life his daughter was living. In his reply Mr. Gray suggested that a lot of money was being spent on pictures, which produced the following broadside from Mr. Ruskin.

London
27 December 1851

'I would not have troubled you and Mrs. Gray on the subject had I thought the merely moving in the circle which Effie and John were in was the occasion of all the expense, but my impression is that, good as their society was, it would have been still higher and better had Effie's taste been for less gay colours. The Highest Ladies in London are remarkably sensitive about quiet colours, especially out of doors. They have quite a dread of Red and Yellow and Effie can by her gifts of nature afford to be as quiet as a Quakeress. I can easily believe, when she dressed on £30 a year, that she was remarked on for dressing well. I know my own taste would have more approved of her then. I believe the error, if it be one, of her later style of dress may arise from no mere love of extravagance but from considering it called for by the position, and the fault is partly her husband's as he inclines to Turner's colours which for Ladies I do not. You are quite right in guessing that my son's purchases of pictures would form the heaviest item in account and that it would be hard to throw so heavy a share of blame on Effie if in my own power to check the grievance, but allow me to tell you that I pay for all John's pictures myself.'

After several more passages about the extent of his financial assistance to his son, he revealed the real reason for his attack.

'Perhaps I was a little annoyed at having £930 paid for a house only dwelt in 18 months and a dislike shown to this place which up to a certain period, had been readily come to and no dislike shown to either House or Inmates—however I will not open old grievances here, the young people will not be asked to come again under any circumstances.'

He was certainly, as Effie had discovered, a master of duplicity. Not only had it been arranged that his son and Effie should live at Herne Hill on return from Venice, and thus be closer than in Park Street, but Mrs. Ruskin was constantly reminding John of her yearning for him.

'I would not have you in England while you feel and think as you do at present if I could bring you at this moment by a wish, but I cannot feel as I do when you are near me . . . however sad I have felt I must in justice to myself say I have not let it operate to the discomfort of others—though there are times when I feel a heart-sickening impatience to see and hear and speak to you, not easily concealed. I am not quite satisfied about the state of your health—is your appetite regularly good.'

Effie was righteously indignant when she heard that the Ruskins were accusing her of extravagance. Ever since their arrival in Venice she had been endeavouring to persuade John to curb his expenditure on unnecessary things, and at the same time cutting down her own expenditure to a minimum.

Casa Metzler
January 1852

'I have remonstrated with him', she wrote in January, 'but in vain. He only replies "Just think what treasures these would be to the British Museum were the Austrians to blow down St Marks some day". I say "Yes, if we had money". He says "Oh, we have plenty for that and I must always have everything proper for my work, even if we live in a garret".
' "Well" I said "I shall not assist you. I shall give up my modelling master" which he willingly assented to. I also wished to give up my music lessons which he decidedly refused. This is the only expense I have. I have wished him to send away the gondola and Carlo, who receives a weekly wage for being with John about two hours a day, but no, he says, he must have him.
'But the Ruskins do such strange things and show no ideas of economy, Mr. R bought the other day another new Turner for £170. John was angry and said it was worth to him about

£80. Then Mr. R writes that when they come abroad in May
to travel in Switzerland and perhaps Italy that it would be so
sad to cross the water and land at Calais without John and that
I might stay with you a couple of months. I said to John "Just
fancy the expense of our crossing the Alps twice and for what
good". Never mind, says John, it must be done—it does not
signify if it is folly or not if they want it. What will you do, he
said. I said I would do what was most economical and that I
had quite made up my mind a year ago never to return to
Perth (much as I should like to be with you) unless he accompanied me. Nor would I ever again permit him to be travelling
months with his parents without me. He seemed satisfied and
pleased. Are they not strange people.'

In a later letter in January she again refers to the extravagance of the Ruskins and to their ruinous influence on her life
with John. She had just heard that her mother was ill.

Casa Metzler
January 1852

'I wish May were here and George in Perth to relieve you, or
to return to the old story that I had been the Boy and never
left you—which I believe in the end might have been better
for all parties. For then the Ruskins would not have had me to
grumble at and I would always have been with my mother
and you, amongst the places I shall always love best. But then
poor John would not have been so happy as he is with me and
it is always something that he thinks me perfect—as long as
he is not with the old people. Every time John is with them
without me his mind is poisoned. Thank you for your remarks
about our expenses which is only another form of Mr. R's
continued and neverceasing disappointment of John's marriage
with me instead of Miss Lockhart or some person of higher
position and more fortune. How he can accuse me of extravagance is to me too strange. He never accuses frankly and
openly but I have seen it in some of his letters to John for a
week past. They have given John most expensive habits which
added to his generous mind entails on him the loss of quantities
of money. He has a perfect mania for buying old books to aid

him in his book on Venice which I know Mr. Ruskin will lose
a great deal on, as it is not selling at all and the beautiful plates
which cost £30 to £50 each and are invaluable as records of
architecture are not sold, as the public are not inclined to give
£12 for a work in which they are not interested. These losses
annoy and disappoint Mr. R, not much I believe really for the
money, as that he is exceedingly proud and cannot bear to
think that the fame of his son is declining, which is only in the
natural consequences of things, as no author enjoys continued
popularity. But John is more vigorous than ever before, and
that will pass.'

In February she heard for the first time of the old Ruskins'
plan to buy a house for them close to Denmark Hill, which she
knew would once and for all shatter any remaining hope she
had of holding John.

Casa Metzler

24 February 1852

'Mr. R and Mrs. R send the most affectionate messages to me
and all the time write *at* or *against* me and speak of the hollowness of worldly society and the extravagance of living in large
houses and seeing great people—all of which perfectly true if
it applied to us, which it does not, for as I have said before I
have spent nothing in dress and the gondola is kept for John
not me. They always put themselves in the position of the
injured party who give up everything to please us or rather *me*
and then they have got so much power over John by knowing
his disposition so well, and always declaring how old they are
and touching his feelings. They arrange and manage everything and Mr. R has been looking at all the houses near to fix
us down beside themselves. They say they think society ruinous for his mind and health and when I ventured to say that
I ought at least to have been consulted John said he *never*
intended as long as they lived to consult me on any subject of
importance as he owed it to them to follow their commands
implicitly. At present they annoy me little but were I to settle
down only amongst them and no others I'm afraid my equani-
mity is not great enough to endure such an existence with
happiness. . . . Mr. Newton is going to Mytelene by Malta and

wants John to meet him at Corfu. John is enraged and wont
write to him. He says "The idea of my leaving my work and
go to Corfu" and then Mr. Ruskin writes "For Heaven's sake,
my dearest John, never whilst I live dream of going into a
vessel with steam in it. Ever since the Amazon burning I have
never had it out of my head. Pray write us directly a long
account of your health, your pulse, meals and sleep, perspiration etc" I am sure that will make you laugh and when I tell
you this kind of thing comes nearly every day interspersed
with lines from Mrs. R in a style almost of amatory tenderness,
calling John her beloved and Heart's Treasure and a variety
of other titles.'

The taking of the house at Herne Hill gave Mr. Ruskin an
opening for renewing his sly attacks on Effie through her
father. He told Mr. Gray of his plan in March:

Preston
30 March 1852

'We have been induced to take the house for the reason of my
son requiring in pursuit of his Literary Occupations to be near
London for a few years to come, and also, as his Mother and I
are getting old, my son inclined to give us a share of his
company, but from Phemy not being happy or comfortable at
our house he could best do so by living *near* us and not *with* us.

'I confess to you that I have great misgivings as to the
propriety of trying the scheme at all. John merely dropped a
few words in a late letter that Phemy did seem a little melancholy at the prospect of a quiet suburban villa near London.
You know the life they have been leading and the society they
have enjoyed, especially Phemy who has daily taken advantage
of the good company in her power. I confess I have great fears
of Phemy being able contently to live at Herne Hill. . . .
Phemy is young and society likes her and she loves society and
I have no hope of her yet leading a very domestic life. . . . My
object in writing to you is to ask the favour of your candid
opinion of our plan.

'John's mother thinks that an only son should do something
for his ageing parents, on the other hand there seems to exist

some idea that the young people, in order to be quite happy,
should be let alone—that any interference on our part does
harm. . . . They never appeared to me to have more than a
decent affection for each other, John being divided between his
pictures and his wife and Phemy betwixt her husband and
her dress.'

Mr. Gray raised no objections to the plan, but once again
suggested that the young couple should be left alone, a suggestion that always incensed Mr. Ruskin.

Liverpool
2 April 1852

'From your light way of treating the subject', he wrote to Mr.
Gray, 'and from the tone of your letter I have no great hope
of your lending your aid in bringing about the change which
may be wanting. However dark my views may be of many
things—it does not alter facts. The young people spend nearly
double their income in a ceaseless round of dressing and
gaiety. . . . I see Phemy as yet very young and being beautiful
and admired and an ornament to society, naturally fond of
being much in it. She does not lead the life I could have wished
my daughter in law to lead but she may come to do so. She will
get tired of her present life and in the meanwhile my son is
not unhappy—he is proud of his wife and pleased to see her
shine in society. . . . If you will not also treat the matter as of
no importance I would solicit the use of all your influence with
John, as you are likely long to survive me, to convince him of
the inutility if not dangers of personalities in his writings.'

He goes on to refer to John's letters to *The Times* in which
he attacks Disraeli and other public men.

In his reply, Mr. Gray reminded Mr. Ruskin that it was he
who had urged John and Effie to seek the best society in London, which drew from the old schemer an unusually verbose
letter charged with self-recriminations.

It is idle to speculate on the effect of a refusal on Mr. Gray's
part to agree with the plan. The Ruskins had made up their
minds that Denmark Hill was once more to be John's real
home, and John was entirely in their power.

By the end of June, John had roughed out the greater part
of the second and third volumes of the *Stones of Venice*, and it
was time to return home. Shortly before leaving, he and Effie
suffered a great disappointment when the Trustees of the
National Gallery turned down John's offer to procure for the
Gallery two pictures by Tintoretto for £12,000. It was Effie
who mooted the proposal.

Casa Metzler
1 May 1852

'Talking of pictures puts me in mind that I dont think I told
you that about a month ago I told John that I thought he
might try to buy some of the Tintorettos, going to ruin here,
for England, and that he ought to write to Sir C Eastlake and
at the same time to Lord Lansdowne for a bequest from the
National Gallery or the nation of £20000. John did not like to
write to Lord L but I insisted as I knew Lord L is fonder of
the Arts than politics. I wrote him a letter myself accompanying John's more business like one.'

Lord Lansdowne's answer to Effie shows the warm place
she had won in the hearts of her friends.

'I assure you that I feel indebted to the Tintorettos for having
procured me a letter from you and, though I have written to
Mr. Ruskin on the subject, I must say that your eloquent
pleading in their favour adds greatly to the desire that I feel to
see them, if it can be accomplished, the property of the British
public, whose taste requires frequent refreshing from such
quarters to keep it straight and sound, amidst all the vagaries
into which it is apt to run—as you will find if, as I hope, you
will return to London in time to see all our annual Exhibitions
now about to open. Our friend, Lady Davy, after a long
hibernation at Bournemouth, has just come into full blow in
town and is exerting herself as usual to promote society. You
must really not allow the lapidary charms of Venice to retain
you there much longer. Whenever you arrive you will find
friends impatient to see you and none more than myself.'

Effie had enjoyed her second winter in Venice. In the sun-
shine and the company of happy and interesting people, she

was able to forget for a time the shadows cast over her life by the old Ruskins, and John had been kind and attentive, and pleased to go about with her.

But her spirits sank lower and lower with each milestone on the road to Calais. John was returning full of eagerness to get to work and to sun himself once more at Denmark Hill. For her there was nothing to look forward to but maintaining an outward appearance of friendliness with her in-laws and, once again, seeking some happiness alone.

CHAPTER XII

The Order of Release

EFFIE found nothing to revive her spirits when she saw her new home at Herne Hill. It was

'a small, ugly, red brick house, partly furnished in the worst possible taste and with the most glaring vulgarity'.

Though it was his parents who were responsible, John was so upset that he at first refused to enter the house, but Effie eventually calmed him down.

She was now, to a great extent, cut off from her friends in London, but her father-in-law lent her his brougham occasionally. 'How I wish it was a gondola', she wrote when the winter fogs descended. She and John were expected to dine nearly every night at Denmark Hill, and Mr. Ruskin assured Mr. Gray that 'we go on very well', though unable to resist adding,

2 August 1852

'I dont like that young Ford, a sort of man about town, coming calling but I should not make mischief by interfering. I think it proper however to give you and Mrs. Gray my thoughts.'

He had brought mischief-making to a fine art. His efforts to fix the blame on Effie for the large overdraft at the bank were brought to naught when he and his wife examined John's account book for the preceding year and, finding that their son had spent as much as £150 on books in six weeks, they begged Effie to take charge of all income and give John an allowance. She went to one memorable dinner in July, given by her friends the Fords.

Herne Hill
22 July 1852

'We had a large party—Lord and Lady Mahon, Mr. Panizzi, Sir William Molesworth, some gentlemen who I did not know and Mr. Henning (the flea as Lord Brougham calls him) who professes to be a great admirer of mine, an odious little man who makes lots of mischief but is very clever. He said he was so charmed to see me again that the sound of my voice was quite refreshing. I said something to him at dinner about his making some bitter little hits at people. He said so coolly, to be heard by everyone "that's the great secret of my success in society. There is nothing people like so much to hear as ill of their neighbours, nothing is so popular." We were all seated at dinner when the Duke of Wellington was announced. I was very agreeably disappointed in his appearance and would yet have known him anywhere from his family likeness. He has a very good face and fine brown eyes but is short and squarely built—quite different to what I expected. . . . When the gentlemen came into the drawingroom Mr. Ford brought the Duke direct up to me and we had a long talk about Venice and Marmont. He recounted to me how it was that Marmont's arm was saved at Salamanca. The arm was condemned but they were forced to make so hasty a retreat that the arm was un-cared for and grew well. He said he would have liked much to have known him. He could not understand how I could live a year at Venice without dying of ennui and want of exercise, and that it would be a very unsuitable place for him as he was Master of the Horse.

'We were talking of fiction and he asked me if I ever read novels. I answered that you had permitted me to read as many novels as I liked when very young, thinking truly that that folly would early cure itself, and that since I was twelve I had hardly read any. He said that was pretty much his own case in regard to novel reading, but that, Alas, he had had many other follies which had not been cured so soon.'

The Duke invited her to Apsley House, and that was the last time she saw him.

He died in September, and the same week Effie wrote:

Herne Hill
18 September 1852

'We paid an agreeable visit to Lockhart who is so delightful although he looks so sad and heartbroken, poor man, and they say that he is much annoyed with his son-in-law, who if he can wishes to turn Abbotsford into a Monastery! I do not see how it is possible but it is said. There we met one of the Doctors who had been at Walmer to the poor Duke. We heard much that was interesting about him. It appears he had been subject to epileptic fits and had been perfectly well with a large party of friends in the Castle and *tending his flowers at five* on the morning. Tuesday he took ill when five of these fits came one after another. The last carried him off. Only last Saturday he went to Folkestone to see a sick friend of his and Lockhart's, Admiral Croker, and stayed with him five hours. They had been great friends in early life and Admiral C often wrote down their conversations and on Saturday last was so struck with what he said that when the Duke left him he wrote it all down and sent it in the evening to Lockhart, who told us that he considered it very remarkable. It was 16 pages closely written and full of anecdotes about Spain, his interviews with the Royal family of France and his opinions about the present state of politics in England. Lockhart thinks his death even now will be a very serious thing for us abroad as we are so unpopular.

'All hope that they will have the sense to put Prince George in his place as he is such a first rate officer. I saw Ld. George Paget yesterday which shows they are back from Berlin so that the Prince is at hand, unless the Queen is so silly as to wish the appointment for Prince Albert which would do a great deal of harm.'

But during that winter there was little to help her forget her hidden sorrows; she could only occasionally get clear of the Denmark Hill atmosphere, but managed to see something of her closest friends.

The new year brought fresh troubles with a new form of attack from Denmark Hill.

Herne Hill
25 February 1853

'The Ruskins are bothering me now because I won't visit without John or go to balls alone. How is one to please them? I have never asked John to go to a single place nor told them of many of the kind invitations I have had, yet they know from John I get them. What should I do? If I do go I must

THE ORDER OF RELEASE
By Sir J. E. Millais, BT., P.R.A.

spend money in carriage hires and go alone. If I don't, they say that it is my own fault if I have not society and that I may go wherever I like or do what I choose provided I don't *degrade* John by taking him into society. In fact they don't care any of them what becomes of me or what I do so that they are left to enjoy themselves selfishly alone. I never saw such a trio; if I had book making powers I should certainly write about them. . . . For my own part I would much rather not go out at all. It subjects me to many inconveniences. . . . They use all their influence against me. They will be kind to me but then I must be their slave in return. I must praise them as three perfect people and be treated as a fool or a child whichever suits them best, but then I must never complain or else get a torrent of insults in return.'

That was in February, but before March was out the strange trio had made an entirely fresh set of plans. John, who hoped to complete the *Stones of Venice* by April, and who was much exhausted, was to go into society during May so as to make acquaintance with

'everybody who has Turners or Missals and get invited to their houses, and after that to go for an extended holiday to Scotland'.

Effie was delighted with the prospect of escaping from the old Ruskins for a few months, and meanwhile had a fresh interest in life as Millais had asked her to sit for his picture 'The Order of Release'.

She found him a hard task master, and had to pose from immediately after breakfast till dinner, and then all the afternoon till dark.

Herne Hill
20 March 1853

'He found my head like everyone else who has tried it immensely difficult and he was greatly delighted last night when he said he had quite got it! He paints so slowly and finely that no man working as he does can paint faster.'

The picture created a great sensation, and was the first ever hung on the walls of the Academy which required a policeman to move on the crowd.

Mr. Andrew Lang wrote that

'as a piece of realistic painting it may challenge comparison with anything else in the world'.

Millais's biographer, his son John, wrote:

'The head of the woman, painted from my mother, was a perfect likeness of her in 1853, except only as to the colour of the hair, a golden auburn, which was changed to black, in order to contrast with that of the child.'

Westall, the famous model, posed for the 'Highlander'. He was a deserter from a dragoon regiment, and was arrested one day in the studio of Mr. Cope, R.A., and tried by court martial. A subscription was raised by artists to buy him out of the Army after he had served his sentence.

Exhibited in the 1853 Royal Academy, it was bought by a Mr. Arden for £400; in 1878 Mr. Renton bought it for £2,853, and on his death it was bought by Sir Henry Tate for 5,000 guineas.

A letter written by D. G. Rossetti at this time shows that Millais's backgrounds were attracting much attention:

14 Chatham Place Blackfriars Bridge

'Your enquiries about the picture I am beginning have succeeded in haling me up to the scratch, without brandy, and indeed the brandy here cannot be drunk.

'I am starting the landscape of my picture in the most lamentable style, owing to a conspiracy of wretched weather, not time to spare for it, and deficient practice in painting that sort of thing.

'I have done as usual a good many things since I saw you, which make as usual precious little when put together.

'I have designed, and written, and made great exertions to be lazy. I devote my evenings at present to translating the pre-Dantesque poets, and have done upward of 50 poems from them. I hope to have the book out before long, having been encouraged by Patmore who says there can be no doubt of my finding a publisher. The original poems are most wonderful things. I calculate on the triumph of being the first man in

England who was ever beforehand with the Germans in translating any important work. On running over what I have
written above I find it is full of Is and stinks altogether of
identity.

'I want horribly to see your backgrounds, the fame whereof
is in men's ears. Hunt's is tremendous.

'We have no companions here except a serene cat, a mezzo-
tint from Murillo, an ideal head of Charles 1st as a martyr, and
the injured ghost of Sir Hoshua Kennels—not to mention the
hatred of Frank Stone, which abideth for ever.'

But Millais was worried about the deadening of his colours
shortly after his pictures were finished—'chilling' John Ruskin
had called it in his letter on 'Ophelia'—and he sought the
advice of John Thomas Linnell, R.A., who wrote:

Red Hill, Reigate
15 January 1854

'I think the grounds you paint on must be too absorbent for I
remember your saying that your picture of the "Huguenot"
deadened in the same way and I have found that when a
picture is painted on such a ground it requires varnishing a
good many times before it will bear out. I think you will find
that all your pictures require is re-varnishing. So far from
Canada Balsam causing a deadness of surface it is calculated to
do just the reverse, for a glossy surface is one of its characteristics.'

That this was good advice is attested by the colour, substance
and surface of his pictures today, which are as perfect as on the
day they were painted.

In April, the prospect of a short season in London for John's
benefit lost some of its glamour for Effie as she fell ill, but she
determined to see it through:

Herne Hill
10 April 1853

'I shall just struggle on and go into town as I might be a little
better, and I would be only too glad to get John out a little, and
everyone seems very anxious we should go in for the month
of May. It is not of much consequence whether I go out or not

to parties but I think it would be right to encourage John to go
as much as possible. . . . I have no faith in Doctors and I know
they would only order me change of air. I only complain of
weakness and pains but it is sad sometimes to pass days without
doing a single thing of use. . . . Mr. and Mrs. R seem to be
aware in spite of themselves that I am not well and Mrs. R
says it is a good thing, if I do feel ill, that in losing my strength
I do not lose my looks. Mr. R who is without exception the
most extraordinary man alive, on my marriage day hinting
disagreeable things at me all dinner time and was in a very bad
humour, but as I suppose I was too careful and too weak to
resent anything anybody might have said on the Monday,
when at Liverpool at the Inn, he wrote me a letter which is
unique and if I could only send it for your inspection I think
my father and you would think it as extraordinary a produc-
tion as I did. He said he had taken pen in hand to John to
expatiate on my perfections of appearance and manner, that in
his life he had never seen anything so perfect as my attitude
as I lay on the sofa the night before and that no wonder
Millais etc. etc. But it sickens me to write such nonsense as I
could spare such writing and excuse it from a fool but from
Mr. R it sounded to say the least I thought unnatural and
almost suspicious.'

Effie no doubt preferred his rudeness and abuse to this maw-
kish display of sensualism, and it is not surprising that she was
suspicious.

They found a house in Charles Street for their reappearance
in society, and invitations soon were pouring in. Of the many
parties described in her letters, one at Stafford House is of
interest:

6 Charles Street
June 1853

'The other day there was great let off at Stafford House and it
was much grander than Royalty. The dinner was made for the
Duchess of Kent and Duke of Genoa and it is a fact that the
morning of the party the Duchess of Sutherland, when bidding
the Queen goodbye at Windsor, the Queen said to the Duchess
"Will you have room for me today" and of course the Duchess

was too proud, and rushed up to town made further prepara-
tions and the Queen, Prince and suite appeared in due course.
The whole house was lighted up and thrown open and crowds
were pouring out and in of the D's *bedroom* where they
admired with all their eyes the point lace hangings and her
brushes with silver backs studded with turquoises. The ladies
were all astonished and so were the gentlemen at the appearance of Frances, Ctess Waldegrave and Lady Desart with their
heads powdered with gold and it was thought hideous. It fell
on their necks and stuck to their cheeks and Lady Cowley has
just come from Paris and reports that the Empress has given
up wearing her hair turned back for everybody has copied her
and she now considers it vulgar.'

During May, Effie was busy preparing for the holiday in the
Highlands. Her husband, who had a profound admiration for
Millais, and knew that he was also contemplating a holiday,
asked him to accompany them. After some disappointments
the Ruskins found rooms in the schoolmaster's house at Brig
o'Turk in Glenfinlas and Millais and his brother rooms at the
New Trossachs Hotel a few hundred yards away.

Effie wrote to her father:

6 Charles Street
30 May 1853

'As far as I can understand John, we shall want our rooms for
the end of the first week in July and he intends to be all the
time in one place and remain until the weather breaks as he
will like to be as long in the company of Millais, and I hope
Hunt with Millais's brother will form our party. The Edinburgh people want John to give some lectures there in November and if the season proves fine I would try and keep him all
the time in the North. But of course the Ruskins will try to
prevent that if they can.

'I fancy John and the two Millais and Holman Hunt will be
very busy sketching and walking over the mountains and I
shall occupy myself in trying to make them all as comfortable
as I can.

'It would amuse you to hear the Pre-Raphaelites and John
talk. They seem to think that they will have everything for the

o

asking and laugh at me for preparing a great hamper of sherry and tea and sugar.'

Holman Hunt found he could not accompany them north, and in her letter informing her parents Effie makes her only personal reference to Millais who she describes as

'extremely handsome, besides his talents, that you may fancy how he is run after'.

Whatever Millais's feeling may have been for her after those long sittings for 'The Order of Release' they had, as yet, found no response. It was John who was so anxious for Millais's company; every mile on their northward journey was another mile away from Denmark Hill, and that and the adequacy of the hampers was all that occupied Effie's thoughts.

CHAPTER XIII

Glenfinlas

ALL Ruskin's and Millais's biographers give prominence to their joint expedition to the Highlands in the summer of 1853.

Not only did Millais paint his famous picture of Ruskin in Glenfinlas, but their appreciation of each other's powers, expressed in letters, has always attracted the attention of authors of books about the period.

Then, again, Millais who never missed anything humorous, made many amusing sketches of the party at work, fishing, playing indoor games, and at morning service, which have been reproduced in several books.

William Millais's description of the morning service at the Free Kirk, which was the subject of the sketch reproduced here, is most amusing.

'The service was to us somewhat comical, and we could hardly stay it out. The precentor was a little very bow-legged man, with the wheeziest of voices, and sang the first line of the paraphrase alone, whilst his little shaggy terrier, the image of his master, joined in the piteous howl.

'The other lines were sung by the congregation, assisted by a few collies. I afterwards tackled the little precentor, and asked him why he didn't have an organ. "Ah, man, would you have us take to the devil's band?" he replied.

'When the sermon came, it was most amusing to us to watch the old men passing their ram's horn snuff-mulls to one another, and putting little bone spades full of the pungent material up their noses to keep them awake. In front of us were two well dressed young girls, in all the newest fashion and when the shallow offertory box was poked towards them, they put in a farthing. We afterwards saw them take off their shoes and stockings and walk home barefoot.'

Biographers, too, have indulged in speculation about Millais and Effie, who were so much thrown together at Glenfinlas, and concluded that their interest in one another was at least heightened if, indeed, it did not become of serious import.

Though it was Ruskin who proposed the expedition, there were many who, at the time, believed it was the old Ruskins who were responsible.

Effie's brother, George, as already noted, had long before come to the conclusion that deliberately leaving Effie so much to herself and urging her to go out alone was part of a plan to regain sole control of their son through divorce proceedings of a normal kind. Miss Douglas-Boswell, who was often with Effie during John's absences, wrote after the annulment:

'I never doubted the taking of John Millais to the Highlands was a regular deep laid scheme, which doubtless J. R. imagined could not fail, judging the world by his own wicked self. But a good God watched over the unsuspecting victims and putting grace into their hearts prevented his malicious designs.'

Miss Douglas-Boswell's views must, however, be treated with some caution, as it is evident from her letters that she detested the possessive, morbid mother and the sanctimonious father, and that the son repelled her.

Whatever the truth the party remained outwardly on the friendliest terms during the four months at Glenfinlas, though their hopes of fine weather were dashed by nearly continuous rain. They made the best of it, and in the evenings discussed art, and Effie held forth on Scottish history, in which she was well learned.

Millais wrote to a friend in August:

'Finding all my friends writing letters, I have just crossed the bog that separates us from them to send you a bulletin of our health and doings. Our patience has been most sorely tried and has stood proof tolerably well. Cannot you see us, one by one, and hour by hour, with anxious faces, trying to read the sun through Scotch mist and rain.

'If you have leisure to read, get Ruskin's two last volumes of the Stones of Venice, which surpass all he has written. He is an indefatigable writer. We have, in fine weather, immense enjoyment painting on the rocks and having our dinner

KIRK AT GLENFINLAS

TOURIST'S HIGHLAND REEL
Sketches by Sir J. E. Millais, BT., P.R.A.

brought to us there and in the evening climbing up the steep mountains for exercise, Mrs. Ruskin accompanying us.

'We went to church and took a delightful walk to a waterfall of seventy feet, where we had a bathe, my brother and self— he standing in the torrent of water, which must have punished his back as severely as a soldier's cat-o'-nine tails whipping. It is quite impossible to walk by these mountain rivers without undressing and jumping in.' (*Life and Letters*)

Ruskin found:

'Millais a very interesting study. But I don't know how to manage him; his mind is so terribly active, so full of invention that he can hardly stay quiet a minute without sketching either ideas or reminiscences; and keeps himself awake all night planning pictures.'

Millais kept up a regular correspondence with John Leech, who, in one of his replies, bewails the lot of the comic artist.

'I have taken a most unfair advantage of your confidence and have adorned the pages of a certain popular periodical with one of your sketches. Of course I have not mentioned your name in the matter to the public, but have left the drawing to speak for itself, and uncommonly well it speaks itself. It is quite clear you must leave all your pursuits and become a regular contributor to "Punch". I have no doubt you have enjoyed yourself mightily in the Highlands, and sometimes I have been inclined to envy you your holiday. I would give something to have a month or two rest but, alas, there is no repose for the funny man, and therefore, perhaps it would be better for you to devote yourself to that branch of art which allows you some leisure. . . . Like yourself, I have had but little of the sport I am afraid we both like, for the only fishing I have had that I can call to mind was to secure some bloaters the other day (for a consideration) out of a shop in the Haymarket and afterwards leaving them in a cab, and they are now most probably carefully packed away at the General Hackney Carriage office with ladies handkerchiefs, opera glasses, parasols and other articles usually left in Hack vehicles.'

In August, Ruskin was turning his mind to lectures he was to give in Edinburgh in November, and Millais joined forces with him and became absorbed in the subject matter.

'Ruskin and myself', he wrote to a friend, 'are pitching into architecture; you will hear shortly to what purpose. I think I was intended for a Master Mason. All this day I have been working at a window, which I hope you will see carried out very shortly in stone. In my evening hours I mean to make many designs for church and other architecture, as I find myself quite familiar with constructions, Ruskin having given me lessons regarding foundations, and the building of cathedrals etc.'

In a later letter he writes:

'We are busy making drawings for the lectures.'

Meanwhile, whenever the weather permitted, Millais was at work on his portrait of Ruskin.

Early in July he had, in Ruskin's words,

'fixed on his place, a lovely piece of worn rock, with foaming water and weeds and moss, and a noble overhanging bank of dark crag; and I am to be standing looking quietly down the stream; just the sort of thing I used to do for hours together. He is very happy at the idea of doing it, and I think you will be proud of the picture, and we shall have the two most wonderful torrents in the world, Turner's St. Gothard and Millais' Glenfinlas.'

Ruskin's diary is full of the picture, and he recorded the exact time of every sitting.

It was not completed until the following January.

At the end of October the party broke up, the Millais returned to London, and the Ruskins went to Edinburgh for the lectures.

On the surface friendship had been maintained despite the test imposed by the bad weather, but during those months the Millais brothers had been profoundly disturbed by Ruskin's conduct to Effie.

Millais occasionally corresponded with Effie, which was perfectly natural between close friends, and Ruskin raised no objection, but as soon as he was again in thrall to his parents a sinister construction was put on this correspondence which came to the ears of Effie's mother.

Millais's two letters to Mrs. Gray, written in December, reveal the strong currents that, unknown to Effie, were running under the calm surface of life at Glenfinlas.

> 83 Gower Street, Bedford Square
> 19 December 1853

'I have no time to answer your letter as fully as I would wish as it is nearly 5 o'clock—the only Post whereby you could receive this, when you will be expecting it—I have been delayed by a friend calling—

'Believe me I WILL DO EVERYTHING YOU CAN DESIRE OF ME, so keep your mind perfectly at rest—I should never have written to your daughter had not Ruskin been cognisant to the correspondence, and approving of it or at least not admitting a care in the matter—If he is such a plotting and scheming fellow, as to take notes secretly to bring against his wife, such a quiet scoundrel ought to be ducked in a mill pond—His conduct is so provokingly gentle that it is folly to kick against such a man—From this time, I will never write again to his wife, as it will *be better*, and will exclude the possibility of his further complaining, although sufficient has passed to enable him to do so, at any time he may think fit. One is never safe against such a brooding selfish lot as those Ruskins—His absence in the Highlands seemed purposely to give me an opportunity of being in his wife's society—His wickedness must be without parallel, if he kept himself away, to the end that has come about, as I am sometimes inclined to think, altogether his conduct is incomprehensible, he is either crazed, or anything but a desirable acquaintance—

'The *worst of all is the wretchedness* of her position, whenever they go to visit she will be left to herself in the company of any stranger present, for Ruskin appears to delight in selfish solitude. Why he ever had the audacity of marrying with no better intentions is a mystery to me, I must confess that it appears to me that he cares for nothing beyond his Mother and Father, which makes the insolence of his finding fault with his wife (to whom he has acted from the beginning most disgustingly) more apparent—I shall never dine at Denmark Hill again, and will not call at Herne Hill to see either, but will leave a card which will suffice—I shall be out of England next year, so that there can be no more interference from me—If I have meddled more than my place would justify it was from the flagrant nature of the affair—I am only anxious to do the best for your daughter—I consider Ruskin's treatment of her so sickening that for quietness' sake she should as much as possible prevent his travelling, or staying a summer in company with a friend, *who cannot but observe* his hopeless apathy, in *everything regarding her happiness*. I cannot conceal the truth from you, that she has more to put up with than any living woman—Again I must promise you that I will never more give occasion for the Ruskins to further aggravate her on my account—*Everything on my part will be as you wish*—I have scarcely time to sign to save post. I will write tomorrow more intelligibly.

'I think the Ruskins must not perceive too great a desire on your part to keep quiet, and submit to anything, as they will imagine it to be fear;—she has all the right on her side and believe me the Father would see that also if he knew all—'

*   *   *

83 Gower Street
21 December 1853

'I am afraid my answer to your kind and judicious letter was dreadfully incoherent, but now I will endeavour to reply more satisfactorily—

'Although you know John Ruskin's odd propensity for roaming away by himself from all human creatures and their habitations, yet you cannot be aware of the abstracted way in which he neglects his wife—It is utterly impossible for a friend to sojourn with them for any length of time, without absolutely being compelled in common courtesy to attend to her—I assure you that Ruskin only expressed approval and delight at perceiving that your daughter and myself agreed so well together, and when *I spoke to him about his extraordinary indifference to her attractions* (which could not be but excessively unpleasing, and conducive to her unhappiness) he only apathetically laughed and said, he thought all women ought to depend upon themselves for engrossing employment, and such like cold inhuman absurdities—There was something so revolting to me about this sickly treatment of her just cause of complaint and discontent, that I never again ventured to speak on the subject, as I could not depend upon keeping my temper.—When she and my brother visited Bowerswell, he was all for my accompanying them, and returning with her, which I refused to do, although I knew he would have been quite as happy without my society. In fact he appeared *purposely to connive at the result*—seemingly callous, and methodically writing all that he himself brought about, to his parents, like a boy of ten years of age—He is an undeniable giant as an author, but a poor weak creature in everything else, bland, and heartless, and unworthy,—with his great talents—of *any* woman possessing affection, and sensibility—Do not imagine that I am induced through circumstances to speak thus depreciatingly of him, or that this is a hasty conclusion of his character. An open enemy is preferable to a cool friend, and Ruskin is one of the latter order and therefore odious in my sight—I think his Inquisitorial practice of noting down everything which could forward an excuse for complaining against his own wife, is the *most unmanly, and debased proceeding I ever heard of, but* even that is nothing in comparison with his aggravating unsociability which she has to put up with—You were kind enough to be plain spoken with me in your letter, and I will be the same with you, it is of no use conventionally disguising my opinion from you, however biased it may be and however painful I cannot resist unreservedly avowing it— You will avert many disagreeable casualties, and greatly increase your daughter's comfort by *permitting always one, or other, of her sisters to be with her*—It is a sufficient inducement (not to speak of her appearance) that these cunning London men detect neglect, and unconcern, on Ruskin's part, and her

unhappiness, to make them impudent, and importunate—
With a companion this evil can be greatly frustrated, as she
would not be left by herself to receive strangers, and gallant
rakes, who can always find an excuse for calling, and who look
upon Ruskin as a kind of milksop,—I have met many of these
fellows even before I knew Ruskin, and have heard them
circulating over dinner tables the most unwarrantable insinuations, and now I find myself continually questioned
regarding my experience of their married life—

'I believe you will have every reason to be satisfied with me,
as your desire is not more earnest than mine to hasten the
interests of the Countess.[1] My intention is simply to call and
leave a card at Herne Hill and the same at Denmark Hill after
which I will carefully avoid, (if they should invite me) dining
there, by managing to get engaged elsewhere. When the
summer comes I shall, I trust, be away on the Continent, after
completing Glenfinlas, which I would leave as it is, had not
Ruskin spoken about it since, to the effect, that he should
consider it an insult to his Father, besides himself, if I did not
finish it. Of course I cannot obviate or foresee the chances of
meeting the Countess in society, but as she rarely goes out, and
myself as seldom, I don't think such a meeting likely. I have
written a letter, (the last I will write) telling her I will *not call
and see her*, as proposed, to escape the suspicion of the Father
and Mother, who will naturally enquire whether I have been
there or not, and will think it strange after our intimacy.
Should *she, and yourself*, consider it more prudent for me to
call as though nothing had happened I will do so—I regret very
much, (in spite of the wonderful advance my pupil has made
in her drawing) that I had not taught her more, as I am convinced she will find it one of her greatest, and most absorbing
recreations. I will take care to send her sketches and engravings
to copy, which she can return by Crawley, by this means a
kind of friendship will be continued which will satisfy the
curiosity of most people who will imagine I go there as before—
Sometimes I uselessly wish that I never had accompanied
Ruskin to the Highlands. I may be beneficial in the end to
their position, in regard to each other, as it has disturbed the

[1] The Millais brothers gave Effie this name one day, and it stuck to her

settled dullness of their existence, *and any change was prefer-able* to the life they have been living, (I should rather say the life that she *has been* ENDURING), for I believe he is com-placent, and happy enough—I have seen nothing but the most placid and patient submission on her part to his will, and yet there is a *stealthy*, bad, dissatisfaction in his nature which is very trying, and disgusting—I sincerely hope that all this is not so new to you, but that you will, (from previous knowledge) be prepared to hear what is so distressing for me to recount, and that this unfortunate business may blow over, like all the other calamities and grievances that have gone before us—If I have not answered as you desired pray let me know, as I am only anxious to accede to your wishes.'

Ruskin, apparently oblivious of the resentment of his friends, wrote in his last letter from Glenfinlas:

'I have stopped all this time to keep Millais company—to keep him up to the Pre-Raphaelite degree of finish.'

His biographers say that he was *very dense* where human relationships were concerned and did not resent Millais's and Effie's growing friendship!

Much, however, happened after the Ruskins returned to London which can only be ascribed to disappointment at the failure to ensnare Effie, for the strange trio intensified their efforts to make her life intolerable.

Whilst at Glenfinlas John received the usual stream of unwholesome letters from his mother and she tried to prevent him lecturing at Edinburgh.

Denmark Hill
15 August 1853

'Mr. Gray of Perth mentions that you have some purpose of giving a course of Lectures in Edinburgh. I cannot reconcile myself to the thought of your bringing yourself personally before the world till you are somewhat older and stronger—perhaps superstition may have something to do with it—I do not say to your father anything about it but I should I think be better satisfied if you continued to benefit the public by writing until you are turned forty two—pray do not let anything I write about this annoy or irritate you. You know dearest that what you think you ought or is right to do. I should be grieved beyond measure were any thing I write to make your task less pleasing. Your father tells you how we have read your vol.[1] I rejoice and am filled with thankfulness —I would rather be your Mother than the mother of the greatest of Kings or Heroes past or present. You know how all you think or feel, or say or do interests.—take care of heavy weights—I take my walks with the same untired delight as far as walking and loving nature goes but I want you to enjoy with me.'

This letter failed in its purpose and the lectures were a triumphant success.

---

[1] 3rd or 4th vol. *Stones of Venice*

CHAPTER XIV

Escape

'I WILL write you a word of Effie's health; but I fear I shall have little cheering information to give you. She passes her days in melancholy, and nothing can help her but an entire change of heart.'

So wrote Ruskin in December. It was to be his last letter to Mrs. Gray. No wonder Effie was unhappy for, though feeling extremely ill in Edinburgh, she had summoned up her strength to attend all the functions for lionizing her husband and now was back under the deepening shadow of Denmark Hill.

Her friends—the Dean of St. Paul's and Mrs. Milman, the Eastlakes, Lord Glenelg, the Murrays—gave her a warm welcome, and Cecilia Northcote, now Mrs. Bishop, pressed her to spend part of the summer with her in Germany but all the kindness of her friends could not assuage her fears for the coming months. Millais had still some work to do on Ruskin's portrait which she knew would add to her difficulties but well as she now knew the Ruskins, she can hardly have anticipated the malevolent nature of their next assault on her peace of mind which was engineered through a child of ten. Mrs. Gray had taken Millais's advice that one of Effie's sisters should always be with her and sent Sophie to London for the winter.

Millais in one of his letters describes her as extremely beautiful and very shrewd. Few children of her age can ever have had such strange experiences as she now met at Denmark Hill.

On her first visit—and Mrs. Ruskin insisted on her visiting them frequently—she found Mrs. Ruskin fondling John in the study. A few moments later a visitor was announced and, after John and his mother had settled on a suitable lie to turn the visitor away, she was told to creep out of the house as she might make a noise and give them away.

On her next visit Mrs. Ruskin threw caution to the wind and after smothering her with kisses told her that her mother was a weak ignorant woman and Effie a poor silly creature simply raised into respectability by John's talents.

Effie, she said, thought herself very clever and people made much of her, but it was John's great abilities and she was merely a Scotch girl with bad manners.

John, too, found in this child, an instrument for exploiting his growing dislike of his wife and told Sophie that he was going to begin harsh treatment when Effie returned from Germany, as there was not time for it to take effect before she went away and that he intended to try what harshness would do to break her spirit. Effie was so wicked he assured her, that he had been warned by all his friends to have nothing to do with her, but that she was so bold and impudent and made such advances to him that she had thrown her snares over him in the same way that she had done to Millais, and that she was so in love with Millais that she thought of nothing but him, and he really thought she was, with the exception of Mrs. Gray, the most intriguing woman he had ever known and that he would write a book about her conduct and get a divorce.

He could not endure his wife and did not mind whether she was ill or well, but he watched everything she did. Mrs. Ruskin frequently told Sophie that she was not to repeat to her sister what she heard at Denmark Hill, knowing perfectly well that every word would reach Effie's ears.

Effie only wrote the truth to her mother when she said it was perfectly disgusting to corrupt a child's mind in this way. She was nearing breaking point and at the end of February wrote to her mother.

Herne Hill
27 February 1854

'He has told Sophie that he watches everything I do or say, therefore it is impossible I can talk about anything that comes uppermost—I do not know what on earth they are such fools for especially John, as were it not for the pain of exposure I have him most completely in my power. I must tell you all these things just to show you how impossible any behaviour is to help things straight for all our sakes, when their object is to get rid of me, to have John altogether with them again, at any price they are resolved to do this, but they seem to wish if possible to disgust me to such a degree as to force me—or else get me—into some scrape—John has been trying again to get me by taunts to write to Millais—He accepted that St. Agnes drawing &c, it now hangs before me and then he said " Didn't I still write to him and where was the harm if he gave me drawings"—I said the drawing was his as much as mine and to send it back if he liked. I suppose by autumn something will be done by the R's—do not think any manifestation will come from me. It is impossible for me to tell you all until I am obliged to seek my Father's advice—but I feel better in my health and as it is impossible by any means of mine to stop their folly—I will just go on as I am doing—Jane Boswell will soon be here and then we go for some days to Oxford and then abroad so that I trust the summer will come and go without anything. It troubles me excessively to write to you about all these things but my position now admits of no other plan and I leave it to your judgement whether or not to give Millais any hints. I wish that picture of John was done.'

This St. Agnes drawing was constantly used by the Ruskins to fan the flames of discord; one day Effie was told to send it back and the next day to keep it.

Determined not to put herself in the wrong she would not write to Millais and yet was terribly anxious about the consequences of Millais hearing from Sophie, or other sources, of her dreadful position.

Her next two letters to her mother show how rapidly the sands were running out.

Herne Hill
28 February 1854

'And what will you write to Millais for really he must know—and be told something of all this or else he will commit some indiscretion from John's false manner to him, and if I let Sophie go and see him she will tell him everything and then he will be put in a passion. I cannot shut my eyes to the Ruskins' wish to draw me into scrapes. It is quite impossible for either you or my Father to advise a submission which might end in their success, since they are perfectly blinded by their selfishness. Don't trouble about me but advise me—I cannot do wrong that good may come. I hope and think I am doing right and I feel better for it.'

*   *   *

Herne Hill
5 March 1854

'I think you see John's plan clearly in regard to Millais—If I cannot go on with the Ruskins, I will do so at least till I see you in autumn or before it—but about Millais there is no doubt that he (John) is acting in a most decided manner to get me into a scrape. About this drawing of St. Agnes, he most completely as far as I can learn from Sophie encouraged him to send it, telling him that it was the finest thing he had done and that I would not know how to thank him &c. Well! Millais I have no doubt takes this for permission, knowing how much pleasure the drawing would give me. He sends it and writes John a most kind note telling me to accept it—John asks me what I thought of it and wasn't it the finest thing I had seen, such an ornament to my room &c. It was hung up and he expressed himself highly pleased with the position. Well! last night I just thought, as I am now so accustomed to his ways, that notwithstanding all his approval that he might lead me into a mess and Millais too, and I said "now you are going to Millais tomorrow what are you going to say to him from me. Do you really quite approve of my having this drawing and are you to tell him so." "No!" said he, "I do *not* think you should take it—but you and Millais must settle that between yourselves." I said that was quite impossible as I did not hold any intercourse with him—He looked incredulous and I said I will send the drawing back in the morning quite coolly.

'He told Sophie that he knew that when he treated me harshly next winter—it would he thought force me to write and complain to Everett and what did he care? It is quite horrible to be obliged to think such things of one's fellow creatures but it is quite impossible not to see the R's settled

ST. AGNES
By Sir J. E. Millais, BT., P.R.A.

wish and idée fixe is to impute something to me which will give them power, and, as they have nothing, their malice is next to insane and if I do not act on the defensive I have no preservative to my honor, for to please them is to destroy myself—John sees all the worth of securing Everett's good opinion and Everett knows my position so well that he is most anxious to promote my happiness in the only way he properly can, by encouraging me to draw. I wish he was gone—I cannot bear to think of what he must endure painting John, —when I think of all his double dealing I wonder how I can speak to him at all and his conduct to Sophie is too detestable. I would rather do anything than that his name should be dragged before the public, and I agree with you that towards winter, after he has gone and no intercourse between us, that if they do not behave better I must then do something without any disadvantage to either of us. For however much he wishes from his regard for me to help me it would be an irreparable misery to himself, although he would try not to feel it, it would hurt his independence. His character stands so de-servedly high that as the founder of a new school and in a great position in this Country it would be a lasting sorrow to have that reputation tarnished in the slightest degree. It is a very very important thing for him to keep clear of us altogether and you may tell him not to think it selfish but imperatively necessary and his first duty to go as soon as possible—things may change but he must not hesitate now—I have been so worried that I quite forgot the Milman's dinner yesterday—Only think!'

Mrs. Gray wrote to Millais and in his reply he urged her to take active steps to end Effie's suffering.

83 Gower Street
3 March 1854

'I am very much obliged for your letter as I shall now be more careful than ever. It is only right that I should know of Ruskin's deceit, that I may act accordingly *Something must be done by you* if she continues to be martyred, as it is *grossly sinful* to permit matters to stand as they do—*Nothing more shall be sent by me,* I should never have sent drawings at all had it not

P

been for Ruskin Himself permitting me to do so. I enclose a letter from him received lately which will tell you everything —If I had only myself to consult, I should write immediately and refuse to go on further with the portrait, which is the most hateful task I ever had to perform, but I am so anxious that Effie should not suffer further for any act of mine that I will put up with anything—rather than increase her suffering—

'Surely such a quiet scoundrel as this man never existed, he comes here sitting as blandly as ever, talking the whole time in apparently a most interested way. Do you think I can get off finishing his portrait without doing harm to the Countess? if so I could leave almost immediately, in May, or 1st of June. My family are going to leave this house then, and are perfectly reconciled to my going abroad—

'I have not painted anything since, nor do I think it likely until I get away from hearing about this—It incenses and disgusts me to hear of this matter, and yet naturally I desire to know all—He was sitting here yesterday and mentioned about sending a little girl's head I have painted, to Herne Hill for the Countess to see. *It is my opinion that some steps should be speedily taken* to protect her from this incessant harassing behaviour of the Rs—If they are bent upon obtaining a separation you will be obliged (in pity for her sake) to consent, for human nature can never stand such treatment.

'I am not sufficiently acquainted with Law to know whether something more than a separation could be obtained, but I think you should enquire into the matter.'

Early in March Effie was strongly advised by Lady Eastlake to free herself from her mental prison and after writing to her mother

'these trials have been for 7 years nearly, they might have gone on 27, only it is better that they should have an end before either these people kill me or lead me into a scrape'

she sat down to write the most difficult letter of her life, one in which she at last told her parents the truth about her married life.

Herne Hill
7 March 1854

'My dearest Father—I have received my Mother's & George's kind letters this morning and feel very thankful that I have your and their approval in the course of conduct I have been endeavouring to pursue for some time—and in fact unless matters had become so sad for me as to threaten my life I should not have on any account, but feeling that the necessity for acting in concert with you might, by being longer delayed, cause you and others connected with my life greater sorrow in the end. I, therefore, as I feel now so ill and in perpetual nervous distress, feel that perhaps I may be adding to yours by a silence which I have kept on John Ruskin's conduct to me ever since I left your care, although I have lately and on my last visit home shown you how very unhappy I was. You are aware that since 1848 to this last year I have never made any formal complaint to you—there were many reasons for my silence the principal being of course my great love for you and my dear Mother—fearing to trouble you when you were in great difficulties yourselves, when I tried to look on my unfortunate position as one where whatever I internally suffered—at least removed me from being a burthen on you—and I resolved that no annoyance which I suffered should give you any. I pass over all other discussions and reasons at present till I see you as I could fill Volumes. To come to the present moment, when even now I was unwilling to tell you all, fearing your anger against John Ruskin who has so illtreated and abused me and his Parents who have so seconded him, although so far they are innocent not knowing the gravity of the offence with which I charge him and from which proceeds all the rest. But they have been most guilty in the education they have given him and ought not to have treated me as they have done—I wish neither to be uncharitable nor to take advantage of any of them, but I am so ruined and nervous in both mind and body that, as they are so anxious to get rid of me and I have not the satisfaction of feeling that any one is the least the better for my forbearance and suffering, I have duly considered the step I am about to take in telling you all. Feeling very ill last week and in the greatest perplexity about my duty to you—I went and consulted Lady Eastlake and also partly Ld. Glenelg, the two persons in London for whom I have most respect. I did not open my mind to the latter as I did to the former, but as I could perfectly rely on their prudence and wisdom I took the advice of Lady E. to permit her to make the necessary enquiries of How the English Law would treat such a case as mine.—You may perhaps at first wonder that I should apply to anyone in preference to yourself—but I was still unwilling to ask you to act for me until I saw I could not avoid giving you trouble and that of a most serious nature. I enclose Lady E.'s most kind and noble letter, it will best show you what she is, as well as perhaps help you, although cases of this description may have come under your own knowledge in the course of your life. I have therefor simply to tell you that I do not think I am John Ruskin's Wife at all—and I entreat you to assist me to get released from the unnatural position in which I stand to him—To go back to the day of my marriage the 10th of April 1848. I went as you know away to the Highlands—I had never been told the duties of married persons to each other and knew little or nothing about their relations in the closest union on earth. For days John talked about this relation to me but avowed no intention of making me his Wife—He alleged various reasons, hatred to children, religious motives, a desire to preserve my beauty, and finally this last year told me his true reason (and this to me is as villainous as all the rest) that he had imagined women were quite different to what he saw I was, and that the reason he did not make me his Wife was because he was disgusted with my person the first evening 10th April. After I began to see things better, I argued with him and took the Bible but he soon silenced me and I was not sufficiently awake to what position I was in—then he said after 6 years, he would marry me when I was 25. This last year we spoke about it, I did say what I thought in May—He then said as I professed quite a dislike to him that it would be SINFUL to enter into such a connexion as if I was not very *wicked* I was at least insane and the responsibility that I might have children was too great, as I was quite unfit to bring them up. These are some of the facts—You may imagine what I have gone through—and

besides all this the temptations his neglect threw me in the way
of. If he had only been kind, I might have lived and died in my
maiden state, but in addition to this brutality his leaving me on
every occasion—His threats for the future of a wish to break
my spirit—and—only last night when he wished to put his
arm round me (For I believe he was cold) I bade him leave me
he said he had a good mind to beat me, and that he had never
admired Romanism so much as if he had a Confessor for me he
would soon bring me to my senses. I don't think, poor creature,
he knows anything about human creatures—but he is so
gifted otherwise and so cold at the same time that he never
thinks of people's feelings and yet with his eloquence will
always command admiration. I cannot bear his presence.—
Once this year I did threaten him with Law, but I really did
not know myself about it, as it was in Edinburgh and he said
"Well, and if I was to take all the blame". I think he might
not oppose my protest—In point of fact, could He?

'I should not think of entering your House excepting as free
as I was before I left it—All this you must consider over and
find out what you can do. Thank God for all his goodness to me
which has enabled me to Live up to this time in his fear and in
I trust a virtuous Life—the glory is all his and under him I
have been kept from sin by the remembrance of the example
you and my dear Mother have ever shown me. If I have not
written you clearly enough you must put it down to illness and
agitation for you will hardly wonder this keeping up of
appearances makes me often sick.'

Millais heard that Effie had at last broken her long silence
and wrote to Mrs. Gray.

83 Gower Street
16 March 1854

'I confess, in spite of the distress it must occasion, that I am
glad that you know all—I think the most generous way of
looking upon his behaviour is to believe him partially out of his
mind—It is needless for me to say how deeply I sympathise
with you in this miserable affair and how I pity her in her
present position which I trust will be changed.'

Mr. Gray, at last aware of the truth, did not hesitate and told Effie he was coming to London at once and would first see Mr. Ruskin.

But Effie and Lady Eastlake, who was a rock of support during these stormy days, pleaded caution.

Herne Hill

30 March 1854

'These two or three mornings', wrote Effie on March 30 'I have come down quite exhausted for John has found out a new method [Here comes a break where the sheet has been torn away, so here two whole pages are missing].

'Papa must be very decided and quite prepared for all sorts of eloquence of this kind to screen his own conduct and as he fears nothing, says the public are fools and that he daresays I have gained their good opinion by my pretty face, and also that I am too cunning to lose my character and not have some steady friends, he will perhaps do some unheard of thing since he seems to think himself quite perfect and really to believe it and me quite mad. It is quite fearful to go on this way—he is naturally quite loathsome to me but of course I did not abuse him for not having married me as just at present he might worry me more than he does. Is he not perfectly awful?'

They advised Mr. Gray not to see the Ruskins but instead to establish beyond doubt the legal position.

Meanwhile Effie kept calm and aloof in the presence of the Ruskins and aroused John to the pitch of telling her that she wanted a good beating with a stick.

Early in April Effie again warned Mr. Gray to be cautious as she knew that if old Mr. Ruskin thought he would lose caste, he would be capable of every form of iniquity, and on the 7th she wrote to her mother.

Herne Hill

7 April 1854

'This is the most important event of my life upon which all my future depends. Everything now is but a choice of evils but the thing must be done—if I am left and the Rs. work farther on

my understanding I fear the result would end in their triumph
—My Father and you would never be happy if I had any
illness which left me in the state they would not be very sorry
to see me in. I am to have a meeting at Lady E.s tomorrow
upon this subject and will give you the particulars.'

Three days later she begged her mother to come to her.

'You really must come here. I think when Jane goes and things
begin to be arranged, it would be most improper for me to be
here alone as I am quite afraid of John and you do not know
what he might not do. Brown thinks him quite mad, although
he says he may have a method in his madness and suggests
that the Grandfather's suicide has still its effects in John's
conduct—I am very ill and so nervous that I cannot meet these
coming events without yr advice and presence as well as
Papa's.

'This day six years ago, we anticipated very different
results, God will defend the right—I am quite decided that to
live on any terms with this man is to continue in sin—'

Effie and her parents planned to leave London on 19 April
ostensibly so that she could be at Bowerswell whilst the Ruskin
trio went on a tour abroad. This fitted in well enough with the
Ruskins' plans, as they had long before told Effie that they did
not mean her to accompany them, whether or not she went to
Germany with Cecilia Northcote. But the legal aspect of a case
of such an unusual character was causing difficulties and the
lawyers asked the Grays to delay their departure for another
week. Lady Eastlake meanwhile did everything possible to
counter gossip that would injure her friend.

7 Fitzroy Square
18 April 1854

'My darling Child' she wrote to Effie,
    'You have been my waking and sleeping thought since I
last saw you, and the thought that I shd not see your sweet
face again, and that no love, not even that of your admirable
parents, could take this cup from you, has drawn many a bitter
tear from me—But it does comfort me, as I know it comforts

your dear mother, that you have been kept in purity and honour, and that no shadow of sin rests on your young brow. Your letter this morning comforts me, tho' it wrings my heart. I could hardly part from your mother yesterday—I felt that she was part of you—I cannot tell you the comfort I feel in *knowing* your upright excellent parents—I am convinced now from my own observation that you cannot be in wiser hands—The legal tidings she brought me were very welcome. God is surely working out some course for you in His love and wisdom, which will enable you hereafter to look back on this troubled time and acknowledge that all did really work together for good to those who love Him.

'I saw Lady Davy late yesterday—she was very anxious to see me on this matter, and though with many digressions she showed me that the whole intent of her heart was to serve you to the utmost of her power by securing the immediate adherence of a few influential friends—Lady Westminster—her niece Lady Octavia—&c. I only begged her not to let anyone think that they were admitted to this knowledge for the sake of gossip, but for the sacred privilege of assisting a much injured long-suffering fellow creature—Also not to speak of it until you should really be gone—

'Your friends will gather together by a strong sympathy and by the need of mutual comfort. I told my dear husband before I saw yr parents—I felt that the time was come—and his manly indignation has only added strength to my own feelings. You may be sure of his voice.'

On the 25th John Ruskin accompanied Effie and her mother to the station, unaware that it was the last time he would see his wife; that afternoon a Citation was served on him. Millais knew the day before that the legal difficulties had been overcome and wrote to Mrs. Gray.

83 Gower Street
23 April 1854

'I felt much inclined to pay you another visit, but think it perhaps better to see no more of you at present—I must however repeat the delight it gives me to think that the Countess is likely soon to have a substantial "Order of release" for herself, which I trust will occasion as much satisfaction as the reverse incident gives her in the picture. Altogether this business is quite incomplete without the stage accompaniments of muslin fairies and blue lights. When you get back to Perth the poor illused Countess (who has been imprisoned so many years) must return to her former happy life, playing, dancing, and *drawing*, and never for a moment permit her thought to rest upon the tragic farce, in which she has so patiently played a suffering part—I assure you the knowledge that she is going home has a most beneficial influence upon me, as I now begin to feel unloosened from a dreadful thought which had taken up all my attention since I was in the Highlands, to the destruction of all painting—I don't think any number of years would have restored in me a sensation of quiet if it had always remained as it was—'

In such a case the question of producing medical evidence when it came before the Court had to be considered and Mrs. Gray was relieved to hear that Dr. Lee, the famous obstetric physician, was 'thunderstruck with the case, had read Ruskin's books and thought him a Jesuit, now thought him mad, shuddered at what Effie must have endured' and had no doubt Dr. Locock (later Sir Charles Locock, F.R.S.) would support him at the proper time.

In a book called *The Tragedy of John Ruskin*, Effie is said to have left without a word, save the traditional note on the pincushion. It must have been a big pincushion because this was the letter.

Herne Hill
25 April 1854

'My dear Mrs. Ruskin

'You have doubtless been wondering why I did not, as was usual with me, pay you a visit at Denmark Hill to bid you goodbye before going to Scotland, but I felt that owing to the circumstances which induce my addressing you this letter that rendered it not only impossible for me to see you now or indeed ever again—but also required that I should state to you the reasons of my sending you my Keys, House Book, wherein will be found a statement of this year's account—together with an explanation of the money received and spent by me and also you will find enclosed my marriage ring which I return by this means to your son, with whom I can never hold farther inter-course or communication. You are aware that I was married by the Scottish form in my father's house on the 10th of April 1848. From that day to this, your son has never made me his wife, or wished to do so, as he at first overcame my judgment, which was ignorant on such points, by a variety of arguments which, even showing him the words of Scripture, did not refute or cause him to change his opinions in the least about. Whilst we were at Salisbury when you caused me to be put in another room on account of an illness, which he told me his Father supposed to arise from his recent connexion with me, He used to laugh & say his Father was imagining things very different to what they were. His conduct and manner went from bad to worse until I felt I could no longer submit to his threats of personal cruelty and desires to get rid of me in any manner consistent with *his own* safety and comparative freedom, I always resisted the idea of a *separation* and would take no steps in such a matter, and threatened him with the course I have now pursued if he did not treat me in a becoming manner, he said "Well what if I do take all the blame, you would make a great piece of work for your Father and go home and lose your position".

'I have gone through this winter and thought at last that I must either die or consult my parents to take proper steps to ascertain what relief could be got, since your son almost daily heaps one insult upon another, more especially accusing me of *Insanity*. My Father and Mother came instantly they knew what I suffered to Town and are only sorry I have lived in such an unnatural position so long. I believe you have been all along in total ignorance of this behaviour of your son—The Law will let you know what I have demanded, and I put it to you and Mr. Ruskin to consider what a very great temporal loss in every point of view, your son's conduct has entailed upon me for these best six years of my life. Your son first said he wd marry me when *I* was 25—then on arriving at that age last year—I enquired on what terms we were to live, he said I was quite

mad, quite unfit to bring up children, and beside did not love
or respect him sufficiently. I said *that* last was quite *impossible*
after his perpetual *neglect*—but that I never would refuse to
gratify his wishes. He then put it off again and said he should
try and break my spirit to induce me to leave him and return
to Perth as I bored him. I think *he* will be glad I have taken this
step. I hear that our affairs are perfectly known in London
society; and nothing more will be said, since the fact of our
marriage not having been consummated was known to *many*
and your son's personal neglect of me *notoriously condemned*—
this has likewise been the case in Perth—My parents have
entirely approved of the steps I have taken and my Mother
accompanies me to Scotland.

'I remain yours truly

'Euphemia C. Gray.'

As the train sped northwards the burden of secret sorrow that
had blighted Effie's young life gradually lifted and after a few
days at Bowerswell surrounded by her young brothers and
sisters she was able to write to Rawdon Brown that

Bowerswell

'feeling that I am really away from those wicked people fills me
with such thankfulness that already a quiet happiness has
settled on my spirit and I feel that I have everything to be
grateful for in having been preserved through such years of
misery.'

Old Mr. Ruskin, fearful of losing caste, stormed and raged
and threatened to cut Millais's portrait of his son with a knife,
but this tragedy was averted by John hurrying the picture away
to Rossetti's studio.

He lost all sense of decency when in the presence of his
friends or when writing them his long verbose letters.

He told W. H. Harrison, for instance, that his son, attracted
by a pretty face, had allowed himself to be led into a matrimonial engagement with a most artful woman, who concealed
for months that her father was totally ruined by railroads, that

she had continued in a course of shameful extravagance and wasted many thousands of his property, and that her falsehoods and ingratitude exceeded all he had ever seen or read of.

These rambling and ridiculous accusations, in which the old miser always emphasized the financial aspect, must have caused many a smile to those who knew Effie Gray when she first came to London and had heard from Mr. Ruskin's own lips his determination that John was to shine in London society whatever the expense.

John took it all very calmly.

'You can be of no use to me at present' he wrote to a friend 'except by not disturbing me, nor thinking hardly of me, yourself, you cannot contradict reports; the world must for the present have its full swing. Be assured I shall neither be subdued, nor materially changed, by this matter. The worst of it for me has long been past.'

It was later when he was required to give his proctor an account of his married life that his hatred of the woman he had so grievously wronged broke through his pose of indifference and exposed an ugly side of his character.

There are no letters from which to draw Mrs. Ruskin's reactions but there can be little doubt that she was the one completely happy person of all those involved. She had from the very beginning known what she wanted and now her efforts had met with triumphant success. There would never again be a competitor for her John's affections if she could help it, and she could look forward to long hours with him, fondling and flattering to her heart's content.

CHAPTER XV

Martyrdom Over

As soon as it was known that Effie had left her husband a flood of gossip was let loose in London social, literary and artistic circles.

There were two camps, those who, unaware of the truth, took Ruskin's part and those who, either aware of the truth or confident that Effie was incapable of wrong doing, took her part.

Effie's supporters formed the great majority and letters poured into Bowerswell from them.

Jane Boswell wrote:

> The Vivary, Taunton
> 26 April 1854

'I got your note last evening, and rejoiced over its contents, not a little: now, I wd be among the first to congratulate you on your *Release*. It has just struck me that picture has been a forerunner of coming events. You have gone through fearful ordeal, my darling, and God has indeed mercifully sustained you: The future no doubt looks dark and aimless at present, but God will have a wise end in it also, & to Him I would humbly and confidently commend you. I am all curiosity to know what the R's will say—I cannot think they will pass it over un-noticed. Dr. and Mrs. Kinglake were truly astonished, and he, like all other men, never heard of a human being so un natural.'

Lady Eastlake wrote:

> 7 Fitzroy Square
> 27 April 1854

'Much as you were loved and respected you were never so much so as now—not by me only but by all whom this sad tale has reached and who know not only what you have suffered, but *how* you have borne it. My dear husband calls you "a heroine of the best kind" and occasionally he *gratifies* me by sentiments of somewhat opposite kind regarding one who I wish could be struck out of your memory as utterly as he will be and already is out of the respect of all good people.'

She was indefatigable in letting all Effie's friends know the truth and their reactions show the extent to which they were stirred by the surprising news. Mrs. Murray 'hid her face in the sofa to conceal her sobs—all sympathy and pity—and, amidst all, the sorrow for the loss of you'. Mr. Boxall, the painter, said 'you interested him more than ever and the good man was not ashamed to weep before me—anxious, like a true knight to fight your battles if fight should be required'.

Good Lady Lewis, with all the woman in her eye, greedy for information, thinking of nothing else. Her husband, Sir Frankland Lewis, who had at one time been a Vice-President of the Board of Trade and Treasurer of the Navy, 'full of few but manly words of respect, anxious to express them to you himself'.

The Fords told her 'it was being taken with but one voice and that against the blackguard—they disputed a little as to the term—but both agreed as to the meaning'.

Mr. Lockhart 'expressed himself in curt, grumbling phrases and hissed out something like "beast"—said there never could be a word said against Effie for whom he was much afflicted and felt the sincerest interest'.

Mrs. Milman's 'heart was full of tenderness and anxiety', and her husband, the Dean of St. Paul's, was longing to hear about his young friend.

At a dinner-party attended by many well-known figures in the literary world, all applauded: 'It's all very well to agree about the writings bit. What do you intend to do with the man —surely when women are banished from society for their faults you will never admit such a villain as that'.

To modern ears these unrestrained demonstrations of affection, grief and anger will seem strange but the London of 1854 was very different from the London of today.

The social, literary and artistic world was relatively a small one. Everybody in it knew everybody else and there were constant parties at the houses of the leading London hostesses where rank, fashion and intellect met and discussed both public and personal affairs.

Letters of the period—and everyone then wrote long letters—are always full of details about how this or that person was dressed, how they were looking, and what they said.

In such a community a case involving a famous man and a popular and beautiful woman naturally aroused the greatest interest particularly as there were not a few who had already guessed the secret of their married life.

After Lady Eastlake's visit Mrs. Milman wrote to Effie.

Deanery, St. Paul's
10 May 1854

'At first I could scarcely believe that one who could think and write so beautifully, *could act* so unworthily; yours has indeed been a fiery trial but thank Heaven you have been purified not consumed in it—The Dean and I have always felt a lively interest about you, we now love and honor you, and shall hope to hear from you that you are enjoying in the bosom of your own family a renewal of that peace and health wh have been so rudely and cruelly broken—that best peace, that "wh passeth understanding" must be yours for you have acted rightly under great temptation, looking unto Him Whose grace is sufficient for us.'

False rumours were in some cases spread about because the case presented something not heard of before.

Lady Eastlake wrote:

7 Fitzroy Square
9 May 1854

'Lady Charlemont called on me last Thursday—Mr. Ford had already given her the outline of the sad tale, which I was glad of, for the good lady with all her kind heart seems to have a very confused *head*, and perhaps from her misfortunes has formed such a very low estimate of the male sex that she heaped upon J.R. every possible and impossible wickedness of motive and aim that has characterised the *roué* part in the novels of the last half century—none of them being *his* particular wickedness which was too new for her apparently to comprehend.'

There were many, too, who refused to believe the true reason for the separation and others, like Dr. Acland, a timid, kindly man, who, relying on the scriptures, expressed the view that there never could be any grounds for a wife leaving her husband.

Carlyle vigorously supported this view and told all his friends that a woman had no right to complain of any treatment whatsoever and should patiently endure all misery!

The view that Ruskin was mad met general support and it was not expected that the Ruskin family would show themselves in London again, but, as will be seen from the next letter, written to Mrs. Gray by a friend, Ruskin still had his supporters.

3 June 1854

'Well the more I hear of Mr. Ruskin the more am I confirmed of his madness. I cannot understand a man in his senses could act as he has done and yet he writes so beautifully, such refined and lofty sentiments that one is quite bewildered—his writings and actions are very very opposite—I cannot think how Effie could have lived so long with him and conducted herself as she did—particularly when she had parents to go to who would be willing to receive her. Geniuses take great license—What a strange history altogether and to come within our own sphere—Elisabeth declares he should be imprisoned for life—that he should not be left to go at large— I think with you he will write some *grandiloquent sophistry* to gull the public showing himself as the injured one—I hear that some *young ladies* will not hear a word against him! 'tis a pity they had not been married to him.'

Miss Boswell, who never minced her words, was only expressing the general opinion when she wrote:

24 Bedford Street South, Liverpool
1 June 1854

'How I wish all the London world wd act with Sir Charles Eastlake in denying J. R. admittance and with Panizzi in cutting him: I do believe many of them will, all the right thinking at least—I wish some one wd cut up his letter in the

Times, and himself in the bygoing. I have been strongly tempted to do so, and regret my want of talent preventing me! It might be so well done by a critique (*sic*) in painting. I cannot conceive how any of the tribe can ever set face in London. So others as well as me think old Madam gets *drunk*. I begin to think I am endowed with an *instinct* enabling me to *divine* people's characters! If old Madam was not drunk that night I dined at D. H. I can only say the imitation was excellent—'

The letter referred to was a letter of Ruskin's to *The Times* praising Holman Hunt's picture 'The Light of the World' which had aroused much criticism.

Effie's friends were very anxious that the true facts should reach the Queen and Lady Charlemont, who confessed she had

'too great a fear of the little woman'

to approach her herself, said she would see that it was done. Queen Victoria, however, declined to let Effie be presented or to receive her at court, as Lady Millais. The story had a dramatic ending.

When Millais, then President of the Royal Academy, was dying the Queen sent one of her gentlemen to convey her sympathy and to ask if there was anything she could do for him. He replied, 'Yes, let her receive my wife'. The Queen consented and Effie was presented by Princess Louise, Duchess of Argyll.

There were still many weeks before the legal authorities would be ready to hear the case and as a friend wrote to Mrs. Gray:

'gentlemen retire into corners and talk it over, some expressing grief beyond utterance, placidly imbibing a cream ice, and one man in 20, for the sake of peculiarity, voluntarily acts as counsel for the "author of Modern Pictures" and makes the best of his case.'

The Ruskins, meanwhile, behaved in their own peculiar fashion.

Q

'It is a marvel', wrote Lady Eastlake, 'how any people in the 19th century can conduct themselves in a trying and peculiar position like this as those old people are doing—nothing can be more indecent and vulgar than their affected glee at a catastrophe so disgraceful to their wretched son.'

They still went everywhere and took every opportunity of spreading malicious stories about Effie.

David Roberts, the landscape painter, meeting the trio at an exhibition was amazed when Mr. Ruskin launched into a stream of vituperation against Effie and said that his son had been entrapped into the marriage and might have married a French Countess, and then added:

'Never mind we shall have to pay for it and we shall at least have John all to ourselves.'

Mr. Ruskin must have been hard put to it to invent this story about the Countess. In the letter to Mr. Gray, quoted in Chapter III, he said that he and Mrs. Ruskin could not sanction a union with Romanism and the ample fortune belonging to the lady was no inducement to run the risk of his son becoming a Roman Catholic. Effie was amused when she heard this and wrote to a friend:

Bowerswell
3 May 1854

'The son is too great a coward to say much, but the wicked old man I knew would be angry not to say some ridiculous things which would only serve to show his own dreadful nature and bad heart. The idea of the French Countess made me smile. The lady was only plain Miss Domecq but her fortune procured her a French Baron for a husband of very questionable character, but I understand they have bought an estate and, as they are now older, I daresay she has given up Balls as he has gambling.

'Mama is going to send Lady E some letters which will show you, if *you* care to read them, that the marriage was all made up on their side.

'My Father thinks this necessary as they have thought proper to add this falsehood to the rest.

'I will try to follow your advice and get well and strong again. My mind is quite at peace and I think, please God, when the warm days come, and with all the kindness and happiness of the family, I may get better and perhaps lose, as Sophie says, the expression of pain above my eyebrows, which I used to think it so odd her noticing and putting her finger on the spot. —but I am very weak and could not begin this letter till I had wandered about a couple of hours as sometimes I cannot form a single letter or move the pen.'

One story spread by the Ruskins which was more insidious because more difficult to refute was that Effie's parents had contrived the marriage to help them out of an awkward financial position, hoping to borrow money from Mr. Ruskin who was then a rich man. It was true that, owing to investing his money in railways, Mr. Gray was in sore financial straits at the time that Effie was invited by the Ruskins to pay them a visit, but he recovered again without asking for or receiving help from anyone, and the suggestion that he sent Effie to London to ensnare the son was as preposterous as the imaginary Countess.

But these and similar fabrications died hard and even after the annulment a story that Effie's parents agreed to let her marry Ruskin on his conditions as to how they were to live together was widely accepted and the blame thrown on Effie's mother.

By June, Effie was restored to health and able to write to Rawdon Brown.

Bowerswell

8 June 1854

'I am quite a different creature. In the first place my mind is completely relieved of all anxiety, and I am naturally so happy that I am able to return to any pursuits that are necessary here with great delight. I look upon myself as much to be envied in getting away instead of dying of misery as many a poor woman has to do who has a worthless wretch to drag on with all her days without the possibility of any Release.'

She had, a week before, come through, without faltering, the trying experience of being examined by the doctors in connection with the legal proceedings.

The Lady Chapel of St. Saviour's Church, Southwark, was then used as the ecclesiastical law court for the Archdeacon of Surrey, instead of Doctors' Commons, and there she went through her ordeal, having been taken to London by her father.

Mr. Glennie, her lawyer, thought then that the case would proceed 'in default' as Ruskin had as yet made no move, but there were still six weeks before the first possible hearing of the case, and the Ruskins were always unpredictable.

Though strongly advised by his friends to let the case go by default, Ruskin's hatred of Effie got the better of him and a fortnight before the final hearing concocted for his lawyer a statement about his married life that can only be described as an infamous document.

Carefully suppressed anger at frustration for a moment broke through his attitude of studied indifference.

It cannot be reproduced here because, as explained in the Introduction, Effie's brother, Albert, directed that on his death the copy which was the only one held by her family was to be sent to the Bodleian Library and not opened for thirty years.

But this last effort to emerge from the case as the injured party could not survive exposure in a Court of Law, and on 15 July 1854 a Decree of Nullity was granted to Effie by the Commissary Court.

It is a long document and only the last paragraphs need be quoted.

'Therefore we John Haggard Doctor of Laws the Commissary aforesaid having heard counsel learned in the Law in this behalf on the part of the said Euphemia Chalmers Gray falsely called Ruskin DO PRONOUNCE DECREE AND DECLARE that he the said John Ruskin being then a Bachelor did at the time libellate contract a pretended Marriage with the said Euphemia Chalmers Gray then and still a Spinster but since falsely called Ruskin and we do also pronounce decree and declare according to the lawful proofs made in the said Cause as

aforesaid that the said Marriage howsoever in fact had between
the said John Ruskin and the said Euphemia Chalmers Gray
falsely called Ruskin was had and celebrated whilst the said
John Ruskin was incapable of consummating the same by
reason of incurable impotency WHEREFORE and by reason of
the premises WE DO pronounce decree and declare that such
Marriage or rather show or effigy of Marriage so had and
solemnized or rather profaned between the said John Ruskin
and Euphemia Chalmers Gray falsely called Ruskin was and is
null and void from the beginning to all intents and purposes in
the Law whatsoever and by reason thereof that the said
Euphemia Chalmers Gray falsely called Ruskin was and is free
from all Bond of Marriage with him the said John Ruskin by
this our definitive sentence of final decree which we give and
promulge by these presents.'

John Haggard was a distinguished lawyer who had been
Chancellor of Lincoln and Winchester before appointment as
Commissary of Surrey. The other two signatories were A. F.
Bayford, a barrister, and Robert Phillimore, then enjoying a
large practice and M.P. for Tavistock, and later a Judge of the
High Court and a prolific author of legal works.

With the signing the curtain was at last rung down on the
tragic farce that had been playing for six years.

There was still one of Effie's married women acquaintances
who agreed with Carlyle that a wife should bear all indignities
and mental suffering in silence, and with Dr. Acland that there
never could be sufficient grounds for a separation.

To her Effie wrote a few days after she heard that the Court
had annulled her marriage.

'On Saturday last, the 15th, after the matter had been
investigated by the first lawyers in England and maturely
considered for both parties, the Court found that my marriage
was a pretended one and a *nullity*. It accordingly has given me
my entire freedom and Maiden name as I never had any
lawful right to any other. I do not however feel at all sure that
you will be able to appreciate this information in its proper
light, from the manner you received the first communication

of my wrongs. You are the only married woman who did not seem to understand what my position had been. Every right hearted woman of *all* my acquaintance at once responded in tones of deepest emotion and sympathy for my sufferings— even although they had only heard the bare facts—without knowing my unexampled trials arising from the extraordinary peculiarities of the whole family. I feel I was not only perfectly justified, but absolutely compelled to take the step I did.

'My natural delicacy compelled me to hide my position even from my parents—until he forced me to reveal it by trying to get rid of me in every way his Jesuitical mind could devise.

'It has most certainly been all his own doing. Had he been only tolerably kind instead of absolutely cruel I never would have exposed myself to such unenviable notoriety. I do not wonder that a few very young Ladies do not exactly comprehend, but I must say I wonder at *any* married lady's not comprehending how much unhappiness must be included in the one fact.'

In her letter to her father, in which for the first time she told him the truth about her married life, she said that if her husband had only been kind to her she might have lived and died in her maiden state. Now, four months later, she reaffirms that it was her husband's cruelty, and not his indifference, that drove her to take a step that would disclose to the public the secret that, in her pride, she had kept so closely for six years.

Nevertheless, she does not hold him alone responsible for the disastrous end to her marriage. She justly lays the blame on the whole family, for almost from the day she entered the house at Denmark Hill as a young bride the machinations and strange behaviour of the old Ruskins had alarmed her. She had always known that her only hope lay in freeing John from the morbid atmosphere of his old home, but though for short periods she came near to success the old couple soon shattered her hopes, and in all their plotting and planning to strengthen their domination over their son they found in him a dutiful ally.

CHAPTER XVI

Happy Ending

The postman again carried a heavy bag up the steep hill to Bowerswell when Effie's many friends heard the decision of the Court and one of the first she read was from Millais.

True to his resolve he had not seen or written to her since February but had kept Mrs. Gray informed of the trend of opinion in London.

In May he wrote to Mrs. Gray:

83 Gower Street
18 May 1854

'As I expected, I hear now that my name is mixed up in the affair, and by some in a manner that makes it advisable that I do not, for the present see anybody connected with you—Any personal communication with your family just now would certainly forward the scandal, which has reached the extreme limit of invention. There must be a large proportion of vagabonds in the world to set such rumours afloat—I am so disgusted with London Society that I shall be right glad when I am out of it and breathing the pure air of the country. In another months time the story will be an old one and something else will be the topic of the day—For my part I have scarcely heard anything because I have avoided as much as possible going out where there was a chance of that being the conversation—My late experience has not increased my good opinion of the public goodnature, some of the most barbarous stories have been in circulation regarding my absence from the R. A. walls, and in connexion with my friend Hunt's works, but next year I hope again to resume my place with a still more conclusive result—All the Summer and Winter I intend working very hard.

'I met Thackeray who was speaking on the subject last night, most people look on J.R. as quite mad.'

In some of his letters he returned to his humorous style.

83 Gower Street
10 May 1854

'I can easily imagine poor old Mrs. R. tremblingly going over the habitation of her mistaken boy, it really must have been an affecting scene. Never mind, they have got him now and will keep on either side of him like two policemen, or the two outside horses in the Edinburgh omnibuses, who always suggested the thought that they were taking their companion to the station house—let us hope that this may not be realised in the case of poor J.R.'

Millais, who knew Ruskin better than most people, was always more generous than his friends and Effie's friends.

New Trossach Hotel
25 May 1854

'I have been thinking a great deal about him lately and I am sure many allowances should be made for him for he is certainly mad or has a slate loose. When I call to mind his ways there seems little doubt but what something was amiss in his head.'

That, too, was to Mrs. Gray in May, and two months later, after Effie was free, he wrote again to her mother on his feelings about Ruskin and recanted his earlier belief that Ruskin had asked him to Glenfinlas in order to throw him and Effie together.

The Peacock Inn, Baslow, Chatsworth
27 July 1854

'In regard to my feelings towards J. R. I cannot but think he is more to be pitied than any other man I know, and I confess now, that like Mr. Gray I could pass him without experiencing much feeling beyond pity. He has behaved *most badly*, but he is half mad, and possibly embittered by discovering—when too late—that he ought never to have married. In that case according to his strange education and bringing up he is not to be judged too severely. You know what I thought of him at the time of his wretched treatment of the Countess, but now I hope

to grow every day less intolerant towards him. I am quite hurt
to hear that he appears to be so ill—this may seem strange to
you but I cannot wish him but peaceful and to go on writing as
he likes. Now she is out of his possession I can forgive him, and
I know she will also. If I recall his behaviour the old antipathy
comes on, which is so painful to me that I can only trust for my
own sake to forget it. I *will* not believe that he desired her to
fall, for in the beginning I cannot imagine a man of education
to be such a devil, neither do I think there was any evil
intention in his asking me to accompany him to the Highlands,
but *I do not doubt* that he was more than indifferent afterwards. There was an amount of cool impudence about his
visiting Bowerswell in spite of his insane conduct to Effie,
which at once declares him to be inhuman,—*no man* could
have face enough to confront the family of the girl he had so
awfully ruined. If I was to ponder much on the subject the
thing which would make me most savage would be his brutal
want of generosity to her. I believe that no living woman ever
behaved as she did, if there had been the slightest warmth in
his blood he would have loved her for her endurance.'

This letter was written at the Peacock Inn near Chatsworth
where he was staying with John Leech and, incidentally,
where he did his drawing of Leech which appears as the
frontispiece in Frith's *John Leech, his life and work*, and it was
there, too, that he addressed his first letter to 'Miss Gray'.

Peacock Inn, Baslow, Chatsworth
21 July 1854

'I cannot see that there is anything to prevent my writing to
you now, so I will wait no longer. I consider that I have a
special right to be amongst the first of your congratulating
friends, for no one has been so keenly interested in the trials
you have gone through, or is so happy at this blessed termination—I had so thoroughly convinced myself of the improb-
ability of ever speaking to you again that I find my brains
unable to keep pace with the sudden alteration of affairs, and
that I am writing this in a state of incredulity. I did not hope to
hear of the decision until Novr. and when I came down this

morning I was surprised to find your Mother's letter upon the breakfast table, for I knew at once the news it contained. The best news I have ever received in my life. May God give you health and peace of mind to enjoy the new life you have entered upon, and I think from your late pedestrian performances at St. Andrews you are not wanting in the former.—

'I will say nothing of the past, recalling bygone events can only be distressing to you. You may always feel happy in having done your duty, for you have done John Ruskin even a greater service than yourself. You were nothing to him but an awful encumbrance, and I believe secretly the source of all his sullen irritability—Love was out of the question in such a nature, so that by the separation you have caused him no more pain than a temporary exhibition of grief such as would naturally follow after your living so many years with him.— Now dear Countess do not be distressed with any more backward thoughts but pray to God that the future may be as happy as the past has been otherwise, and that you may not grow less earnest in your appeals to Him than you were in adversity.—

'This time last year there seemed no more chance of what has happened than that the moon should fall, and now you are Miss Gray again—If you could see me I am sure you would Pity me for I am scarcely able to write common sense I am so bewildered, I cannot separate you in my mind from what appeared to be your inevitable doom and when I see you I shall not be able to believe but what J.R. has got a duplicate Countess.

'I have been painting out of doors all day, or rather pretending to paint—so that I might be away from my friends and have some quiet to think upon this wonderful change.

'I must see you before returning to London, *if you will invite me*. Oh! Countess, how glad I shall be to see you again, this is all I can say now, and you must imagine the rest—I can never be sufficiently thankful for God's goodness to me—I really believe that I should have grown a selfish callous fellow if this alteration had not come about.

'Since the time of my first hearing of your intention to separate from Ruskin I have been in a constant state of anxiety, so much so that I am now quite dull in my head. I have been striving nightly to think upon what I must soon be about, but the subject flies from me immediately—however I think I can show poor Ruskin that he cannot write me down in a week. Here I am going off into a wretched bit of bombast; that is not the spirit I hope to work in—When I come to my senses I will tell you about what I am going to set about and every other subject you care to hear.

'If I have done wrong in writing to you take no notice of my letter beyond asking your Mother to write a word in answer.

'I should think you find it rather difficult to return to your old signature—"Effie Gray". You must now grow so fat that cabmen will refuse to take you as a single fare.'

But eight months were to elapse before he saw her. Effie was still suffering from the after effects of her terrible experience and, though she knew that Millais loved her, she was in no mood to contemplate a second marriage.

Lady Eastlake, too, was anxious that she should give time a chance of healing her wound before accepting Millais, and wrote in August:

7 Fitzroy Square
August 1854

'I have passed close to the scene of your former troubled and harassed life and even to be in that neighbourhood gives me pain. But all that is *over*, and another life lies before you, my dearest child—and one that cannot but sparkle brightly to your view,—for your heart, however mistrustful it may have become, is now really engaged. I knew it was so, and can only honour you for having held it in tight subjection at a time and during trials when a little sophistry might have argued you into believing that you were not bound to do so. All I hope and believe is that out of your past sufferings good may have sprung, that all delusions may be powerless upon you, and that you may view your future with *safer* eyes. But don't think more of it than you can help, be sure that you do more than enough for him in letting him look forward to the privilege of making you really happy—and let neither his happiness nor misery disturb that rest of body and peace of thought which you so much need. Think only of *yourself*—it wont be selfishness. I shd have better like to have shipwrecked him— with canvas, colours and brush—on a desert island for two years—and then rescued him. I like him very much, but I do not want him yet awhile. I wanted my Effie to be untroubled till she was fit for this life's work again, knowing all the time that the two dear people were safe enough to come together at last. Now my only refuge is in hoping that you will disturb yourself about his waving locks as little as you can, and give him just the scantiest *parish* allowance to keep him from starving.'

To her firm friend and confidante, Rawdon Brown, she wrote in October:

Bowerswell
9 October 1854

'I am much better, as I am at present gaining health and strength and very happy teaching my sisters. I am not fit to marry anybody believe me, and after what I have suffered could not do so without very much time for thought and deliberation, and you know it would never do to be wretched twice. If I marry it must be to somebody who wouldn't require to live in London. I am very unfit for living in town although I should like to go occasionally. I could not be shut up in a street without pining, then I cannot have a man to be unkind to my dear parents and other important items to leading a quiet life.'

January found her still of the same mind:

'I see you will not be pleased till you get me married—but why grudge me my happy security and quiet life now— patience, my dear friend, for I have lots to do first and am very shy.'

Millais had finally severed relations with the Ruskins during the previous month. Though now utterly distasteful to him,

JOHN RUSKIN
By Sir J. E. Millais, BT., P.R.A.

he felt bound to complete the Glenfinlas picture, and so could not avoid contact with Denmark Hill.

In December Ruskin, who studiously ignored all recent happenings, wrote to Millais:

Denmark Hill,
11 December 1854

'We have just got the picture placed—in I think the very light it wants—or rather—for it cannot be said to want any light—in that which suits it best. I am far more delighted with it now than I was when I saw it in your room. As for the wonderment of the painting there can of course be no question—but I am also gradually getting reconciled to the figures in the way. On the whole the thing is *right* and what can one say more—always excepting the yellow flower and the over large spark in the right eye, which I continue to reprobate—as having the effect of making me slightly squint—which whatever the other faults of my face may be—I believe I do'nt. My father and mother say the likeness is perfect—but that I look bored—pale—and a little too yellow. Certainly after standing looking at that row of chimnies in Gower Street for three hours—on one leg—it was no wonder I looked rather uninterested in the world in general. But the more they look at it the more they come to it. Please send me your proper address, as I may often want to write to you now. I need not, I hope, tell you how grateful I am to you for finishing this picture as you have.

'Faithfully and gratefully yours

'J. Ruskin.'

Millais, free at last of the picture, was also free to terminate the pretence of friendship and replied a week later:

'My address is Langham Chambers, Langham Place, but I can scarcely see how you conceive it possible that I can desire to continue on terms of intimacy with you. Indeed I concluded that after finishing your portrait you yourself would have seen the necessity of abstaining from further intercourse.

'The barrier which cannot but be between us *personally* does not prevent me from sympathising with all your efforts to the advancement of good taste in Art, and heartily wishing them success.'

To which Ruskin replied two days later:

'Sir,

'From the tenour of your letter, received yesterday, I can only conclude that you either believe I had, as has been alleged by various base or ignorant persons, some unfriendly purpose when I invited you to journey with me in the Highlands, or that you have been concerned in the machinations which have for a long time been entered into against my character and fortune. In either case I have to thank you for a last lesson, though I have had to learn many and bitter ones, of the possible extent of human folly and ingratitude. I trust that you may be spared the natural consequences of the one, or the dire punishment of the other.

'I remain

'Your obed^t serv^t

'John Ruskin.'

With the coming of spring Effie's heart softened towards Millais, whom she had not seen for over a year, but who she knew was waiting eagerly for a word from her and he was invited to pay a visit to Bowerswell in April.

Before May was out he was writing to his oldest friend, Holman Hunt, to announce his engagement.

Langham Chambers, Langham Place
22 May 1855

'My dear old friend

'Every week since I wrote to you last I have been saying I will write to Hunt next week. All the hurry and excitement of the R. A. is over and yet I find myself delaying until it is absolutely necessary that I should tell you first that next Month please God

I shall be a *married man*. What think you of this, you must have partly expected it and will not be knocked down by this sudden announcement.

'When you come back you must come and see me. I am afraid I shall not be in London to receive you when you arrive, but I shall hope to see you soon after—How strangely the world is wagging, I wish you would marry too and set down soberly to work until the end,—Apropos of work, my picture this year has been blackguarded more than ever, altogether the cabal stronger than ever against every good thing—such *injustice*, and felonious abomination has never been known before. Fancy *Herbert, Lee*, and old Satyr Cooper as hangers; Charles above the line, in the octagon, Martineau at the top of the Architectural, *your Father's likeness* rejected (in spite of the indignation of several of the best R. A.s), my picture against the door of the middle room, the very mentioning of these disgraceful facts incense me so that I begin to tremble— I almost dropped down in a fit from rage in a row I had with the three hangers, in which I forgot all restraint, and shook my fist in their faces, calling them every conceivable name of abuse. It is too long a story to relate now, but they wanted to lift my picture up, after I had got permission to have it lowered three inches, and tilted forward so that it might be seen, which was hardly the case as it was first hung, oh! they are felons—! no better than many a tethered convict—so let them pass—I am going to be married so quietly that none of my family come to the wedding—Good gracious! fancy me married my old boy. Every day I see greater reason to be tolerant in judging others—We cannot reckon upon ourselves for the safe guidance of a single project. But I must not fill this letter with truisms—I am very anxious about this change in my life as you may imagine, therefore you must forgive me if this letter is full of it. Since I last wrote I have been in Perth to see her, which was indeed a strange meeting, I was there only a few days as I was backward with my work, and had to return in haste, however I saw enough of her to arrange matters to this end. She dislikes naturally coming to London after her life in it, and I much fear it will never cease to live in her memory, and will always affect her spirits, but time will shew. I have so little belief in my own ability to blot out this ruin in her first life that I am often very desponding in the matter, but I cannot see how this marriage could have been otherwise, everything seems to have happened to work out this end, and perhaps I should allow myself to go placidly with the stream, instead of worrying myself about the probable termination. If I omit to tell you anything of interest you may afterwards find out it will be from forgetfulness—Ruskin I have long since finished with, a few letters passed between us, and in his last, in answer to my saying that I must *of necessity* cease to continue on terms of friendship, through circumstances he must be aware of, he replied in an abruptly angry manner, commencing, "Sir" and ending "Yr *Obedt. Servt.*", and so ended all communications between us—I hear of him of course continually, that is one thing which disturbs me, as She will never escape hearing his name mentioned—Well, it is certainly a strangely tragic tale, and I hope the last scene will be a happy one to her, poor body. I am writing this amidst a crowd of callers—Wilkie Collins is here and desires greeting—Tomorrow is the Derby day—Last Epsom I went to we went together with Mike, you remember. I think Halliday is going this year. All London knows now of my marriage and comments upon it as the best thing I *could* do, the *noblest*, the *vilest*, the most impudent &c. &c. &c.

'I am a bad hand at writing, I wish you were here that I might speak with you. I feel the want of you more than ever and *Art wants you home*. It is impossible to fight singlehanded and the R. A. is too great a consideration to lose sight of with all its position with the public, wealth, and ability to help good art. When Lady Chantry dies, the Academy will have funds at its disposal for the purchase YEARLY of the best living works, and all this should be in *our* hands—In my contest with the hangers, I said I would give up my Associateship if they dared to move my picture, which so frightened them I suppose that they didn't touch it afterwards; I WANT YOU BACK AGAIN to talk over this matter of Exhibition. I am almost indifferent about these things now, and yet I think it a duty for other poor fellows like Brown (whose three pictures were rejected) Anthony, Seddon (*turned out also*)—Goodbye old fellow.'

There were to be no favours, satin shoes and junketings this time, but Effie's wedding dress was to remind her of the one happy interlude in the past seven years,

'I do wish I had your facility of expressing what you mean to say', she wrote to Rawdon Brown, 'I cannot do more than *thank you* and say how truly glad I am that my present was of any use to you. *Yours* to me will be marked by an important event in my life. I shall buy my *marriage dress* with this and as it was to be covered with Venetian Lace at any rate, you can think how pleased I shall be to wear it as from you and how I shall remember the trouble I have given you before to procure this delicate fabric for me. What however I shall put on your *robe* you have never seen, but it will all be connected with Venice and I like that. Indeed you are all too kind to me and the recollection of all the kindness I met with from Mr. Cheyney, his brother, and yourself in my trials I shall never forget. I hope I shall be happy. I have the greatest reason to be thankful about everything connected with the future as far as I can see. . . The marriage will be very quiet. I do not wish anybody but my immediate relations and his if they like to come. Neither of us are the strong of the earth, sometimes I feel dreadfully nervous. He is worse but I think this is temporary with us both. I am really much stronger than I have been for years and today walked to the top of Kinnoull Hill.'

Millais's fears that it might not be in his power to make Effie a completely happy woman did not diminish as the wedding day approached and on the last morning he wrote to Charles Collins:

'Everything is prepared, and there is no mistake about it. The room we are to be married in is full of beautiful flowers, and it does not want *four hours* to put me into another state of life —God knows but I trust a better one. There must be I suppose a great deal of vagueness in taking this step. I am completely in the dark, and uncertain about the probable close of the matter, but all seem very happy. . . I am only hopeful it may be the right course I have taken which can only

R

be known from experience. . . This is a trial without doubt as it either proves a blessing or a curse to two poor bodies only anxious to do their best.'

It was to prove a blessing.

They were married in the drawing-room at Bowerswell on 3 July 1855, and the opportunity was taken to baptize, immediately afterwards, Effie's brother, Everett, who was twenty-six years younger.

The superstitious, who were wont to remind their friends that Effie was born in the room in which Ruskin's grandfather committed suicide, were deprived of a second opportunity for gloomy forebodings because the drawing-room this time was not the same room as the one in which Ruskin plighted his troth to love and cherish Effie until death parted them.

There this story ends.

Effie Gray, escaped at last from the shadows cast over her by Denmark Hill and a husband who had never been anything but a stranger to her, entered a life of great happiness and one abundant with promise for a woman of her keen intelligence. Not a word of her first marriage ever passed her lips. It was understood by her friends and family that it was a forbidden subject.

Her house in Palace Gate became a centre of the social, literary and artistic world, and she herself one of the leading hostesses in London, although her activities in this direction were restricted during the earlier years whilst she brought four sons and four daughters into the world.

First came Everett and George who were the two boys in the 'Boyhood of Raleigh'.

Then Geoffrey and then Effie, who married Captain James, Scots Greys, and who sat to her father for many famous pictures—'My First Sermon', 'My Second Sermon', 'Red Riding Hood', 'The Minuet', 'New Laid Eggs' and 'Forget-me-not'. She also sat for the figure of the girl on the horse in 'Nell Gwynne', as Landseer had expressed a wish, when dying, that Millais should complete his unfinished picture.

After Effie came John, the explorer and naturalist, whose *British Mammals, British Deer and Their Horns, British*

Ducks and book on Rhododendrons are standard works, and whose travel books—*Newfoundland and its Untrodden Ways, A Breath from the Veldt, Far Away up the Nile*—are widely read.

Then came Alice, who married Charles Stuart-Wortley (afterwards Lord Stuart of Wortley) and was the model for 'Sleeping' and 'Picture of Health'.

Then Mary who sat for 'Waking', 'The Bridesmaid', and 'The Last Rose of Summer', and lastly Sophie, who married Captain D. MacEwen, Cameron Highlanders, and was the model for 'A Flood', 'Still for a moment', 'Forbidden Fruit', 'Princess Elizabeth' and 'Clarissa'.

With Millais, Effie's rich talents, so long kept in subjection, found full expression. For forty-seven years she helped and encouraged him, freed him from the burden of writing letters when he was absorbed in his work, managed the affairs of her large family, and delighted her husband with her music when he was tired or worried about a picture.

She died at Bowerswell on 23 December 1897.

As long as the memory of English art exists the name of Millais will go down to posterity as among her truest and most individual exponents.

His Pre-Raphaelite pictures, some of his subject pictures of a later period, and his portraits of Carlyle, Gladstone, Bright, Cardinal Newman, Tennyson, Disraeli, Salisbury and Irving are a part of the nation's treasures. He succeeded Leighton as President of the Academy in February 1896, and the flood of congratulations that poured in upon him was quite over-whelming.

'The Millais-nium of art has come', wrote Holman Hunt, 'from P.R.B. to P.R.A.'

But he was already a doomed man and at the opening of the Academy in May he was unable to keep up with the Prince of Wales, who, on learning the cause, insisted on his returning home.

He took up his palette once more to start on a picture to be called 'The Last Trek', but his strength was failing fast and he could not begin it.

He died on 13 August 1896 and was buried in the

Painters' Corner of St. Paul's Cathedral, the pall being borne by
Holman Hunt, Philip Calderon, Sir Henry Irving, Sir George
Reid, Viscount Wolseley, the Earl of Rosebery, the Earl of
Carlisle and the Marquis of Granby.

Three stanzas of the charming and sympathetic poem that
appeared in *Punch* immediately after the funeral give as
faithful a picture of him as any of the many written tributes.

At last Death brings his Order of Release
And our great English painter lies at peace
   Amidst a nation's sorrow
A man in heart and Art, in soul and fame,
By love encompassed, and secure of fame
   Through history's long tomorrow.

The world seems greyer, gloomier, far less young,
For loss of him, the free of touch and tongue,
   Nature's own child in both
By glowing canvas or by rushing stream,
With brush or rod, he was no thrall of dream
   Feebleness, fad or sloth.

English he was, and England best inspired
His skill unfailing, and his toil untired.
   On his strong canvas live
Her loveliest daughters and her noblest sons,
All that to a great age, which swift outruns,
   Its greatest glories give.

John Ruskin continued to pour out his rich prose in books
and pamphlets which are part of his country's heritage.

For two periods he held a Professorship at Oxford. His
immense influence as an art critic remained unabated and the
art literature of his time was largely founded upon him. Even
if his magnificent prose, which once formed public taste of art,
is not so attractive to twentieth-century readers as it was to
those who waited impatiently for a new book by him, his great
crusade to raise the standard of life of the poorer section of the
community ensures him an abiding place in the hearts of the
English people and in their history.

Affection, rampant and unmanageable, was once more to cause him much unhappiness and leave him defeated and exhausted.

In 1858, Lady Waterford brought to Denmark Hill a lovely child of nine, Rose La Touche. She was a precocious child and when Ruskin described her as 'like patience on a monument' and walking 'like a little white statue through the twilight woods, talking solemnly' she was, though only thirteen, subject to melancholy moods.

Two years later he wrote to his friend, George Macdonald, 'I can't love anybody except my Mouse-pet in Ireland who nibbles me to the very sick-death with weariness to see her'. He was now completely obsessed with her and when she was eighteen he proposed to her, but she told him he must await her answer until she was twenty-one.

To a man of his highly strung temperament her decision was almost unendurable. A year later he is entering in his diary that he has many weird dreams and that he is suffering from despondency, sleeplessness and nervous prostration, but he has not given up hope and counts the days to the date Rose's answer is due.

When the date fell due she again postponed her answer. She was not well, very restless, and was now in a state of religious mania. Two years later he again proposed but this time her answer was final, she could never marry him. 'His last words to me were a blessing', she wrote, 'I felt too dumb with pain to answer him. . . I cannot be to him what he wishes, or return the vehement love which he gave me which petrified me and frightened me.'

In January 1875 Ruskin wrote: 'The woman I hoped would have been my wife is dying' (*Fors Clavigera*). She died on 29 May.

In biographies of Ruskin, this strange and morbid story is always given much prominence, but the true reasons for Rose's final decision and the sustained opposition of her parents have hitherto remained obscure. In some account this opposition has been ascribed to the mother's jealousy as she was at one time one of Ruskin's most fervent admirers. It was not a jealous woman but a much troubled mother who wrote to Effie Millais in October 1870, after all other efforts had failed.

In her letter Mrs. La Touche stated that a Mr. Cowper Temple and his wife, who believed all Ruskin's statements and had great influence with her daughter, were endeavouring to persuade Rose that she was bound to reward Ruskin's love and constancy by allowing him to renew his addresses.

Ruskin, she said, denied impotence, and explained that he had lived with his wife as with a sister for six years because there had never been any love between them, and the marriage had been arranged by the parents. He had respected his wife too much to be anything but a protector and companion. Their tastes had been quite incompatible. He had made every effort to make his wife happy, and when he failed to do so had not resisted measures to give her her freedom.

The Cowper Temples believed all this and were urging on Rose that Ruskin's past history had been beautiful, pure and heroic.

She begged Effie to crush the falsehoods that Ruskin was spreading as her daughter, impervious to all other argument, would, she believed, listen to Effie's evidence.

Though Effie had for the past fifteen years been endeavouring to obliterate from her mind her six years of thraldom, she could not turn a deaf ear to this appeal, and wrote a full and frank account of her life with Ruskin.

'I have received your kind letter and I am truly distressed that you are in such trouble about your daughter.

'Mr. Millais is extremely averse to my being brought into contact even by correspondence with your daughter who, if she is still under the mischievous influence of Mr. Ruskin, will not think differently whatever I say.

'If your daughter can for a moment believe such a statement as his that he should marry a girl of 19 without professions of the most devoted kind, how can any words of mine undeceive her.

'He pursued exactly the same course with me as with her; he always took the tone of his love and adoration being higher and above that of ordinary mortals, and immediately after the ceremony he proceeded to inform me that he did not intend to marry me. He afterwards excused himself from doing so by saying that I had an internal disease. His father tried to induce him to believe me insane and his whole conduct was simply as monstrous as his present statements are perfect falsehoods.

'Our marriage was *never arranged* by anybody. There was no inducement but the utmost determination on his part to marry me. Prior to his professions to me he had been devoted to a Spanish lady and broke a blood vessel from disappointment that he did not get her. I do not think she wished it but religion was given as the obstacle.

'But he had quite got over that and on our visiting her years after he had no feeling about her.

'Now that I am a married woman and happy with a family I think his conduct can only be excused on the score of madness, as his wickedness in trying his dreadful influence over your daughter is terrible to think of.

'I can easily understand the hold he has acquired, as it was exactly the same over myself. His conduct to me was impure in the highest degree, discreditable, and so dishonourable that I submitted to it for years not knowing what else to do, although I would have often been thankful to have run away, and envied the people sweeping the crossings.

'His mind is most inhuman; all that sympathy which he expects and gets from the female mind it is utterly impossible for him to return excepting on artistic subjects which have nothing to do with domestic life. It is perfect falsehood to say that I did not agree with his pursuits. No one more so. He not only gave me the opportunity but the means of education when abroad for acquiring knowledge of painting, sculpture, architecture, every branch of the fine arts, a slight knowledge of Latin and Greek, and we read together the works of the ancients and, as I am particularly fond of history, every thing he wanted for his writings of this kind.

'From his peculiar nature he is utterly incapable of making a woman happy. He is quite unnatural and in that one thing all the rest is embraced.

'He always pretended to me to the last that he was the purest and holiest of men and he had a peculiar influence over a young mind in making himself believed.

'I had no idea I could get away up to within a month of leaving him, which I did under the care of my parents and entirely without his knowledge by the advice of lawyers. So far from his conniving at my leaving him it was a great shock to them all; this statement of his is also entirely false.

'He once years before offered me £800 a year to allow him to retire into a monastery and retain his name—that I declined. He was then under the influence of Manning.

'I think if your daughter went through the ceremony with him that her health would give way after a time and she would be submitted to the same kind of treatment as I was.

'It is very painful for me to write all this and be again obliged to recall all those years of distress and suffering, of which I nearly died. But I hope that your daughter may be saved and come to see things in a different light.'

The La Touches were profoundly grateful and in her letter of thanks Mrs. La Touche said that she believed her daughter was now saved. She had promised her father that she would have no more to say to Ruskin and her friends had promised that they would never again name him to her.

In 1878 the first of a series of attacks of madness occurred which left Ruskin very exhausted, but from which he made remarkable recoveries. After the sixth attack he went into complete retirement at Brantwood, on the eastern side of Coniston Water, which he had bought in 1871.

During the next eleven years he was often depressed, sometimes very excited, sometimes speechless and not recognizing anyone, but for short periods quite sane. Collingwood describes those years in these moving words:

'All that I now remember of many a weary night and day is the vision of a great soul in torment, and through purgatorial fires the ineffable tenderness of the real man emerging, with his passionate appeal to justice and baffled desire for truth. To those who could not follow the wanderings of the wearied brain it was nothing but a horrible or a grotesque nightmare. Some, in those trials, learnt as they could not otherwise have learnt to know him, and to love him as never before.'

He died on 20 January 1900, a few days before his eighty-first birthday.

A grave in Westminster Abbey, close to that of Tennyson, was offered by the Dean and Chapter, but his cousin, Mrs. Severn, felt bound to refuse the offer, as he had expressly stated that he wished to rest at Coniston.

*   *   *

I recently walked up Kinnoull Hill, where Effie Gray so often romped as a child, and where she sought solitude when she wished to be left with her own thoughts after her years of fiery trial with the Ruskins.

On my way back I passed the seat at the top of the long walk where she so often sat during the last year of her life, and where I said goodbye to her before sailing for Australia.

For her it must have been a hallowed spot, because it was there that a chapter of her life, which she had always tried to efface from her memory, came to an end, and a new chapter, with memories that could still bring gleams of happiness to her tired eyes, had begun.

As her end approached, she must have found it increasingly difficult to blot out those six grievous years; she was so much alone, and it is the older storehouses of memory that open their doors as the years advance.

When I reached the terraces of the 'Vale of Rest', I sat down and pondered over the strange story I had unravelled. It was hard to believe that the solid, well-proportioned, Victorian house in front of me had been the setting for the drama that had been played out within its walls. The large double door was the same that had opened nearly a hundred years earlier for a smiling, happy couple who, to a chorus of good wishes and a shower of satin shoes, had entered the brougham that was to take them on their first journey together. Many of those who wished them 'God speed' saw them as an exceptionally good looking and highly talented young couple who would seldom be seen again in Perth, as they would soon be shining in the London social and artistic world and when they could tear themselves away would prefer the Continent to a Scottish provincial town. There were, as I now knew, a few anxious hearts behind the smiling faces, because to some of the austere Scottish elders there was something queer, perhaps a little frightening, about the bridegroom.

Seven years later, those doors had opened again for a wedding couple to enter a brougham. This time there were no misgivings amongst those who waved them on their way. The only anxious hearts were inside the brougham.

But they need not have been anxious. The Fates had frowned heavily on her first venture; they were now about to make amends.

They had certainly dealt unmercifully with that young and lovely girl and that brilliant young man. If only his passionate love of beautiful things had been satisfied by pictures and architecture; if only he had been able to control his susceptibility to a beautiful face, and been content to admire or adore Adèle, Effie and Rose from a distance; if, after his uncontrollable passion had led him to the fatal mistake of contracting marriage, those two old birds of ill-omen at Denmark Hill had died; if, indeed, they had died during that second visit to Venice; how different would have been the pattern of his life and the life of the girl, whose noble character preserved her from social disaster and sustained her for six years of persecution by three people who were often hovering in that borderland between sanity and madness.

But how idle to speculate on what might have been! The missing chapters in the story of two men of genius and a beautiful woman, with its Oriental flavour of passion and intrigue, were now completed.

I suddenly remembered Effie's letter from Venice about the firegrate. She had entrusted the purchase of a grate to her husband, and he had returned with some old iron for which he had given five shillings.

'It proves', she wrote, 'that talents have been wisely distributed and that a man who can write the Seven Lamps is not fit to choose a fire grate.'

The distribution had been on a very lavish scale for John Ruskin, too lavish for his own happiness or for the happiness of anyone who loved him.

INDEX

Index